# Society under Siege

# Society under Siege

Zygmunt Bauman

polity

The right of Zygmunt Bauman to be identified as author of this work has been asserted in accordance with the Copyright, Designs and Patents Act 1988.

First published in 2002 by Polity Press in association with Blackwell Publishers Ltd, a Blackwell Publishing Company

*Editorial office*:
Polity Press
65 Bridge Street
Cambridge CB2 1UR, UK

*Marketing and production*:
Blackwell Publishers Ltd
108 Cowley Road
Oxford OX4 1JF, UK

*Published in the USA by*
Blackwell Publishers Inc.
350 Main Street
Malden, MA 02148, USA

ISBN 0-7456-2984-9
ISBN 0-7456-2985-7 (pbk)

A catalogue record for this book is available from the British Library and has been applied for from the Library of Congress.

Typeset in 10.5 on 12 pt Sabon
by Kolam Information Services Pvt. Ltd, Pondicherry, India
Printed in Great Britain by MPG Books, Bodmin, Cornwall

This book is printed on acid-free paper.

# Contents

**Part II   Life Politics**

# Acknowledgements

I am deeply in debt to John Thompson for his initiative, friendly advice and critical comments that led to the composition of this volume – as well as for the title of the book. And to Ann Bone, for her unique combination of empathy, perseverance and care.

# Introduction

Sociology was born as a modern project, and like all other modern projects followed from the start and through all (or at least most) of its history the Comtean triune task of *savoir pour prévoir, prévoir pour pouvoir*. Sociology aimed to know its object in order to guess unerringly where it tends to move and so to find out what could and should be done if one wished to prod it in the right direction. And the object to be known, to be seen through and eventually moulded, was 'human reality' – that condition under which (to take a hint from Marx's famous phrase) humans made their biographical/historical choices from which the condition itself is however exempt (having been for that very reason called 'reality'). It was that exemption from choice that challenged sociological imagination. Modern practice being an exercise in transgression of boundaries and in transcendence of limits, anything resistant to the human power of choice was an offence, a *casus belli* and a call to arms.

One needed to know one's object because knowing one's object was tantamount to disarming it. Stealing the object's mystery was like stealing Jupiter's thunder. A known object would not put up any more resistance; or at least one could anticipate such resistance as the object may put up, take the necessary precautions and pre-empt its impact. This is why reconnaissance is the *conditio sine qua non* of forcing the adversary to submit. Information is the best of weapons, and the more thorough and comprehensive it is the more completely and irrevocably the enemy, robbed of its secrets, will be disempowered. Once known, its assets will become its liabilities.

Modern science positioned itself as the intelligence branch of modern practice, for which the extant reality (read: the as yet unpenetrated, opaque and obscure, and therefore uninterfered with and for the time being unmanageable segment of the action-setting) was the enemy. Throughout the past two centuries, sociology strove to be recognized as a science by joining in the performance of that role and demonstrating that it was capable of doing so.

Practice is what agents do, and it is another agent determined to act that constitutes the adversary, and it is the objective which the agent sets for its action that provides the principle by which relevance is ascribed or denied to the many attributes of that adversary. The gathering of information would make no sense – indeed, would be inconceivable – unless there was an agent engaged in purposeful action: setting objectives and pursuing them. In the case of sociology, such an objectives-setting-and-pursuing agent was the sovereign state, and sociology constituted itself as the intelligence branch of its practice.

Disarming reality in order to render it softer, more tractable and receptive to change was the defining feature of the modern spirit, but the right and ability to do so was a matter of contention between modern institutions; it was also the most coveted prize of the modern power struggle. The modern state had been defined by Max Weber as the institution claiming *monopoly* on permissible ('legitimate', no-appeal and no-compensation) coercion: in other words, as an institution that claims to be the only agency entitled to deploy coercive action in order to force the extant state of affairs to be different from what it has been and would continue to be if left alone.

Action is coercive if and when in pursuing its objectives it takes no account of its object's 'natural tendencies'. In the case of a sensuous and agent-like object, 'coerciveness' of action means that the object's intentions and predilections are rendered illegitimate by being classified as motives arising from ignorance or criminal inclinations. 'Legitimacy' of coercive action means that the agency that applies it denies its object the right to resist coercion, to question its reasons, to reply in kind or sue for compensation. That legitimacy was itself a stake of coercion. No matter how much coercion was applied, though – that legitimacy, and particularly the monopoly of legitimate coercion, was never immune to contest and therefore for most of the time it was seen as an ideal state not-yet-achieved; as an unfinished project and a battle-cry calling to the struggles ahead.

There was an agency, and there was an objective, and there was the determination, and resources, and a reasonable hope of reaching the goal. There was therefore a vacancy for an intelligence unit – and sociology applied for the job.

Whatever form the aspiring state would wish to carve on the found reality, the meta-objective, the condition of the feasibility of any conceivable objective, had to be a certain submissiveness, a pliability of the reality meant to be given another shape. As every sculptor knows, pliability is not the trait of the substance to be reshaped, but of the relation between the toughness of the substance and the sharpness of the carving tools. A successful outcome of the carving efforts depends as much on the power of the tools chosen to perform the set task as it does on the submissiveness of the medium; and so a reliable knowledge of the latter is required to allow for the right choice of the first. When it comes to carving social reality, though, the 'sculpting agency' seldom if ever matches the exclusivity of purpose and the fullness of the authority over procedure that can be found matter-of-factly in a sculptor's studio, even if most of the modern states undertaking the carving job took the sculptor's freedom as a pattern and as an ideal to be pursued.

One needs a powerful and resourceful state to protect the undivided authority of the sculptor in her or his studio; the state had only itself to protect its own authority over the society cast and treated as a sculptor's studio writ large. In the task of that protection, the state was simultaneously the umpire and a party, more often finding itself in Baron Münchhausen's predicament (that is, pulling itself out of the bog by its own bootstraps) than enjoying the sculptor's liberty. Most of the time, there were other would-be sculptors eager to use carving tools in order to engrave on the same substance a different image – and vociferously demanding the right to do so. The major concern of the state had therefore to be the withdrawal of carving tools from the high-street shops and wiping out their cottage industry. Hence the claim to the monopoly on the production and use of the means of 'legitimate coercion' – that objective being explained as the enforcement of the preferred (more rational, more humane or promising more security, and for any or all of those reasons superior to its currently competing or yet likely to be presented alternatives) model of reality.

Enforcement of a preferred shape at the expense of the extant one always means coercion – *readiness* to apply coercion and the *threat* to resort to coercion. But so does all violence – and once the acts are stripped of their definitional wrappings there is nothing left to distinguish 'empirically' one from the other. Any boundary drawn to separate them must be arbitrary – and so the claim to monopoly on the means of coercion boils down to the indivisibility of the arbiter's office. Coercion is legitimate as long as it is approved by the arbiter through the procedure of arbitration that the arbiter has approved. All other coercion is designated as violence, and the paramount mission and most urgent task of the legitimate coercion is to uproot and extirpate it, prevent it from happening and punish it when it happens.

*The right to draw the line between legitimate (permissible) coercion and illegitimate (impermissible) coercion is the prime stake of all power struggles.* On that battlefield the adversaries preaching alternative models for the reshaping of social reality ultimately meet and confront each other. The 'civilizing process' (by which name the activity of the state likes to be known) consists in rendering the battlefields redundant through reducing to a minimum or eliminating altogether the likelihood that the state-promoted boundary between legitimate and illegitimate coercion will be disputed.

The kind of violence most hotly opposed in the process is 'meta-violence' – coercion aimed at undermining the legitimacy of state-approved coercion. The opposition is hardly ever one hundred per cent effective, since violence (that is, coercion blatantly challenging the extant legitimacy, bidding for legitimacy or counting on gaining legitimacy) is a pencil with which the boundary between the legitimate and the illegitimate is drawn and redrawn.

For a greater part of its history, roughly coterminous with the history of the modern state, sociology examined the ways and means by which the resilience or immunity to meta-violence of state-approved coercion is achieved and how the legitimacy of coercion is entrenched through the mobilization of sentiments aimed at the internalization of the state-protected order, or through dissolving coercion in the fabric of daily life. Summing up the explorations of all preceding sociology, Talcott Parsons suggested that the drama daily rehearsed of defusing the potentially disruptive effect of the voluntarity of actors was from its inception its major concern, while unravelling the plot of that mystery was its principal cognitive aim. The history of sociology, in Parsons's rendition, consisted in adding ever more precise and comprehensive footnotes to the 'Hobbesian problem': namely, the possibility of repetitive, routine, regular behavioural patterns and so of harmonious and peaceful cohabitation of actors pursuing their own, ostensibly incompatible interests. On the centrality of that mystery to all investigation of society there was little disagreement between otherwise disparate schools of socio-logical thought. Norbert Elias, no enthusiast of Parsons's grand syn-thesis, saw the condensation in the state of a coercion previously diffuse and scattered all over the network of social interactions as the hub of the 'civilizing process'. The process of 'socialization', defined as the reforging of the 'will of society' (more commonly known under the name of 'common interests') into the motives of its members, and the expedients meant to bar, neutralize or suppress competition to that reforging, stood for many years at the centre of sociologists' attention and constituted, in its numerous incarnations, the bulk of sociological investigation.

The ultimate outcome of the legitimacy contest seemed through-out the solid phase of modernity a foregone conclusion. There was but one competitor with a realistic chance of victory: the alliance of the emergent nation and the emergent state, of the nation legitimiz-ing the state's demand for discipline and the state aiding and abet-ting the integrating/assimilating/repressive ambitions of the nation. The globe was divided into the realms of nation-states, and the territories belonging to none of the extant realms were 'no man's lands' waiting to be annexed and incorporated. For all practical intents and purposes, 'sovereign power' and 'nation-state' were synonymical.

Giorgio Agamben, following the clue contained in Otto Schmitt's definition of 'sovereignty' ('Sovereign is he who decides on the state of exception'),[1] suggests that the true defining feature of sovereignty is not so much the right to determine the law but the right to exempt from the law; it is the capacity to denude its subjects of the repressive/protective envelope of the law that makes power fully and truly sovereign. The 'sovereignty', we may say, means the right to issue 'Wanted – dead or alive' posters that designate easy prey for bounty hunters. The true subject of the modern state – of any modern state, regardless of its political regime – was 'bare life', life positioned permanently on the tenuous line separating inclusion from exclusion.

In modern politics, the 'realm of bare life' 'gradually begins to coincide with the political realm'.[2] 'Only because politics in our age had been entirely transformed into biopolitics', Agamben suggests, 'was it possible for politics to be constituted as totalitarian politics to a degree hitherto unknown.' The same transformation explains 'the otherwise incomprehensible rapidity with which twentieth-century parliamentary democracies were able to turn into totalitarian states and with which this century's totalitarian states were able to be converted, almost without interruption, into parliamentary democracies'.[3]

As Karl Marx observed a long time ago, casting an anticipatory look from the threshold of the modern era: the rulers' ideas tend to be the ruling ideas. They turned out to be also the sociologists' ruling ideas, or more exactly they ruled the sociologists' thought and practice. No wonder, as what passed for Émile Durkheim's reality of 'coercive social facts' was the reality perhaps shaped already, but certainly intended to be shaped, by the coercive practices of the sovereign nation-state's rulers. Bent on cracking the mystery of the 'social reality effect', sociologists could not but discover the sovereign/legitimate power of the state as its both necessary and sufficient condition. The sensation of coerciveness was a side-effect of the absence of competitors likely to approximate, let alone to match, the superior powers of the champion whose demise for that reason could seem only a sheer fantasy. The forms of rule could be a matter of contention – but not its sovereignty and its identification with the state, where all threads of social integration and trajectories of social reproduction originated and to where they returned.

The point is, though, that (as Jean-Pierre Dacheux aptly put it) 'all those unthinkable things that primed the fixing of the frontiers deemed stable and impassable'[4] gave way under a double pressure – from above (globalization) and from below (biodiversity that ultimately defied the attempts to dissolve it and blend it inside the framework of the state-nation). One wonders to what extent the felicitous and for a long time successful marriage between nation and state still holds.

At the threshold of the modern era, the republican descendants of jaded and fading holy empires abandoned the principle *cuius regio, eius religio* and chose divorce from their respective churches, having proclaimed religious faith to be a private matter of no concern to the political sovereign; but only to take the nation as their wedded partner soon afterwards and to proclaim the promotion of patriotism to be the task of the sovereign state and the public duty of its subject. What new era may be signalled by the separation between state and nation, if this is indeed what is currently happening?

The divorce hearings, to be sure, proceed in fits and starts, and whether a decree nisi will or will not be granted in the end and the separation be final may still seem a moot question. Time and again, here and there, the orthodox type of state patriotism erupts seemingly unscathed – as if it has merely been dormant for a while, and has lost none of its passions and mobilizing powers. We have witnessed recently such a great awakening of the old-style, state-focused, patriotism in the United States of America – in the aftermath of the terrorist assault and the sudden discovery that the state-provided shield against the dangers emanating from the outer world has not guaranteed the personal safety of Americans, that it can be easily pierced and that more, much more needs to be done to make it tight and impermeable if the dream to make it such can be ever fulfilled. That outburst was sufficient to arouse an uncharacteristically unanimous support for the state's initiative to dispatch the professional navy and air force on a military expedition, and to trigger a quite old-fashioned jingoist hue-and-cry against the few dissenting voices (as Susan Sontag, for instance, learned the hard way, while most journalists and reporters escaped that lesson seeking shelter in 'emotional correctness'). Even so it remains anybody's guess whether it would be enough to prompt and sustain a readiness for the massive self-sacrifice that an equally old-fashioned universal conscription would require, and only time may tell how long the gust of patriotic emotions would last without being spurred by more and yet more shocking shocks and reinflated by new panics. On a smaller scale, explosions of patriotic emotions occur regularly and routinely around sporting events, with the worldwide sports establishments specializing in the supply of outlets, and with mostly commercial promotion companies cashing in on the flag-waving custom.

Demonstrations of national loyalty and manifestations of unity proceed, however, after the pattern of a swarm – a massively copied style of individual behaviour – rather than that of a coordinated conduct of a stable and tightly knit community, or a conduct conducive to the merging of a 'whole greater than the sum of its parts', a whole for the sake of which each part is ready and willing to sacrifice itself. Besides, such demonstrations tend to acquire the character of carnival events. Like all carnivals, they serve as safety valves for accumulated emotional steam, but otherwise are short-lived and hardly affect the flow of everyday life – underlying, if anything, the progressively reduced role of patriotic emotions in 'ordinary' day-by-day pursuits, including the routine reproduction of mundane order.

In daily life, the nation coterminous with the state is but one of a large set of imagined communities vying for loyalty and to be focuses for communal emotions. The composition of the set varies over time, and the battlefronts between competitors are constantly on the move. Whatever priority a particular emotional engagement may take over its competitors is seldom absolute and never guaranteed to last as long as it takes to perform the set task. All engagements come, as a rule, prepackaged with exit kits, even if in the midst of the emotional outburst the termination of engagement may seem inconceivable. The economics of emotion-based loyalty has all the bearings of Richard Rorty's 'campaign', rather than 'movement', politics. The positions ascribed to diverse 'imagined' (or postulated, or peg[5]) communities in the collectively or individually composed hierarchies of loyalties move up and down or vanish altogether from one event to another in lives lived as a succession of relatively self-enclosed episodes.

The aspect of such a perpetual 'musical chairs' game of loyalties particularly relevant to the present topic is the ever more evident, and perhaps irretrievable, loss of the privileged (and *unassailably superior*) position enjoyed or claimed by the nation-state. The state, stripped of a large part of the once comprehensive, 'total' sovereignty, exposed more often than not to a 'there is no alternative' situation rather than exercising free choice of policies, and buffeted by outside forces rather than the democratically expressed preferences of its own citizens, has lost most of its past allure as a location for secure and profitable investment.

Nationalism in its modern form would have been unthinkable were it not for the credibility of the modern state's bid for total sovereignty and is unlikely to survive the collapse or the withdrawal of that bid. That bid is nowadays seldom repeated, even less frequently pursued with a modicum of earnestness, and if heard sounds more like a pep-talk, a desperate yet only half-hearted attempt to dust off the long shelved memories in hope to recover their rudimentary powers of inspiration – rather than a declaration of intent, let alone a call to action or marching orders.

It is often said that the fading of the nation-state, and particularly the looming divorce between state and nation which neither of the partners can be sure to survive, is a local phenomenon, confined to a comfortable, well-off part of the globe, jaded and lulled by its genuine or putative security deemed to be safely anchored in its economic power and military superiority. In the rest of the world – so the story goes – the turbulent era of state-aided and abetted nation-building is still ahead. It is only now that in faraway lands (not 'Western', or not sufficiently 'Westernized' – stopped or delayed on the road to the 'Western' form of life) nationalisms are born and prepare to go through the motions acted out by the nations of the 'West' in the past. The story does not hold much water, though. It can be questioned on a number of grounds.

To start with, all the similarities between cultural crusades of the early modern states and the present-day intertribal warfare, mass murders and spasms of ethnic cleansing are purely incidental. Or perhaps not incidental after all – resorting to an orthodox vocabulary to account for unorthodox actions, or explaining unfamiliar and essentially different phenomena as repetitions of the possibly irrelevant, but familiar precedents, is after all a widespread and difficult to defy inclination. Not incidental, therefore – but misleading all the same. Tribal wars may bear some superficial resemblance to the early stirrings of inchoate European nationalisms – but first and foremost they are a vivid testimony of the bankruptcy of the nation-state experiment. They are products of putrefaction; tribal flowers sprout and flourish on the nation-state grave.

The nation-state was a grand vision of a nation blended into the polity; the communal interests dissolved in, and becoming indistinguishable from, *raison d'état*. Survival of the nation being identical with the unsapped and intractable might of the state, love of the nation manifested itself most fully in the meticulous observance of the law of the land and faithful service to whatever had been presented and recognized as being in the state's interest. The state could claim the undivided loyalty of all its citizens and override all other interests – 'particularisms' when viewed from the perspective of the sovereign totality of the state. Cultural peculiarities, religious disagreements, linguistic idiosyncrasies or any other discrepancy in beliefs and preferences should not matter. Above all, they should not stand in the way of unswerving loyalty to the state, common to all. In case of conflict, priorities were unambiguous and the line of duty one for all.

That model of the nation-state was to remain, as it were, an 'unfinished project' even at the height of the nation-state's glory years. Most nations most of the time were frail coalitions of but partly compatible forms of life. The assimilatory pressures and cultural crusades were an indispensable accompaniment of all nation-building, but they seldom reached their projected goal of a sameness-based unanimity. The unity was hardly ever foolproof and free from centrifugal forces, and its perpetuity was never seen as fully guaranteed. According to the famous reminder of Ernest Renan, nation was a 'daily plebiscite'. The citizens' effort to put the 'Germanhood' or 'Frenchness' above all other values and loyalties was seldom considered zealous and whole-hearted enough. The principle of 'my country, right or wrong' had to be, and was, hammered home untiringly – and yet stopped short of universal approval. And yet what held national unity together through thick and thin, carrying it round successive awkward corners, was the continuous might of the sovereign state – the sole force capable in principle, even if not in practice, of assuring joint security and welfare and of resolving conflicts as they arose. The marriage between nation and state (as the largest, most powerful, durable and densely institutionalized modern incarnations of Victor Turner's *communitas* and *societas*) could be in many cases, particularly during periods of courting and through extended honeymoons, a union of love (more correctly, Anthony Giddens's 'confluent love' – mutual attraction prompted by an anticipated satisfaction); but mutual convenience cemented it more solidly than admittedly capricious love ever could.

The new 'imagined communities' are formed against the state, its territoriality, its claims to total sovereignty, its inborn tendency to draw and fortify borders and to impede or arrest border traffic. They situate themselves in the same extraterritorial space into which power, fallen from the weakening hands of states, has flown. They strive to establish themselves in the ongoing battle against state boundaries and the state-promoted right to territorial self-separation. There is some grave symbolic significance in the fact that the terrorist force that took it upon itself to call the bluff of the self-reliance and invulnerability of the most self-reliant and least vulnerable state of the world acted from a territory which has long ceased to be a state, having turned into an incarnation of the void in which global power floats. And similarly symbolic is the ineptitude of the response that mistakes that new, global variety of violence, with its new, global aims and stakes, for the interstate conflict of yore and reduces the 'war against terrorism' to the task of bombing out of existence an already non-existent 'rogue state'.

Having stripped the state of a good deal of its former powers, globalization cast a huge question mark on the benefits the partners may derive from their 'marriage of convenience'. It has become much less clear than before, and certainly has stopped being immediately obvious, what an imagined community may gain (that is, apart from the mostly symbolic trappings of a separate identity, that could also be obtained in many an alternative way) from a be-what-may, till-death-us-do-part union with one and only one political unit. 'Connecting' into a network of global forces may be a risky but also a more promising step to take, offering more opportunity and much wider room for manoeuvre.

In a world of fluid and temporary coalitions (ruled, as Paul Virilio suggested, by the 'aesthetics of disappearance'), durable and un-breakable engagements wrapped into a dense web of institutions portend an uncertainty of fate, rather than security of status. This applies to all unions, as the endemic volatility of engagements renders the convenience for whose sake unions are entered frail and transient. The orthodox union of state and nation has, however, its special reason to lose a good deal of its past allure.

Having 'outsourced' many of its most demanding functions (eco-nomic, cultural, and to a growing extent also social and biopolitical) to manifestly non-political, 'deregulated' market forces, the state has only limited and no more than occasional use for the awesome mobilizing potential thanks to which nations used to be such a wel-come, indeed indispensable companion of the state struggling for legitimation. Most of the remaining functions are performed by selected professional units guarded by restricted entry and official secrets acts. Mass conscription and its necessary accompaniment – the mobilization of popular emotions – are definitely out.

On the other hand, the emaciated sovereignty and waning powers of the state with which it developed in the past a 'special relation-ship' deprive national identity of its privileged position among im-agined communities that could serve as a meeting point for diverse and diffuse interests and as sites of their condensation into political forces. As far as the solidity of institutional foundations is con-cerned, the advantage of the nation over its potential alternatives, such as for instance ethnicities or imagined communities woven of religious, linguistic, cultural, territorial or gender differences, has been considerably reduced.

As an effect of all that, sociology, much like society, its long-time object, even if for different reasons, found itself in a double bind: *it lost its natural(ized) object together with its self-evident client.* As the state abandoned the bid for a monopoly on legitimate coercion, and as the coercion administered by the state lost its privileged place among the many coercions of varying, but essentially contested degrees of legitimacy that operate on the two separate yet recipro-cally dependent battlegrounds of cyberspace and life politics, the identification of 'society' with the nation-state lost much of its past self-evidence. As a matter of fact, so did the identification of 'soci-ety' with any, complex perhaps yet coherent, set of 'structures'. It takes now a lot of imagination-stretching to visualize 'social real-ity' as administered and managed – either by tangible, bodily agen-cies or their shadowy replicas like 'value syndromes' or 'ethos of culture'. Drawing boundaries of self-contained and self-sustained 'totalities' that would make postulating such sets plausible defies imagination.

The world is full.

All similarity to the familiar expression 'full house' is purely fortuitous – a syntax-insinuated fiction. When you see such a notice in front of a cinema or a concert hall, you know that there is no room left here, in this building, now, on this evening; and that you need to make some other plans for where to go and how to spend your time. This 'full house' is, though, just *one small place among many*. And when you read the notice, you stand *outside* the house that is full. There are other buildings you can go to, and if you insist on entering this particular house in front of you, you may be able to do so at some other time.

This is not however the case of a 'full world' – for the simple reason that *il n'y a pas hors du monde*...there is no 'outside', no escape route or place to shelter, no alternative space to isolate and hide in. Nowhere one can claim with any degree of certainty to be *chez soi*, free to follow one's own ways, pursue one's own goals and be oblivious to all the rest as irrelevant. The era that started from building Chinese or Hadrian's walls and ended with the Berlin Wall is over. In this global planetary space, one can no longer draw a boundary behind which one could feel fully and truly secure. And this is final – for today and any other future day one can think of. Every conceivable site one occupies at the moment or may yet move into is *inside* this world and bound to stay there for whatever counts as 'forever'. Of this full world we are all insiders and permanent residents with nowhere else to go.

Of that fullness you know from the inside. That fullness, is not just another item of information. You *feel* that fullness, you *live* it daily, and whatever you do or may yet do, that experience of fullness won't go away. Woe to those who try to forget it or feel conceited enough to trust their power to opt out. The awakening may be devastatingly cruel, just like that morning of 11 September was for those among the New Yorkers who might have believed that things that happened 'out there', on the other side of the well-protected border, did not and would not affect their well-being, that all the pencils needed to draw the boundary between good and bad fortune could be found on this side of the border and that soon the state-of-the-art anti-missile shield would make the sealing of that border complete and foolproof.

'Globalization' is the term commonly used to account for that uncanny experience of the 'world filling up'. With the velocity of transmission (also of action-triggering signals) approaching its limit – the speed of light – the near instantaneity of the cause-and-effect succession transforms even the largest distance into proximity, and in the end puts paid to the cause–effect distinction itself. For all practical intents and purposes, we are all now in the close, indeed intimate vicinity of each other.

Because it involves drawing speed to its limits and reducing distance to an ever more negligible factor in the calculation of action, globalization is unlike any other territorial expansion of the past. As Paul Virilio put it, 'we live in a world no longer based on geographic expanse but on a temporal distance constantly being decreased by our transportation, transmission and tele-action capacities.' 'The new space is speed-space; it is no longer a time-space.'[6] Virilio suggests that speed is no longer a means, but a milieu; one may say that speed is a sort of ethereal substance that saturates the world and into which more and more of action is transferred, acquiring in the process new qualities that only such a substance makes possible – and inescapable. We may say that the most radical novelty brought about by the near liminal speed of action at a distance is not so much the suddenness of arrival/appearance, as the instantaneity of *disappearance* (or even the absence of the actor from the scene of action, the actor's presence *sous rature*, erased – appearance and disappearance, so to speak, rolled into one). The new speed renders the action momentary and thus virtually unpreventable, but also potentially unpunishable. And the mirror reflection of the action's impunity is the potentially unbounded and incurable vulnerability of its objects.

One of the possibly most consequential effects of that new situation is the endemic porosity and frailty of all boundaries, and the inbuilt futility, or at least the irreparably provisional nature and incurable revocability, of all boundary drawing. All boundaries are tenuous, frail and porous. Boundaries share in the new facility of disappearance: they are effaced as they are drawn, leaving behind – as the Cheshire cat its smile – only the (similarly volatile) memory of drawing. Geographical discontinuity no longer matters, as speed-space, enveloping the totality of the globe's surface, brings every place into nearly the same speed-distance from every other and makes all places mutually contiguous.

More than two centuries ago (in 1784) Immanuel Kant, in his *Ideen zu einer allgemeinen Geschichte in weltbürgerlicher Absicht*, recorded a prophetic vision of the world to come: 'die volkommene bürgerliche Vereinigung in der Menschengattung' – a 'perfect unification of the human species through common citizenship'. That would be, Kant noted, the fulfilment of 'was die Natur zur höchsten Absicht hat' – of 'Nature's supreme design'. That must have been, in Kant's view, Nature's design from the start: since the globe we inhabit is a *sphere*, you cannot increase your distance without ultimately cancelling it, the surface of the globe on which we live bars 'infinite dispersion' and in the end we must all be neighbours simply for having nowhere else to go. The surface of the earth is our shared property, none of us has more 'right' to occupy it than any other member of the human species. And so, ultimately, at the time the limits of dispersion make themselves felt, there will be no recourse but to live together and to support each other.

Such a time must finally have arrived, since Kant's philosophical meditations on the future of mankind that for two centuries quietly gathered dust, unread except by a handful of the *Ideengeschichte* experts, have suddenly surfaced back from the depths of oblivion in which they were sunk, bursting right into the centre of political debate. Theorizing the art of living on the surface of a spherical planet might once have been a luxury best indulged in far from the madding crowds, in the secure parochiality of a provincial Königsberg; it is now – as the globe's inhabitants are already learning daily the hard way and the politicians will need in the end, however reluctantly, to realize – the item at the very top of the agenda of human survival.

The *ancien régime* of which Alexis de Tocqueville wrote in the aftermath of the French Revolution was a collection of localities – villages, townships, parishes – from which the ruling dynasty zealously creamed off their surplus product, but in which it otherwise expressed little interest, refraining from the running of their daily affairs and seldom interfering with their self-propagating routines. That regime was replaced with a new kind of power – introducing a law uniform for all to replace a variegated collection of burdens and privileges, intending to level up the differences between regional usages and standards of life, and above all actively interfering in the way the production and distribution of (now seen as *national*) wealth was conducted. We may say that the French Revolution initiated the integration of society on a new supralocal level of the state, now wielding, or struggling to obtain, a power that 'reached the parts which former powers could not and did not wish to reach'; a process that took Europe at least a century to accomplish and other continents a century more.

That effort started by the French Revolutionary governments was the response to the inability of municipalities, guilds and other forms of local government to contain and control powerful economic forces that rose above local level and moved beyond local control – the only control in operation. Entrepreneurs of the time complained and fulminated against 'silly local constraints' that cramped economic initiative and arrested progress – just as today's multinationals complain about 'economically absurd' national attempts to keep watch on, monitor and correct economic activity on national territory. To express their dissatisfaction they used a vocabulary strikingly similar to that known to us from the writings and speeches of the prophets and advocates of the emancipation of global economic forces 'of progress' from the 'retrograde parochiality' of nation-states...

Just as then, the present-day institutions of democratic, political and ethical control, territorially confined and tied to the ground as they are, are no match for increasingly extraterritorial and free-flowing global finance, capital and trade. Just as then, the task now is to create and entrench such institutions of effective political action as can match the size and the power of the already global economic forces and bring them under political scrutiny and ethical supervision. The alternative is the continuing, and deepening of the currently disastrous effects of the 'venture capital' licence: the growing inequality and polarization of the globe, the massive destruction of livelihoods, the impoverishment of entire lands and populations, the revival of tribal sentiments and animosities with all their murderous, often genocidal, consequences.

The brute fact is that – on the planet we all share – many different ways of being human coexist and more still emerge daily out of the 'reconnaissance wars' only to be expected in the 'frontier-land' into which the global 'space of flows' has turned. Unless we decide to exterminate all infidels and manage to achieve our purpose, we can do pretty little to change it. At least in a short run...No shortcuts here, no quick fix of the discomforts born of polyvocality and the clash of good-life models.

In the long run this is an altogether different story. In this globalized world of ours, we all live closer to each other than ever before. We share more aspects of our daily life than ever before. We have the opportunity to know more about each other's customs and preferences than ever before. And since our weapons become ever more

murderous and have already reached the power to destroy the
planet, including the homes of those who invent, produce, market
and launch them – there is more than ever before reasons, for all of
us, to put talking to each other above fighting each other. Let us
take up this unique chance; and I hope that through many a trial
and error we will indeed take it up, once we finally understand, or
be forced to understand by the boomerang effects of our ignorance,
that there is no acceptable substitute for a dialogue.

But to engage in such a dialogue, we all need to feel secure, have
our dignity recognized and our ways of life respected, looked upon
seriously, with the attention they deserve. Above all, we need to feel
that we are all given an equal chance in life and an equal possibility
to enjoy the fruits of our shared achievements. Most of those conditions are either missing or suspected to be missing in that 'new
world disorder' that emerges out of the 'deregulated', one-sided process of globalization. And so there is a temptation to resort to violence rather than negotiate; to wage endless 'reconnaissance wars' in
order to find out how far the 'adversaries' can be pushed back, how
much they can be forced to give away. Fluid conditions, like all
liquids, do not keep their shape for long – and so many people are
tempted to find out how much they can do to reshape them in
their own favour. To frighten the 'adversary' by displaying one's own
superior, or at least nuisance-making force seems to many, and with
good reason, the best way to achieve this effect.

Sooner or later, served daily with the evidence of our interdependence, we will have to realize that no one can claim the earth, or any
part of the earth, as their own indivisible property. In view of our
interdependence, *'solidarity of fate' is not a matter of choice*. What
does depend on our choice is whether that shared fate will end up in
mutual destruction, or generate solidarity of feelings, purposes and
action. Regardless of our diverse, often sharply distinct and sometimes hotly antagonistic political or religious creeds, we all wish to
live in dignity, not to be humiliated, to be free from fear and be
allowed to pursue happiness. This is a wide and solid enough
common ground on which to start building solidarity of thought
and action.

Reforging solidarity of fate into solidarity of purpose and action
is one case in which the verdict of 'there is no alternative', so often
abused in the case of other choices, can be legitimately pronounced.
Either we draw proper conclusions from our global interdependence
and turn it to the benefit of all, or it will turn itself, with our overt
or tacit support, into a catastrophe after which few if any people

will be around to count the merits and demerits of any one of the conflicting ways of life or to quarrel about the differences between civilization and barbarism. *Tertium*, quite simply, *non datur*. The choice, as Hannah Arendt already warned forty years ago, is between solidarity of common humanity and solidarity of mutual destruction. No rhetoric and labelling exercise will chase that choice away.

On this planet, we are all dependent on each other, and nothing that we do or refrain from doing is indifferent to the fate of everyone else. From the ethical point of view, this makes us all responsible for each other. Responsibility 'is there', put firmly in place by the global network of interdependency – whether we recognize its presence or not and whether we take it up or not. Whenever we deny its presence, play down its practical significance or just refuse to be bothered, claiming our impotence, we assume the attitude of 'bystanders': people who see evil and hear evil (as we all, courtesy of the World Wide Web and worldwide television network, do now – and do 'in real time'), sometimes speak of evil, but do nothing at all or not enough to arrest it, to thwart and to frustrate. But in the new frontier-land of the full planet, evil – any instance of evil, wherever it is gestated and whoever may be its intended or 'collateral' victim – affects us all. A global world is a place where, for once, *the desideratum of moral responsibility and the interests of survival coincide and blend*. Globalization is, among other things (perhaps above all), *an ethical challenge*.

Being stuck in the role of a bystander is not a pleasurable condition. Moral scruples are reason enough to be tormented. But at the ever more frequent moments when our mutual dependency and universal frailty and vulnerability are dramatically, shockingly forced into everybody's awareness, another agony is added: that of the humiliating, infuriating awareness of helplessness. Not just ordinary people, admittedly relegated to the care of their private troubles and duly immersed in their private concerns, but those in high offices and in the limelight, leaders and experts meant to attend to the public tasks and to care for the well-being and security of all, are also caught unprepared and confused. They seem to be groping in the dark like the rest of the nation do, finding all trusted routines singularly unfit for the fast changing conditions and desperately seeking new and hopefully more effective stratagems – only to discover that the effects stop far short of the expected and the promised. The more thoughtful among them refrain altogether from promising speedy and watertight solutions, thereby admitting that 'at the top', just like here, 'at the bottom', there is nothing that could match and withstand the enormity of the dangers; that like the rest of us they have been cast in the position of bystanders, and that the skills they have, the strategies they design and the resources they command would not suffice to lift them out of that position and up to the rank of resolute and effective actors.

That agony of personal helplessness, magnified and multiplied by the spectacle of ineffectuality at the top, stems ultimately from the discovery and growing certainty that our ability to act (to act collectively as much as singly or severally) is not on a par with the new planet-wide interdependency/vulnerability of the human species. In that frontier-land that spans the globe and sprawls over the 'extraterritorial territory' of the 'space of flows' high above the familiar world of the law of the land and of the police who are supposed to make sure that such law is observed, *everything may happen but nothing can be done* – at any rate not with any degree of self-assurance and certainty of the results. The other side of the bystander's plight is the horrifying sense of a world that is neither managed nor, as far as one can see, manageable: no divine providence, no cunning of reason, no invisible hand to insert logic in the apparent absurdity and to assure a happy end to the seemingly endless succession of disasters; no sages either who would (or indeed could) take matters in to their hands and send the events rolling on a more palatable, but above all consistently predictable, route. The first, instinctual reaction is to try an escape from this impenetrable wilderness of the 'masterless' world back into the cosy world of stern, but resolute and 'knowing their jobs' managers carrying sovereign territorial powers secure behind their seemingly impermeable borders, or even farther yet into the world of quasi-communal swarms secure in their routinely believed and observed, no-appeal-allowed dogmas. But the way back is cut off – *there are no local solutions to global problems*, however tempting their prospect could feel. While there is no livable 'forward' into which this or that escape strategy could conceivably lead.

Almost two centuries ago, in the midst of the first great secession and from the inside of the frontier-land it spawned, Karl Marx charged with the error of 'utopianism' such advocates of a fairer, equitable and just society as hoped to achieve their purpose through stopping advancing capitalism in its tracks and returning to the starting point: to the premodern world of extended households and family workshops. There was no way back, Marx insisted; and on this point at least history proved him right. Whatever kind of justice and equity stands a chance of taking root in social reality needs to start now, as it needed to then, from where the irreversible transformations have already brought the human condition. This ought to be remembered when the options endemic to the second secession are contemplated.

Retreat from the globalization of human dependency, from the global reach of human technology and economic activities is, in all probability, no longer on the cards. Answers like 'stand the wagons in a circle' or 'back to the tribal (national, communal) tents' wouldn't do. The question is not how to turn back the river of history, but how to fight the pollution of its waters by human misery and how to channel its flow towards a more equitable distribution of the benefits it carries.

There is also another point to remember. Whatever form the postulated global control over global forces may take, it can hardly be a magnified replica of the democratic institutions developed in the first two centuries of modern history. Such democratic institutions have been cut to the measure of the nation-state, then the largest and all-encompassing 'social totality', and are singularly unfit to be inflated to a global volume. Let us recall that the nascent nation-state was not an extension of communal mechanisms either. It was, on the contrary, the end-product of radically novel modes of human togetherness and new forms of social solidarity. Nor was it an outcome of negotiation and a consensus achieved through hard bargaining among local communities. The nation-state that in the end provided the sought-after response to the challenges of the 'first separation' made that response work *in spite* of the die-hard defenders of communal traditions and through *further erosion* of the already shrinking and emaciated local (derisively renamed 'parochial') sovereignties.

An effective response to globalization can only be global. And the fate of such a global response depends on the emergence and entrenchment of a global (as distinct from 'international', or more to the point interstate) political arena. It is such an arena that is today, most conspicuously, missing. The existing global players, and for obvious reasons, are singularly unwilling to set it up. Their ostensible adversaries wishing to draw on the time-honoured but increasingly ineffective art of interstate diplomacy seem to lack the needed ability and indispensable resources. Truly new forces are needed to re-establish and reinvigorate a truly global forum adequate to the globalization era – and they may assert themselves only through bypassing *both* kinds of players.

This seems to be the only certainty – all the rest being a matter of our shared inventiveness and political trial-and-error practice. As Reinhard Kosseleck indefatigably reminds us, the kind of settlement that emerged at the distant end of the long struggle to tame the forces unloosed and running wild was not just unpredictable, but unthinkable – for the lack of adequate concepts. Until they reach the peak, people who climb a mountain pass have no hunch of what lies on the other slope; they cannot even venture to offer a credible description of the landscape on the other side of the crest. In the midst of the first secession, few if any thinkers could envisage the form which the damage-repairing operation would ultimately take. What they were sure of was that some operation of that kind was the paramount imperative of their time. We are all in debt to them for that insight.

And so the top has been torn off or has fallen off from the im-agined/postulated totality which in the past was referred to when-ever the sociologists of the past century used the concept of 'society'. As a result, the orthodox referent of the concept has lost its clearly (institutionally) drawn boundaries. No boundaries, how-ever generously sketched and however ample and resource-rich might have been the part of the globe they circumscribed, contain today the self-sustained and self-perpetuating 'totality' which the kind of society constituted through the sociological narrative was thought to be. But the planetary population as a whole and the globe it shares do not resemble such 'totality' either. The most we can say is that something global in volume but more or less corres-ponding to the sociological idea of 'society' is still *in statu nascendi*, and in a very preliminary stage of that transitory and admittedly open-ended 'state of becoming'. In a concise summary of the pre-sent-day situation, Constantin von Barloewen suggests that the glob-alization of communication and finance goes thus far hand in hand with 'political fragmentation and balkanization' and nation-states 'fast losing their sovereignty as a result of the virtualization of the world economy', with homogenization and differentiation running parallel.[7]

The top fell off – but so did the bottom, and for reasons closely linked. The softened, weakened, increasingly porous shelf of the nation-state does not hold its contents as tightly as it used to. With joyful abandon, the state sheds its past ambitions and cedes the functions it once jealously guarded against extant or budding com-petitors. 'Deregulation' is the motto, 'flexibility' (read: no long-term commitments) the catchword, 'cutting public expense' the substance of the state's vocation. Gone are the tempting images of the 'good society' the state was hoped, and promised, to construe. The buck of happy life has been passed from the state's offices, to stop in the countless individually owned desks and private bedrooms. *The tasks of which modern State Politics (invariably with a capital 'P') was once proclaimed to be in charge have fallen into the domain of life politics.* Even more incongruously than searching for local solutions of globally generated problems, biographical solutions to socially gestated troubles are encouraged to be sought and expected to be found.

Vacated by state politics, the public stage falls an easy prey to life politics. The new electronically operated public scene serves as a magnifying mirror in which life politics, blown up far beyond its naturally confined proportions, fills the whole frame, leaving the rest of the picture out of sight. The pursuit of happiness and meaningful life has become the major preoccupation of life politics, shifting from the construction of a *better tomorrow* to the feverish chase of *a different today*. A chase never grinding to a halt, lasting as long as the succession of days crying out to be made different.

The first part of this book is dedicated to the exploration of the new 'speed-space' – waiting, thus far with mixed (to say the least) success, for the nascent global politics. The second part deals with the setting in which life politics, with similarly mixed success, is conducted. Throughout the book, a third protagonist is obtrusively present, though visible mostly through absence: the void extending between the two spaces. As it happens, this void has been left by the 'disappearing act' of the very space on which sociology, the faithful companion, self-appointed counsellor, scrupulous chronicler and voluble story-teller of modernity in its 'solid' phase, focused its attention and in which for almost two centuries it invested its hopes for a better world, a world more suitable for human habitation. In this black hole, the concerns and the ambitions of sociology, 'solid modern' after the pattern of its object of study and practice, have sunk and vanished.

This does not mean, though, that sociology has completed its course and reached the time to retire. Since the inception of the modern era, sociology tied its fate to the self-assertion of humanity. That prospect remains today as distant as it was at the beginning – though in those heady times the distances between decisions and their fulfilment seemed to be shorter than they do now and the sobering truth that horizons tend to recede faster the quicker you approach them was not yet discovered. We know now that the self-assertion of humanity is not a one-off project, but humanity's way of being-in-the-world. That self-assertion creates its own challenges – more formidable yet with each successive link added to the chain of its (always partial) successes. The challenges posited by the modern era entering its 'liquid' phase are, arguably, the most awesome of all. Or perhaps they seem so awesome since we are only beginning to appreciate their volume and since few if any of the instruments in our toolbox are fit to tackle them.

There are at least two reasons for sociology to acquire an importance of which past generations of sociologists could only dream.

The first is liquid modernity itself. Sociologists always averred, most of the time counterfactually, that this world of ours is 'human made' and so it can, in principle, be remade by humans. At no other time in modern history was that proposition more true than it is today, at a time when melted solids are reluctant to set and petrify, offering, thanks to the perpetual fluidity of shapes, a standing invitation to human ingenuity and good will.

The second is that the only 'settlement' on the cards on our full planet is that of humanity's reconciliation with its own incorrigible diversity. The sole feasible chance of a settlement stands and falls by our acceptance that it is precisely from such diversity that humanity's powers to transcend present horizons and to draw new ones derive, and that whatever form the ultimate settlement may assume, the road to it leads through a coherent effort to reforge the human diversity that is our shared fate into a vocation of human solidarity. As hardly ever before, the self-assertion of humanity (sociology's continuing *raison d'être*) appears, in addition to being one of the noblest ethical dreams, also as the *desideratum* of our survival; and, above all, as despite all odds a *realistic* proposition, and the very next chapter in the unfolding story of humanity.

This book has been conceived as a modest contribution to an inventory of the challenges, rather than as a portfolio of blueprints for the tools to tackle them. Before the right tools are designed, we first need to know the shape of things, the soil on which they sprout, and the conditions in which they incubate. Once we do, the obsoleteness of the means with which we respond to the alarming threats our condition goes on gestating will be more visible, and perhaps easier to repair.

# Part I
# Global Politics

# 1

# Chasing the Elusive Society

Now, as in C. Wright Mills's times, the job of the sociological imagination is a simultaneous reciprocal translation between private and public stories: translation of individually faced and privately tackled problems into public, collectively confronted issues, and of public interests into individually pursued life strategies. Since its inception, the place of sociology has been in the *agora*, that private–public meeting place, where (as Cornelius Castoriadis kept reminding us) the *oikos* and the *ecclesia* come face to face, hoping to make themselves understood to each other through a principled yet benevolent, and above all attentive dialogue.

The raw stuff processed by the sociological imagination is human experience. The end-product of the sociological imagination called 'social reality' is cast of the metal smelted from the ore of experience. Though its chemical substance cannot but reflect the composition of the ore, the product's contents also bear the mark of the smelting process which divides the ore's ingredients into useful product and waste, while its shape depends on the mould (that is, the cognitive frame) into which the melted metal has been poured.

The products of the sociological imagination, imagined social realities, may therefore vary in composition and shape even if the same experience supplies the raw material for the processing. It is not just any social reality, though, that can be melted and moulded from the given ore of human experience; one may expect contemporaneous products, however different they might otherwise be, to carry a 'family resemblance' betraying their common origins. But we can also suppose that once the deposits of a certain kind of ore are depleted and a different type of ore is fed into the furnaces, the smelting techniques would sooner or later be modified and the moulds recast.

I suggest, and I wish to argue, that the roots of the present-day reorientation of sociological inquiry, the shifts in our understanding of the products to be sought and the techniques likely to lead to their finding, are best understood if traced to the seminal change in the common experience of being-in-the-world.

## The managerial imagination

The kind of imagination destined to lead to the 'orthodox consensus' (so dubbed by Anthony Giddens) which still prevailed in most sociological departments a couple of decades ago was triggered and set in motion by the experience of life carried on (to quote Talcott Parsons for a change) inside a 'principally coordinated space'. Following the habit of Minerva's owl, known to spread its wings by the end of the day (that is, not very long before the sun rises on not just another, but a different, day), Parsons summed up the history of social thought as a consistent, even if overly long, vitiated and contorted, effort to crack what he considered to be the principal mystery of all human existence, first hinted at by Hobbes: how come that the actions of *voluntary* actors are nevertheless not random, and that out of the yarn of individually motivated actions regular and lasting *patterns* are woven? As if following Karl Marx's maxim that 'the anatomy of man is the key to the anatomy of the ape', Parsons was also to rewrite the history of sociology as a long pilgrimage towards a preordained destination, namely his own discovery of the 'system' as the desperately sought ultimate and conclusive answer to the Hobbesian query. A 'system' with two strong arms: one (the 'structure') gripping actors from outside and setting limits to their freedom; the other ('culture') reaching into the actors' interior, that place where wishes and purposes are sown and incubate, and kneading free will into a shape which makes the steeliest of structural grips feel like a comfortable, caring embrace.

To that 'system' Parsons imputed a purpose, and that purpose was the system's own survival: staying alive for as long as possible in a form as little changed as possible. Whatever else the system could be ostensibly concerned with, it aimed first of all at its own stability over time. For this purpose, the system 'maintained its pattern' by managing – defusing and neutralizing – the tensions which threatened it. Whatever served this task, whatever helped to preserve the status quo and its immunity to tangential or shearing forces, was 'functional'; whatever contravened the managing efforts, pressed for change and so added tension was 'dysfunctional'. The system was in a good state of health (defined by Parsons as homeostatic 'self-equilibration') if and only if it successfully cultivated the first category of attributes and fought back the second. Structure and culture were the principal contraptions serving the twofold task. They operated differently and used different tools, but converged on the same target. They cooperated and complemented each other in the ongoing war of attrition waged against randomness and contingency, as well as against mutations of the pattern. Both were essentially conservative forces, meant to keep things in a steady shape.

However odd that picture of social reality may seem to us who happen to live in the 'software' rather than 'hardware', 'liquid' rather than 'solid' phase of modernity, it did square rather well with the society imagined after the pattern of an administrative office. In the 'hardware', 'solid' phase of modernity, much of the experiential evidence pushed imagination in that direction. The main pressure to which men and women of that society were likely to be subjected was the requisite of conformity to standards and of following the routines ascribed to the allotted statuses and roles. That kind of society might have had little time and even less sentiment for inherited constraints and shown little restraint in sweeping them out of the way, but it was bent on constructing 'new and improved' constraints of its own and at any rate did not take lightly any *individual* tinkerings with the norms. The borderline between norm-following and deviation was clearly drawn and well guarded. Antiquity of custom might have been devalued as a title to authority, but new routines were brought into being – meant to bind tighter yet, and unlike the dilapidated and putrefied routines they came to replace, bind for a very long time to come. Individual human plants might have been uprooted and forcibly 'disembedded' from the beds in which they had been left to germinate and sprout in the *ancien régime*, but solely in order to be 're-embedded' (and earnestly seek 're-embedment') in the beds laid out in a better planned and rationally designed societal garden.

Modernity was a response to the gradual yet relentless and alarming disintegration of the *ancien régime* with its archipelago of loosely linked and essentially self-reproducing local communities, capped by supralocal powers known for their enormous greed but fairly limited managerial ambitions and capacities. That was, in Ernest Gellner's memorable phrase, a 'dentistry state' – specializing in extraction by torture. By and large, the managerial skills of princes were confined to the creaming off of surplus produce; they stopped well short of intervening in its production.

The 'wealth of the nations' – if that idea cropped up at all – was viewed by the rulers of the premodern state as something one may enjoy or suffer, but should placidly accept in the way one did the other inscrutable verdicts of Providence. It only came to be seen as a task, and so an object of scrutiny, concern, design and action, at the time when the monotonous self-reproduction of the conditions under which goods used to be produced – and above all the solidity of what came to be viewed as the 'social', as distinct from the divine, order – could no longer be relied upon. As Alexis de Tocqueville demonstrated, the *ancien régime* collapsed well before the French revolutionaries boldly went where no one dared to go before, or thought it necessary or rewarding to go – into the heretofore unexplored territory of legislating a new, artificially designed, monitored and administered, man-made order into messy and unwieldy human affairs.

Modernity was born under the sign of such order – order seen as a task, as a matter of rational design, close monitoring and above all pernickety management. Modernity was bent on making the world manageable, and on its daily management; the zeal to manage was whipped up by the not altogether groundless conviction that when left to themselves things will go bust or run amuck. Modernity set about eliminating the accidental and the contingent. If the notorious 'project of modernity' can be adumbrated at all, it can only be envisaged as a retrospective gloss on a firm intention to insert determination in the place where accidents and games of chance would otherwise rule; to make the ambiguous *eindeutig*, the opaque transparent, the spontaneous calculable and the uncertain predictable; to inject the recognition of purpose into things and then make them strive for the attainment of that purpose.

Reflecting, recycling and reprocessing the modern experience, social science, itself a modern invention, set about exploring the mysterious ways in which free will is deployed in the production of regularities, norms and patterns – those 'social facts' of Émile Durkheim: external, coercive, blind to individual tussle and deaf to individual yearnings. In their practical application, so the incipient social science hoped, such findings would be of use in the construction of new and improved regularities, norms and patterns and in making them stick and hold once they had been put in place. Social thought shared with the rest of modern science the urge to 'know nature in order to master it' and so make it more suited to the needs of the human species; in the case of social science though, 'mastering nature' meant primarily mastering the human species itself, and that meant guiding and streamlining the moves of every and any individual member of that species.

I remember being taught social psychology half a century ago mostly by the results of laboratory experiments with rats, in which hungry rats were sent through twisted corridors of a skilfully constructed maze in search of food, while the speed with which they learned, through trial and error, the shortest way to the target was carefully monitored. The less time they took to reach the pellet of food which was their reward, the more successful their learning process, the royal road to survival, was concluded to be. I was lucky to have had sensible teachers and none of them suggested that 'rats are like humans'; but there was tacit agreement among us all, teachers and students alike, that from the rats' behaviour in the maze we could learn a lot about the logic of our own human life in our own maze-like world; not because the rats were 'like humans', but because the maze constructed in the experimenters' laboratory seemed so similar to the world in which we, the humans, searched for, discovered and learned our ways in our daily life. Like the maze, our world seemed to be made of solid, impenetrable and impervious walls that could not be broken through and that would last without change of shape if not forever, then surely for the duration of our learning; like the maze, our world was full of forking paths and crossroads – each one with a single turn that was right but many seductive yet deceptive turns leading to a blank wall or away from the target; as in the laboratory maze, the reward for finding the right passage was, in that world of ours, placed each time in the same spot; learning the way to that spot and then following it with relentless monotony was apparently the sole art that needed to be mastered.

To cut a long story short: the laboratory maze was a miniature replica of the 'big world' of humans; more exactly, of the visualization of that world by the countless humans who experienced it daily. Constructors of the maze were 'within reason', or at least not wide of the mark, when they insisted that whatever goes on in a rat's head cannot be established with any degree of certainty, but that this is only a minor irritant, since the mysterious things called thoughts or emotions can be left out of account without damage to the precision with which the learning process can be measured and the course of streamlining, regularizing and routinizing the learning creatures' behaviour can be modelled. Taking a shortcut from the stimulus to the response might have been dictated by technical necessity, but no harm is done once that shortcut is taken to be the sole thing which counts as the quantifiable relation between 'input' and 'output' – the forces operating 'out there', in the world, and the learners' reactions to such forces.

Émile Durkheim, the advocate of 'external' and coercive 'social facts' as the genuine driving force of individual conduct, and Max Weber, the advocate of an 'understanding sociology' bent on 'explanation at the level of meaning', might have suggested and deployed cognitive strategies in many ways incompatible, but there was an underlying agreement between them on at least one point: individual actors are not good judges of the causes of their own actions, and so their individual judgements are not the stuff of which good sociological accounts of 'social reality' can be made, and are better left out of account. What really makes individuals tick, including their genuine, not self-assessed, motives, is located in the world outside and more often than not eludes their grasp. According to Max Weber:

> In the great majority of cases actual action goes on in a state of inarticulate half-consciousness or actual unconsciousness of its subjective meaning. The actor is more likely to 'be aware' of it in a vague sense than he is to 'know' what he is doing or be explicitly self-conscious about it. In most cases his action is governed by impulse or habit. Only occasionally, and, in the uniform action of large numbers, often only in the case of a few individuals, is the subjective meaning of the action, whether rational or irrational, brought clearly into consciousness...
>
> [I]t is the task of the sociologist to be aware of this motivational situation and to describe and analyse it, even though it has not actually been concretely part of the conscious 'intention' of the actor: possibly not at all, at least not fully.[1]

While according to Durkheim, the representations which we, the ordinary and sociologically unenlightened folks, 'have been able to make in the course of our life' of the 'facts properly so called',

> having been made uncritically and unmethodically, are devoid of scientific value, and must be discarded. The facts of individual psychology themselves have this character and must be seen in this way. For although they are by definition purely mental, our consciousness

of them reveals to us neither their real nature nor their genesis. It allows us to know them up to a certain point... [I]t gives us a confused, fleeting, subjective impression of them, but not clear and scientific notions of explanatory concepts.[2]

Each one of the two great codifiers of the rules by which the game of sociology was to be played for many years to come might have ignored the significance of the other codifier's propositions and failed to acknowledge his participation in the same game, and yet both saw eye to eye when it came to the dismissal of the effectively independent role of individuals as autonomous agents. That dismissal was, after all, what the project of the modern order was about, and the role of sociology, overtly proclaimed or tacitly presumed, was to smooth the way to the implementation of that project in practice. The sociologists' bird's-eye view – external and thereby 'objective' and *wertfrei* – of the springs, causes and effects of individual actions can be seen in retrospect as a theoretical gloss over the managing agencies' treatment of society at large, the whole of society as well as its variously cut-out segments, as *objects of normative regulation and administration*. The strategy of sociological work had to be legislative and monological if the promise to render that work of any use to managerial needs was to be held to – but also to retain its credibility: its reasonable correspondence with daily reiterated lay experience.

The founders of modern sociology had their doubts as to the wisdom of the project they examined and described as social reality. Sometimes, not unlike God who was unsure about the quality of His man-making experiment and uncharacteristically abstained from describing it as good, they were haunted by a dark premonition that something of ultimate value was left out of account once humankind embarked, or had been pushed, on the road on which the ordering/rationalizing zeal had kept it moving ever since. Weber famously agonized about the slow yet relentless erosion of individuality; Durkheim equally famously bewailed the threats to the ethics of solidarity.

Not so, though, the lesser minds who followed the path which the founders, prudently, spattered with warning signs and used intermittently both the bright and the sombre colours of the palette to sketch. The managerial perspective which the founders studied in the fashion of entomologists examining the bizarre ways of an insect species was whole-heartedly embraced by most of their followers and made their own. Paul Lazarsfeld's sole worry was that sociology, presumably because of its youth, was not yet fit to raise human society to the level of reliability and predictability of a machine – the idea which he expressed with exemplary clarity in his 1948 speech to Oslo students (as quoted by Mills):

> [S]ociology is not yet in the stage where it can provide a safe basis for social engineering....It took the natural sciences about 250 years between Galileo and the beginning of the industrial revolution before they had a major effect upon the history of the world. Empirical social research has a history of three or four decades.

For Talcott Parsons, on whose work, in his own conviction, the history of social thought, barring a few regrettable errors and silly deviations, converged with implacable logic, system management was already the essential truth of social reality, and therefore unravelling the secrets of managerial wisdom as embodied in the system's daily works was the prime task of sociological theorizing. In C. Wright Mills's translation from Parsons's notoriously esoteric language into plain English, that wisdom consisted in supplying the system with all the means needed for self-equilibration, that is for remaining steadfastly, come what may, identical with itself:

> There are two major ways by which the social equilibrium is maintained, and by which – should either or both fail – disequilibrium results. The first is 'socialization', all the ways by which the newborn individual is made into a social person...The second is 'social control', by which I mean all the ways of keeping people in line and by which they keep themselves in line. By 'line' of course, I refer to whatever action is typically expected and approved in the social system.[3]

Not everybody among the practising sociologists, to be sure, kept themselves 'in line' with this recipe for sociology as a science and art of 'keeping in line'. Robert S. Lynd, for instance, was deeply annoyed and repelled by the general tone of *American Soldier*, a study celebrated in sociological departments across the US and elsewhere as the pattern for future sociology to emulate:

> These volumes depict science being used with great skill to sort out and to control men for purposes not of their own willing...With such socially extraneous purposes controlling the use of social science, each advance in its use tends to make it an instrument of mass control and thereby a further threat to democracy.[4]

Mills's own verdict left no room for doubt: 'To say that "the real and final aim of human engineering" or of "social science" is to "predict" is to substitute a technocratic slogan for what ought to be a reasoned moral choice.'[5] Of voices of ethical concern there was, indeed, no shortage. They would not by themselves, however, muster a power of conviction strong enough to shift the sociological establishment in its tracks. To give sociology a chance to follow the course suggested by the moral critics' reprimands and exhortations something more needed to happen.

And it did.

## The collapse of social engineering

The last part of the twentieth century happened to be the time of what deserves to be called the 'Great Transformation Mark Two': a departure which took trained sociologists, as much as the sociologically uninitiated, by surprise – and unprepared. Just as most of the members of the sociological profession were busy polishing off the finer details of scientific management masquerading as 'behavioural science', just as they discovered the 'corporatist state', the 'administered society' and the 'Fordist factory' as the shape of things to come, just as they followed Michel Foucault into selecting Jeremy Bentham's Panopticon as *the* prototype and ultimate enbodiment of modern power – social realities started to run wild and flow away from their carefully woven conceptual net, and with fast accelerating speed.

The substance of the current Great Transformation Mark Two is the collapse of 'social engineering' ambitions and agencies willing and able to make them flesh. Before François Lyotard could declare the demise of 'grand metanarratives', the decline of grand models of a predesigned and closely and comprehensively administered 'societal order' had started in earnest; a truly watershed-like shift in social practices began, best captured (with the benefit of hindsight) in Peter Drucker's pithy proclamation of 'no more salvation by society'.

The 'managerial revolution', at its peak when James Burnham discovered it and presented it as (what else?) another historical inevitability, has all but met its own counterrevolution and restoration and gone into reverse. These days the art of management increasingly relies on the refusal to manage and on leaving yesterday's subjects of management to find, as currencies do in the present-day deregulated exchanges, 'their own level'. Domination has now found lighter, less burdening, less awkward and less constraining strategies than continuous and ubiquitous surveillance, meticulous minute-by-minute Taylorist-style regulation and dense nets of sanctions, all calling for bulky administrative offices and the setting of permanent garrisons on the conquered territory. It looks as if the chapter of Panopticon-style rule is about to be closed. Following the lead of 'Fordist' factories and the mass-conscript army barracks, the clumsy, unwieldy, troublesome and above all exceedingly costly panoptical structures are being phased out and dismantled.

It is no longer the job of the managers to keep their subordinates in line and guide their every move; and if it still is their job here and there, it tends to be resented as counterproductive and making no economic sense. It is now up to the subordinates to capture the eye of the superiors, to vie with each other for their attention and to make them wish to *purchase* services which once upon a time the superiors, in their past avatar of bosses, supervisors or foremen, *forced* them to provide. As the Sorbonne economist Daniel Cohen points out, 'there are no more white collars who give orders to blue collars – there are only collars of mixed colours who confront the task they have to resolve.' Not much is left of the managers' management once it is up to the managed to prove their mettle and convince the managers that they won't regret hiring them. Employees have been 'empowered' – the endowment which boils down to bearing responsibility for making themselves relevant and valuable to the company. 'It is no longer the company which supervises its employees. It is now the turn of the employees to demonstrate [their usefulness] to the company.'[6]

This fateful departure has been greeted by many with panegyrics inspired by unqualified enthusiasm. The dissolution of the managerially designed routines has been proclaimed to be a historic act of 'empowerment', the ultimate triumph of individual authenticity and self-assertion which modernity in the first period of its history abominably failed to deliver – turning out instead, and in huge volumes, the obedient and cowardly, dull and conformist mentality of the 'other-directed'. The presently occurring departure might have been everything its worshippers and panegyrists repute it to be – but it also, as Boltanski and Chiapello have explained,[7] portends the end of the security once associated with status, hierarchy, bureaucracy, fixed career tracks and tenure. The void left by security and long-term visions and planning is filled by an accelerating succession of episodic projects, each one in the case of its successful implementation offering not much more than a slightly enhanced chance of 'employability' in other, as yet undisclosed and in principle unadumbrated, but equally short-lived or explicitly fixed-time projects. Projects are blatantly short-term and until-further-notice; and so it is their profusion, their ever growing supply, preferrably excess, that is deemed and hoped to compensate for the lack of durability and secure prospects.

Integration-by-succession-of-short-term-projects needs little, or no control from the top. No one has to force the runners to keep running; as far as the fitness to stay in the race is concerned, the burden of proof has shifted decisively to the runners and to all those who wish to join in the race. Speaking in terms of costs and effects (the sole way of speaking that 'makes economic sense'), no other form of social control is more efficient than the spectre of insecurity hovering over the heads of the controlled. That spectre reminds them of what Ralph Waldo Emerson observed a long time ago – that 'in skating over thin ice, our safety is in our speed.'

The 'new and improved' power relations follow the pattern of the commodity market which put allurement and seduction in the place once occupied by normative regulation and substituted PR for command, and needs creation for surveillance and policing. It is true that the orthodox techniques of power-assisted integration, by and large discarded now as the means of keeping the mainstream on course, go on being deployed in keeping the 'underclass' of the excluded, of those who are blind to seduction and deaf to publicity, or too poor or indolent to properly respond to either, at a distance or in secure confinement and out of mischief. But for most of us the new techniques of power offer an often exhilarating experience of an enhanced freedom to choose and a chance to make choices rational (according to some sociologists quick to recast the new form of domination into social-scientific wisdom, we are now all 'rational choosers' and we have been all along, though like Molière's M. Jourdain we failed to notice in the past). As Ulrich Beck pithily put it, 'how one lives becomes the *biographical solution of systemic contradictions*.'[8]

The new techniques of domination result in an endemic inconclusivity of choices and all too often in their inconsequentiality – so that one choice will not pre-empt other choices that are yet to be confronted, while all choices resent being fitted into a 'whole life' project, which a few decades ago was still perceived as a 'must'. And no wonder they resist, since from the 'system', now deprived of a headquarters with a fixed and permanent address, only diffuse and confusing, controversial and mutually contradictory signals keep coming daily, and in daily growing quantities. A flexible identity, a constant readiness to change and the ability to change at short notice, and an absence of commitments of the 'till death us do part' style, rather than conformity to rough-and-ready standards and staunch loyalty to ways once selected, appear to be the least risky of conceivable life strategies.

These are indeed profound changes; social reality is no longer as it used to be at the time when the founding fathers of sociology set about cracking the mystery of society disguised as human fate; and not as it used to be for a while later, when George Orwell and Aldous Huxley penned down the nightmares of their times, the first of a bare-faced totalitarianism, and the second of a totalitarianism masquerading as a universal obligation of strictly rationed happiness; and not even as it appeared later still to Hannah Arendt, who ascribed to modern society an endemic totalitarian tendency, or Michel Foucault who picked Bentham's Panopticon as the key to understanding the clockwork of social reality. And so life is not as it used to be for its users in those now largely bygone times. The context of human life and the meaning of a reasonable life strategy have changed; but will sociology, dedicated to the study of that context and that strategy, follow suit?

There is no certainty that it will; and still less is it sure that it must. But in as far as sociology remains an ongoing commentary on human experience, the profound shift in the composition of that experience prompted by the departures signalled above needs to find sooner or later its reflection in sociological concerns and strategies.

Life challenges, life tasks and life pursuits tend to assume today a colour and shape quite different from those they bore half a century ago. They used to be, essentially, responses to the order-design and order-building-and-maintenance concerns of power. They are today, again essentially, responses to the fading and demise of such concerns. They can be understood and so become amenable to genuine conversation only if they are put in the context in which they belong – that of the retreat of the agencies striving to substitute predesigned and ready-made routines for individual choices, and the steady pressure to seek and adopt biographical solutions to the unpredictability, incoherence, and often inanity of a socially constructed condition constantly 'on the move'.

Of what needs to be done to re-establish and reinvigorate the link between sociological work and the social agenda, we may take a clue from Franz Rosenzweig, one of the more insightful yet less often read modern thinkers, who suggested many years ago a sharp distinction, indeed, an opposition, between 'logical' and 'grammatical' modes of thinking, both firmly entrenched in the practice of intellectual work.

The first, 'logical' mode 'means thinking for no one else and speaking to no one else'[9] – and so enjoys a good deal of independence from those it thinks about. This mode, we may comment, is a tempting option, since it offers a welcome shelter from the confusion with which the messy life of the hoi polloi is fraught, and the risks and anxieties to which any engagement with that life may lead – while the high and mighty are likely to lend a sympathetic ear to a thought that thrives on the hoi polloi's silence and does nothing to make them audible. This kind of thinking has been in Rosenzweig's view a dominant feature of the extant academic philosophy, a symptom of 'apoplexia philosophica'[10] which secured for that philosophy an astonishing longevity but also rendered it totally irrelevant to human life. Let me add that much of orthodox sociology can be, with little distortion, and particularly in its current 'zombie', posthumous phase, put fairly and squarely in the same category.

The second, 'grammatical thinking', is described by Rosenzweig as having a structure akin to speech:

> 'Speaking' means speaking to someone and thinking for someone. And this someone is always a quite definite someone, and he has not merely ears...but also a mouth...Speech is bound by time and nourished by time and it neither can nor wants to abandon this element. It does not know in advance just where it will end. It takes its cues from others. In fact, it lives by virtue of another's life, whether this other is the one who listens to a story, answers in the course of a dialogue, or joins in a chorus...In actual conversations something happens.[11]

## Surfing the network

In an interview conducted a decade ago, Ed MacCracken of the Silicon Graphics company spelled out some basic assumptions on which a new business philosophy, in his view badly overdue and so urgently needed, needs to be built:

> The key to achieving competitive advantage isn't reacting to chaos: it's producing that chaos...Our feeling is that this rapid, chaotic rate of change will continue forever and will continue to accelerate... Irreverence is important in a highly creative environment...Fun and

irreverence also make change less scary...For example, we recently replaced two old divisions with five new ones. We brought a New Orleans band and held a wake on our Mountain View campus. We filled two coffins with paraphernalia from each division and then buried them. This ceremony reinforced our philosophy that we must view life as it is and how it might be rather than how it was.[12]

Norman Augustine was summing up the strategy already followed by the most successful business companies and aimed at by all the rest when he suggested that 'the most important lesson became self-evident: there are only two kinds of companies – those who are changing and those who are going out of business.'[13] Change has become a must and its own purpose, needing no other justification. As Richard Sennett noted as the case in contemporary America, 'perfectly viable businesses are gutted or abandoned, capable employees are set adrift rather than rewarded, simply because the organization must prove to the market that it is capable of change.'[14] Staying put invites disaster – and so does, by implication, the intention to capitalize on past achievements instead of running after new ones, to stick to the forms and methods of action that proved effective in the past but are of no more use, to entrench and fortify what has been gained and proved profitable. Transience and inbuilt obsoleteness turn into assets, certainly the source of instant and short-term gains – but short-term gains are the only gains that count in a world no longer ruled by norms which have any more than a sporting chance of outlasting the actions that abide by them.

In the short term, asset-stripping makes 'more economic sense' than asset-building; taking apart what was there before is more expedient and promises more profit than the laborious job of putting things together. Andrei Schleifer and Larry Summers explained how that comes about:[15] during corporate takeovers, mergers and reshuffles, 'outsourcing', 're-engineering' and 'rationalizing' bouts, profits are derived from breaches of contract – from getting rid of costly commitments like old and highly paid staff, liquidizing local investments while leaving hosts of less resourceful 'stakeholders' in the lurch, in short, from taking money and running away. Breaching contract is in the short term a highly profitable step to take for the powerful – those mobile, volatile and versatile enough to take it. (George W. Bush, one of most business-attuned presidents in American history, has recently applied this tactics to state politics as well.) But because such steps are being taken, and because the 'stakeholders' know only too well that they may be taken at any place and time and without warning, confidence – that adhesive which holds together the known present and imagined futures, the substance which cements scattered actions into long-term trajectories – that trust is waning. Entering long-term commitments, just like relying on other people's long-term commitments, acquires more trappings of irrational conduct as it ever more spectacularly jars with the evidence of day-to-day experience. On the other hand, friability of contracts, volatility of commitments and temporariness of engagements look increasingly like 'rational choices'. Aided and abetted by rational actors, they become self-propelling and self-accelerating.

The frames for life projects, that experiential stuff of which images of 'society' as lasting and solid totality used to be woven, turn brittle and fragile; however useful at the moment, cognitive frames can no longer be reasonably assumed to outlast concerns with the tasks-at-hand. The fragility of frames becomes, in its turn, the experiential premise of what François Dubet dubbed the 'disappearance of society'.[16] Whatever 'totality' is imagined instead is (as Boltanski and Chiapello suggest) composed solely of the mosaic of individual destinies, meeting in passing for a brief moment only, and solely in order to drift away again on their separate ways, with enhanced vigour, a moment later.

Using Gary Becker's distinction between the types of 'capital' which individuals, cast adrift, can count on to keep themselves seaworthy, and adding to Becker's 'general' and 'specific' human capital a third, 'biographic' capital, Daniel Cohen points to the daunting inadequacy of all three:

> Working in the Fordist factory of old, a worker is always a worker ('providing he does not drink', as Ford said), whatever trajectory he follows. In the world starting today, the risk of 'losing everything' is permanent. The high-class professional, owner of 'unique' knowledge, may brutally descend into incompetence with the appearance of a new technology; a 'specific' worker is, by definition, one that risks everything in case his company goes bankrupt or decides to make its employees redundant. Finally, the third kind of capital, collected in the course of individual life, can be lost when the workers are permanently excluded from the labour market and fall into the vicious circle of poverty and desocialization.[17]

Having examined a long series of declarations of faith made on various occasions by contemporary business leaders, and using gods of Greek mythology as metaphorical headings for their classification, Hatch, Kostera and Koźminski suggest that Hermes – 'the archetype of decentralized communication and change as a positive value'[18] – is the most common type among the emergent business elite. Nigel Thrift confirms this finding when noticing the remarkable change in vocabulary and cognitive frame which marks the new, predominantly global and exterritorial, business elite.[19] To convey the gist of their own actions, they use metaphors of 'dancing' or 'surfing'; they no longer speak of 'engineering', but instead of cultures and networks, teams and coalitions, and of influences rather than of control, leadership and management. They are after looser forms of organization, such as can be put together, dismantled and reassembled at short notice or without notice. It is this sort of fluid, endemically unstable form of assembly which best fits their view of the surrounding world as 'multiple, complex, and fast-moving, and therefore "ambiguous", "fuzzy" and "plastic"', 'uncertain, paradoxical, even chaotic'.

Today's business organization has an element of dis-organization deliberately built into it: the less solid and the more fluid it is the better. Like everything else in the world, any sort of knowledge, skills and know-how cannot but age quickly; and so it is the 'refusal to accept established knowledge', the unwillingness to go by precedents and to recognize the wisdom of accumulated experience that tend to be seen now as precepts of one-upmanship in the ongoing race for effectiveness and productivity.

Boltanski and Chiapello suggest that 'savoir-faire' – know-how, the acquired skills of doing things – is being gradually but relentlessly displaced by 'savoir-être' as the quality most valued among present and aspiring members of the business elite. 'Savoir-être' is turning into the decisive factor of recognition, promotion and enrichment. 'Savoir-être', knowing how to move in the world, means more than anything else the quality of being well connected, capable of communicating easily, and having a wide circle of similarly well-connected people with whom to communicate. One may say that to 'know how to be' is to develop an expanding network of communication with oneself at the centre, or better still to position oneself at the interface or crossing point of a great number of networks. Multiplying the links while refusing to accord preference to any of them, let alone grant to any of them one's own exclusive commitment – this seems to be the strategy most likely to lift its practitioner to the top. Living in a network, moving through the network, shifting from one network to another and back with growing speed and facility, travelling light and being constantly on the move – all this means to be and to stay at the top. The passage from 'savoir-faire' to 'savoir-être' boils down, in other words, to putting the accent on polyvalence, on flexibility of employment, on the ability to learn and to adapt to new functions rather than on the possession of skills and acquired qualification, on the capacity to gain trust, to communicate, to 'relate'...[20]

This shift in emphasis and the associated revaluation of values is according to Boltanski and Chiapello a manifestation of 'the new spirit of capitalism' which finds its fullest expression in the lifestyle of the emergent global business elite. But the other part of the global elite, worldwide academia and the culture industry, follow closely. As Richard Rorty caustically observed: 'Platoons of vital young entrepreneurs fill the front cabins of transoceanic jets, while the back cabins are weighted down with paunchy professors like myself, zipping off to interdisciplinary conferences held in pleasant places.' But, he adds, 'this newly-acquired cultural cosmopolitanism is limited to the richest twenty-five per cent of Americans.'[21]

It is this kind of life experience, shared by the 'richest', or rather the best connected, most at home in the web of global communication and most mobile 25 per cent of Americans and a somewhat smaller percentage of Europeans, which is processed by new sociology into the new image of social reality and recycled into a new strategy of sociological vocation. The new elite's experience of lightness, detachment, hovering, leapfrogging, prancing, surfing and gliding needs a new conceptual net to catch it; such a new language has not been slow in being coined. Pierre Bourdieu and Loïc Wacquant, in a scornful critique of some of the most influential among the current sociological fashions, called that 'newspeak' resorted to by all sectors of the global elite 'la nouvelle vulgate planétaire'.[22] Among many conceptual keys once deployed by sociology to open up hidden compartments of human experience but now falling out of use, diagnosed as too rusty or re-evaluated retrospectively as having been unfit from the start, 'society' is the first term of the sociological vocabulary to be scoffed at and to go, to be replaced by 'network'.

## Society? Difficult to imagine

Few of our contemporaries remember that when it first appeared in the language of the emerging science of sociology, 'society' was a metaphor, and selective as all metaphors are, laying bare certain features of the object to which it was applied while assigning a lesser importance to its other traits. From those parts or aspects of the world to which the sociologists assigned topical relevance and which they set to explore, the metaphor of society drew to the surface and made salient the quality of being a 'company'. According to the *OED*, 'fellowship, companionship', 'association with one's fellow men, esp. in a friendly or intimate manner' are the oldest meaning of the word 'society'. Some other meanings, all preceding the adoption of the term by sociology, were those of 'a number of persons associated together by some common interest or purpose', first recorded in 1548, of 'the state or condition of living in association, company or intercourse with others of the same species' 'adopted by a body of individuals for the purpose of harmonious coexistence or for mutual benefit, defence, etc.' (1553), of 'a corporate body of persons having a definite place of residence' (1588) and 'the aggregate of persons living together in a more or less ordered community' (1639).

There is a common denominator to all such primordial and presociological uses of the word 'society'. All of them, explicitly or implicitly, conveyed images of closeness, proximity, togetherness, a degree of intimacy and mutual engagement. 'Society' could be used as a metaphor because the kind of experience which the sociologists struggled to grasp and articulate was that of a number of people sharing the same place, interacting in many if not all of their activities, meeting each other often and talking to each other on many occasions. Being united in such a way, that quantity of people faced the prospect of living in close proximity to each other for a long time to come – and for that reason the unity of life-setting was capped by the effort to close ranks, to make the coexistence 'harmonious', 'orderly', so that 'mutual benefits', benefits for all involved, might follow.

The choice of metaphors to be used in the narratives of human experience was then, as it is now, the job performed by the thinking and articulate few, and it has always been the *experience of that chosen category* which prompted the articulation, while simultaneously supplying the looking-glass through which experiences of other humans, the human experience as such, was to be examined. Having that in mind, we may say that for the thinking elite of the early modern era the choice of 'society' as a metaphor made a lot of sense. It chimed well with what they knew and felt; the kind of 'sociological imagination' it triggered stayed close to their daily experience.

That was, after all, the time of 'solid modernity', of building tough frames and enclosures meant to last, of integration and unification: of fastening together dispersed workshops into factories, of welding archipelagoes of scattered communal islands into the compact continents of nation-states, of cementing diffuse and variegated dialects, customs and ways of life into one nation of one language, purpose, and government. However split, at odds with each other, antagonistic and quarrelsome the various parts of the new wholes might have been – togetherness, companionship, interaction were the order of the day, as was the awareness of being doomed to share company for a long time to come and the 'we will meet again' feeling. Such parts of the elite as practised *vita contemplativa* as much as their brothers-in-arms dedicated to *vita activa* faced the same predicament, the same destiny and the same prospects: namely, the present and future engagement with the rest of the people enclosed within the boundaries of the nation-state. 'Being in each other's company' was their joint fate, which it would be better to reforge into a joint vocation. Policing social order nationally or locally – the task of political and economic managers – and the cultivation of patriotic or republican sentiments – the task of thinkers reflecting on the task of the managers – were aspects of the same engagement. And the metaphor of 'society' was an insight into the experience of engagement.

Admittedly, society was from the start an 'imagined entity'. But when Benedict Anderson, to the universal joy and acclaim of social science practitioners, coined the concept of 'imagined community', he followed, as most of us do most of the time, the habits of Minerva's owl. The concept was born just when the object it named was about to dissolve in sunset twilights. 'Society' could grip the human imagination because it did not know it was imaginary, and could continue to do so as long as there were no reasons to discover that it was, or to embrace that truth if it happened to be suggested. Society spent most of its life in the garb of *reality*.

This is, anyway, how Émile Durkheim, writing *Les règles de la méthode sociologique* at the threshold of the now bygone century, could still unpack in good conscience the meaning of 'society' while counting on the comprehension and approval of his fellow society members. 'Society' was reality, full stop – and it was easy to argue and demonstrate that it did not differ in any important respect from other objects which we consider real on account of the fact that we can neither wish them away nor try to break through the space they occupy without bruising heads or knees. Reality, Durkheim pointed out, 'is to be recognized by the power of external coercion which it exercises or is capable of exercising over individuals', and that power can be sensed in its turn in the 'existence of some definite sanctions or by the resistance offered against every individual act that tends to contravene it'. In short, you know reality when you see it, and you know it by the pain you suffer, pain caused by its 'imperative and coercive power'.[23] Durkheim did not, and had no reason to, entertain any doubt that the hard proof of society's reality is all on the plate of our shared daily experience. It was that experience that taught each and every human that society is real – sociologists were there only to put that lesson in words and set exam papers.

Metaphors help imagination. And so did the metaphor of 'society'. Without it, imagination would spill all over the vast expanses of anything but cohesive and consistent human experience, desperately seeking a common estuary yet unable to find it. Though imagination hovers above the level of daily experience, it is the images made familiar through that experience which allow us to play the game of reading shapes into the clouds and constellations in the night sky. The reality of society was to Durkheim an *empirical fact*. In his time, it was easy to extrapolate the reality of society from the evidence abundantly supplied by everybody's experience. The kind of experience which supplied the proofs that were most convincing and least contentious was that of coercive power. It was that widespread sense of coercive power constraining individual freedom that set imagination on the move and prompted it to gestate a credible image of a forceful entity that made sense of the experience which started the whole process.

And yet the 'coercive power' on which Durkheim focused his argument was not the only experience that lent credibility to 'imagined totality'. There were others, whose role in prompting and guiding imagination became more protruding in the course of the century and particularly salient as the century ran to its close – together with the experiences which squared well with the image of a cohesive, coherent, 'aware of what it was doing', sense-giving totality at the top. The image of society drew its credibility from the experience of coercive constraint – but also from the sense of collective insurance against individual misfortune, brought about by the establishment of collectively sustained welfare provisions, and above all from the sense of the solidity and continuity of shared social institutions endowed with a life expectation long enough to dwarf the time stretches in which individual life-projects – whole-life projects – were accommodated. All imagination-feeding experiences seemed to lead in the same direction; they converged on the legislating-executive-juridical powers of the state, and it was easy to tie them together in the image of 'society' as 'a whole that is greater than the sum of its parts', a company with wisdom, reason and a purpose of its own and certain to outlast the lifespan of any of its individual members.

The point is, though, that all three types of experience – of consistent normative pressure, of protection against the vagaries of individual fate, and of the majestic longevity of a collectively controlled order – began to fade fast in the last decades of the twentieth century, and to be replaced by another experience, which no longer suggested a 'company', but rather (to borrow Keith Tester's description) a world that was 'separated from individuals', a world that 'has experientially become increasingly like a seamless web of overlapping institutions with an independent existence'[24] – but, let me add, an existence with an undefined life expectation, all too often brief and always 'until further notice'. The 'we will meet tomorrow' feeling, the sense of consistency and continuity suggesting a thinking, acting, quarrelling yet cooperating company cemented by a shared purpose and joint planning, has all but vanished from experience. And short of that feeling, experience can hardly lead imagination to the vision of 'society' in the sense which sociology kept implying over the last hundred years at least, or render that vision credible if it is offered now as a warrant of life logic.

The most common, intense and absorbing experience, the experience most likely to supply the raw material for world-imaging, is that of the consumer: an experience of life as a series of consumer choices made in response to the attractions put on display by competing shopping malls, television channels and websites; but also in public places and inside private abodes increasingly shaped, but above all perceived and 'made sense of', after their pattern.

Harvie Ferguson made an inventory of the context-related impressions likely to be obtained by visitors to any cathedral or chapel of consumption.[25] The multitude of shops and the orgy of commodities vying for attention 'rather than appearing exhaustive, offer a continuously changing point of contact, with the ideally infinite, and therefore uncontainable, commodity world behind it'. 'Any actual display of goods', however, 'can be no more than an arbitrary sample from an ideal set of infinite possibilities.' The set itself is bound to elude vision forever and remain unfathomable – stretching infinitely beyond the reach and defying the powers of imagination. The idea of a 'totality' – not to mention a 'compact totality', a 'whole' – is the last thing that the incurably partial and random sample of the set within vision would suggest. And finally: 'like dreaming, objects are lightly taken up and cast off. None has lasting value.' Objects are to be used as long as, but no longer than, their power to satisfy is untapped or at least not fully exhausted: each object carries a 'use by' date from the start. No permanent link is thereby likely to be built between the object and its user. In the end, 'it does not matter which commodity is chosen' – objects are but samples of a set that cannot and would not ever be embraced in full. And the activity of sampling gains, not loses, from being random.

I have dwelt on the consumer experience, but I do not suggest that this is the *only* contemporary life-lesson that makes 'society' into an unfitting metaphor for the imagined totality meant to tie together the various strands of human being-in-the-world. On the contrary, the power of consumer experience over the imagination is so overwhelming because of the corroboration it receives daily from all other aspects of individualized life: most significantly, from the accumulating evidence of the impotence of the state, that executive organ of society, to shape and monitor the setting in which individual life is conducted and individual problems are expected to be tackled and resolved; from the Houdini-style conduct of managers eager to download off and away the risks of choice-taking and the burden of responsibility for the results; and from the daily reiterated spectacle of vanishing acts performed by familiar signposts, landmarks and orientation points which used to mark life's itineraries and allowed life projects to be plotted.

Imagination has been often censured for its flights of fancy, and imagining a stable core of society behind the flux of apparently unconnected experiences is still conceivable; particularly if the image of 'society' is firmly settled in the vernacular, remains an integral part of an inherited world-image and a powerful presence in collective memory. That image, however, survives mostly thanks to the inertia of the widely shared cognitive frame; unlike in the relatively recent past, it is no longer reinvigorated by fresh evidence. Current experience prompts imagination in a different direction.

The currently 'lived through' experience would rather suggest that the realities of the human world ought to be visualized after the pattern of the late medieval God construed by the Franciscans (particularly the Fratricelli, their 'Minor Brothers' faction) and the Nominalists (most famously, William of Ockham). In Michael Allen Gillespie's summary, that Franciscan/Nominalist God was 'capricious, fearsome in His power, unknowable, unpredictable, unconstrained by nature and reason and indifferent to good and evil.'[26] Above all, He stayed steadfastly beyond the reach of human intellectual powers and pragmatic abilities. Nothing could be gained by efforts to force God's hand – and since all attempts to do so were bound to be vain and only bore testimony to human conceit, they were both sinful and unworthy to be tried. God owed nothing to humans. Having put them on their feet and told them to seek their own ways, He retreated and retired – and even if not in so many words, declared His indifference to human affairs.

In the essay 'Dignity of Man', Giovanni Pico della Mirandola, the great codifier of the Renaissance's self-confident and ebullient ambitions, drew the sole conclusions that could sensibly be drawn from God's retreat. God, he concluded, made man

> as a creature of undetermined nature, and placing him in the middle of the universe, said this to him: 'Neither an established place, nor a form belonging to you alone, nor any special function have We given to you, O Adam, and that for this reason that you may have and possess, according to your desire and judgment, whatever place, whatever form, and whatever function you shall desire... You, who are confined by no limits, shall determine for yourself your own nature...[27]

It is society's turn now to follow the example of the Franciscan/ Nominalist God and to retire. Peter Drucker, that William of Ockham and Pico della Mirandola of the 'liquid modern' era rolled into one, summed up the new wisdom, in keeping with the spirit of the age, in a sound-bite: 'No more salvation by society.' It is now up to human *individuals* to make the case 'according to their desire and judgment', to prove that case and to defend it against the promoters of other cases. There is no point in invoking the verdicts of society (the last of the superhuman authorities to which the modern ear agreed to listen) in order to support one's case: first, the invocation won't be believed since the verdicts – if there are any – are unknown and bound to stay unknown; secondly, the sole thing one can be pretty sure of about society's verdicts is that they would never hold for long and that there is no knowing which way they would turn next; and thirdly, like the God of late medieval times, society is 'indifferent to good and evil'. The retreat of society, like the retreat of God several centuries before, ushered in a time of, simultaneously, cognitive ignorance and ethical doubt.

Deus turned *absconditus* triggered the Pyrrhonian crisis of the sixteenth to seventeenth centuries. *Societas* turned *abscondita* is triggering the Pyrrhonian crisis Mark Two – of the late twentieth and early (?) twenty-first centuries.

## Will the dead rise?

Some gods in the past are known to have been resurrected. The question is, can society perform (or be performed on) a similar miracle?

Unlike the resurrection of gods which is the subject-matter of theology, the prospect of the resurrection of society as a credibly imagined totality is a sociological matter. That prospect translates into a thoroughly sociological question: can individual experience be reborn as fit (and prone) to be reprocessed into the image of society, and what kinds of social conditions must be met for that to happen?

For all we the ordinary and sociologically undrilled people know, we are still as before 'in a company'. The world into which our individual life trajectories are woven is densely packed. Indeed, at no time before were we made daily so aware of the co-presence of such enormous numbers of others: the streets we walk or drive through are crowded, but the screens of the TVs we watch and the computers we use to surf cyberspace are even more so. Physical distance no longer matters: no part of the human race, however remote, is barred access to our experience.

But there are some other things – which we, as long as we stay undrilled sociologically, *do not know* and which we cannot gather from what we experience. Since we hear occasionally that what other people do and what happens to them somehow affect the life we live and the chances of living life the way we would like it to be lived, we guess that we may be travelling, all of us, on board the same superjumbo jet; what we do not know is who – if anybody – is sitting in the pilot's cabin. For all we know, the cabin may be empty and the reassuring messages flowing from PA speakers may be messages which have been recorded at an unknown time in places we would never see by people we would never meet. We can hardly put our trust in the impersonal wisdom of automatic pilots, because time and again we hear and watch yet more disturbing news: that people sitting in traffic-control towers have failed to control, and added to the chaos instead of guarding order. We cannot therefore be sure about the airport to which we are heading – and even less about the one at which we will eventually land. Last though not least, we have not the slightest idea what people like us, the passengers of a superjumbo jet, can do singly or severally to influence, change or improve all that, especially the course of the aircraft in which we are all locked...

This seems to be the crux of the problem – indeed the critical point around which the chances of society's rebirth rotate. What seems to be gone (whether forever or for the time being, remains to be seen) is the image of society as the 'common property' of its members, which at least in principle can be conceivably tended to, run and managed in common; the belief that what each member does or refrains from doing, matters – to the society as a whole and to all of its other members; and the confidence that 'we can do it' – we can do jointly what we jointly think can be done, see it through and watch the results; and the conviction that doing it or not doing it makes a difference, the sole difference that truly counts.

Such images and beliefs and that confidence once rested on the 'mutual fit' between ends and means, problems and the powers required for their resolution. 'Society' armed with the resources of the nation-state could balance the books and provide the measure of security its members needed to exercise their freedom. This, however, does not seem to be the case any more in our fast globalizing world in which power is being evacuated from politics and the most crucial factors shaping the conditions under which individuals conduct their lives are no longer controlled or even held in check by the only agencies of collective action discovered or invented in the history of modern democracy.

The paradox of rising individual freedoms coupled with a deepening sense of public impotence is not exactly new. Many years ago Max Horkheimer was alarmed by 'the helplessness of men before the opaque whole which they keep in existence', which he linked to the junction of the 'continuing irrationality of society' and the poor state of knowledge at our disposal.[28] And he insisted that making the intellectual and situational grounds of historical action 'a topic of study and debate rather than taking them for granted or repressing them into silence' is a necessary condition of 'self-conscious history' – that is, of the recovery of the collective 'public powers' currently missing. The kind of critical reflection which Horkheimer considered to be the means to that end would be itself 'a part of the development of society'.

The separation between individual and society in virtue of which the individual accepts as natural the limits prescribed for his activity is

relativized in critical theory. The latter considers the overall framework which is conditioned by the blind interaction of individual activities...to be a function which originates in human action and
therefore is a possible object of planful decision and rational determination of goals.[29]

The problem is hardly new, then. What seems to be new is the
question of an agency capable of implementing whatever goals
might have been 'rationally determined' and so rendering that 'rational determination' a worthy and sensible, and therefore attractive, proposition. The gradual dissipating of society as such an
'imagined agency', prompted by the experience of a growing gap
between the globality of power and the locality of politics, between
the magnitude of problems and the limitation of the instruments of
action needed to confront and resolve them, is today a most vexing
obstacle to the 'rational determination of goals' and a major contemporary source of the widespread sense of 'public impotence'.

As I tried to argue in *In Search of Politics* and in *Liquid Modernity*, the sense of impotence and the further desertion of the *agora*,
that birthplace and home ground of an effective agency of collective
action and the site where private problems and public issues could
meet and engage in a dialogue, are linked in a vicious circle: the two
phenomena feed and reinforce each other. The less ground there is
to believe that society may change anything that matters in the
plight of the individuals, the less reason there will be to reinvigorate
the *agora*; and the more inexpedient and unenterprising the *agora*,
the more credible the belief that little can be gained from attending
to its health. Weakness of agency tends to be self-perpetuating and
self-exacerbating – and arguably the greatest challenge that con-
fronts sociology at the threshold of the twenty-first century.

I anticipate a question: is there a way back to a self-confident,
lively *agora*, or rather a way forward to a new-style *agora* large
enough to accommodate the enormity of tasks and responsibilities
incubated in a 'company' stretched to the size of the planet? Well, in
lieu of an answer I can only quote after Hannah Arendt – that
supreme practitioner of the kind of *vita contemplativa* endemically
pregnant with *vita activa* – the words which she herself quoted, with
her whole-hearted approval, from Gotthold Ephraim Lessing, one of
her spiritual heroes:

I am not duty-bound to resolve the difficulties I create. May my ideas
always be somewhat disjunct, or even appear to contradict one an-

other, if only they are ideas in which readers will find material that stirs them to think for themselves.

And I can quote Hannah Arendt's own words that come closest to grasping her own personal credo, one that I share:

[E]ven in the darkest of times we have the right to expect some illumination [that] may well come less from theories and concepts than from the uncertain, flickering, and often weak light that some men and women, in their lives and their works, will kindle under almost all circumstances and shed over the time span that was given to them on earth.[30]

# 2

# The Great Separation
# Mark Two

## Aristotelian meditations

How to read Aristotle's *Politics* in a society so unlike the one in which the thoughts this seminal book contains were conceived? This is, admittedly, a moot question.

There are more than enough grounds to reject Aristotle's *Politics* offhand as hopelessly out of date and jarringly at odds with almost all the values that contemporary politics is expected to promote (like, for instance, equality for women, individual freedom, or universality of human rights). It is easy to collect arguments for rejection by quoting sentences entrenched in a totally alien mentality that clashes violently and uncompromisingly with our own *doxa* – that subliminal knowledge, the foundation stone of perception sunk so deep that it seldom if ever rises to the threshold of attention; those thoughts we do not think *about*, but *with*. Consider, for instance, the following: 'Those . . . who are as much inferior to others as are the body to the soul and beasts to men, are by nature slaves, and benefit, like all inferiors, from living under the rule of a master.' Or: 'a man's fortitude is shown in ruling, a woman's in obeying.'[1] These two sentences (and there are many others like them) would suffice to consign Aristotle's *magnum opus* to where it belongs – to bygone ages – and keep it there, leaving it to the exclusive interest of historians, ethnographers and collectors of curiosities.

This is not the only way to read Aristotle, though. Aristotle was not a science-fiction writer, but an acute observer with an exquisitely sharp eye and a diligent recorder of realities with an exquisitely sharp pen. He can be hardly blamed for being unaware of things we know and for perceiving as 'natural' other forms of human life than we do. He did not, and could not stand above the social realities of his time. But he did himself stand out from his contemporaries by piercing through the timebound accidentals and reaching to some permanent, extemporal attributes of human being-in-the-world. Nothing has happened since Aristotle, neither in our experience of the world nor in our story-telling of that experience, that would invalidate his blunt verdict that 'a man who cannot live in society, or who has no need to do so because he is self-sufficient, is either a beast or a god.'[2] Some aspects of human existence are apparently immune to the labour of time, and Aristotle was a grand master of the art of spotting them and articulating them into a kind of 'prolegomena to all future sociology'.

Aristotle's insights into the universal, timeproof, *sine qua non*, indeed transcendental conditions of human togetherness have withstood the test of time in an exemplary fashion. Not, though, because all known forms of human togetherness have risen to their challenge, met and fulfilled the conditions; but because throughout human history those insights have hardly ever ceased to haunt and nag at and prompt human imagination; and so they went on preventing any form of human togetherness from setting itself as the limit of human possibilities and ossifying into an ultimate stage of human history that would disallow all further change. Aristotle's essentials of human cohabitation retain their topicality because they have remained throughout unfulfilled, outstanding, *noch nicht geworden*. They can best be described as sharp knives pressed against the future; or thorns in the flesh of all extant regimes, forms of state, and power hierarchies. It is that permanent *unfulfilment* that has made them, if measured by the yardstick of human history, eternal – and assured their survival.

'Why is man more of a political animal than any bee or other gregarious creature?' Aristotle asked, and answered:

> [M]an is the only animal endowed with speech ... [T]he power of speech is intended to express what is advantageous and what harmful, what is just and what unjust. It is precisely in this that man differs from other animals: he alone has any notion of good and evil, of justice and injustice; and an association of living beings possessed of this gift makes a household and a state.

Why? Because we can, correctly or not, imagine virtue as being individual property and carried by an individual even when alone and unassisted – but we cannot do the same with justice. Justice, Aristotle insists, 'is bound up with the state: its administration, which consists in determining what is just, is the principle of order in political society.'[3]

There is, Aristotle suggests, an unassailable *sequitur* that connects the notion of good and evil (and human creatures, blessed/cursed with speech as they are, cannot but have such a notion) with huddling together into a *polity*. After all, it is only in the state and through the state that the *notion of good and evil* can find its fulfilment in the *just order of shared living*. The urge to reforge the notion of good and evil into a regime of justice, and after that the need to administer such a regime, are the very reasons why 'only beast or god' can do without society. It is the search for justice that makes human togetherness a foregone conclusion, while making of living in a polity the essential condition of humanity – transcendental, one may say, to all historically shaped, always provisional, forms of human cohabitation.

'Justice', though, is an 'essentially contested' concept and for that reason bound to remain permanently open-ended. None of the 'really existing' forms of state (or Aristotle, having surveyed every form he knew and could know) has been spared (nor could be spared) criticism; none can be immune to the eroding impact of critique. Given the intrinsically contentious nature of all and any of the ideal's articulations, none of the ideal's genuine or putative embodiments would emerge from the test spotless. You won't find this in Aristotle, but it can be said that the most salient trace of the pressure that the urge of justice exerts on human societies is precisely that circumstance: the fact that no society can describe itself as 'justice fulfilled', and that all societies think of themselves, or are shown by others, to be not just *enough*. The urge to justice prevents the political body from standing still. A society is just in as far as it never stops criticizing the level of justice already achieved and seeking more justice and better justice.

A polity, the state, is not therefore *any* gathering of people. To form a polity, it is not enough for a quantity of people to inhabit the same territory. It is not enough either, as Aristotle insists, that all such people 'have the right of suing and being sued in the courts'. The awarding of the right to sue is far from enough to meet the stern demands of justice. It does no more than accord to the subjects the protection of the state, and the title to seek redress, in the event that they feel harmed or offended by other subjects and in the case that such harm or offence is disallowed or prohibited by the laws of the state. It says, however, nothing about the nature of those laws. In particular, it is silent about whether the laws of the state agree or disagree, and to what extent, with what the people who form the polity consider to be 'justice'. It says nothing about the duty of the lawgivers to listen to the people's idea of justice. An appeal to the Aristotelian idea of citizenship can be gleaned in the critical observations of Joe Klein, the perceptive political commentator, in the *New Yorker* of 4 June 2001: 'governance has become a form of consumerism, not citizenship: you buy the party that seems to offer a better deal or services.' Using the present-day vocabulary we would say that to be a citizen it is not enough to be a consumer of state services.

Humans who know of the difference between good and evil would not settle for an arrangement, even a comfortable and pleasurable arrangement, that gives them no say in deciding the difference between justice and injustice. To be a member of a polity does not boil down to the use of laws for one's own protection or advancement. It needs to include the partaking of the shaping of the laws, and seeing to it that the laws as already shaped chime well with the idea of justice. Only such a subject of the state as does that may be called a 'citizen'. 'The special characteristic' of a citizen, according to Aristotle, is 'that he has a share both in the administration of justice and in the holding of office', that 'he has the right to take part in the deliberative or judicial administration of a particular state.' For that reason it is right to say that the definition of the 'citizen' is 'particularly well suited to the citizen of democracy'. There is no citizen worthy of this name in a state that has no 'popular assembly' where the laws of the country are considered, critically assessed, discussed and changed.[4] And, we may add, there cannot be a polity worthy of its name without such a 'popular assembly'.

## Politics as critique and a project

The *OED* notes that at the time when the word 'political' was first recorded (in 1449) it conveyed the sense of the 'constitutional', as distinct from (and opposed to) despotic or tyrannical. This usage, however, as *OED* immediately comments, 'is now superseded'. It looks as though Aristotle's legacy has been dusted off and reappropriated at the threshold of the modern era in its original, pristine

essence of the ideal pressed against recalcitrant reality; or a benchmark against which to measure the actual forms of human togetherness, to expose their shortcomings, condemn them, and repair or
replace them. It seems, though, that having performed that task it
did not stand up well to the passage of time.

When first introduced into English vernacular, the concept of 'political' was a war cry and a call to arms. It has lost that meaning
since, like so many other concepts/programmes (for instance, those
of culture or civilization), it was originally coined as critique of reality but later transformed into 'objective description' of reality as its
heralds and missionaries turned into that reality's administrators.

Analysts and theorists of politics have come since then to identify
'politics' with the practices of the 'really existing' political forma-
tions that usurped the name of the 'political process' to attach it to
their own actions while censuring and vilifying as ignoble – pre-
scientific, anti-scientific – the habit of deliberating what politics
should be like but is not. This has been, at any rate, the analysts'
and the theorists' most commonly assumed stance, the *comme il
faut* of political discourse.

The paradox, though, is that when calling for concentration on
the '*objective* description' of 'really existing politics', scientific studies depart from the actual practice of political life which now, much
as two millennia ago, is more akin to Aristotle's vision of an open-
ended, self-critical and self-transcending process – triggered, set in
motion and kept on course by the urge to justice. It is the description of politics as a perpetual (and forever unfinished) chase after
the elusive ideal that deserves the label of objectivity.

*Politics is the ongoing critique of reality.* Politics is a mechanism
of change, not of preservation or conservation. Politics fits Robert
Musil's metaphors from *Der Mann ohne Eigenschaften* – of the train
of events that unrolls its rails ahead of itself, or the river of time that
sweeps its banks along with it.[5] Its course recalls as well the conduct
of Walter Benjamin's Angel of History – who runs 'ahead' with his
back turned towards the future which he cannot see, propelled/re-
pelled by the horrors of past injustices which he cannot but see.

The model of justice pursued by any form of politics is, after all,
not *gegeben* but *aufgegeben*, always a step ahead of the status quo.
Justice is a task looming in the yet-unknown future, a task which
itself needs yet to be posited, faced and confronted, prompted by
present suffering condemned as unjust.

Not all human suffering stands condemned as such. In order to
be seen as unjust and for that reason resisted and earmarked for

rectification, it needs to be seen as *amenable to alteration*. More to the point, the sufferers need to believe that it is within human power to remove this particular kind of suffering. They, and the witnesses to their misery, must be confident that things can be made different from what they are, and that it is human action that can make them different. They need to trust the practical ability of citizens to change the status quo if they find it not to their liking.

To sum up: whether or not the state may serve the purpose (urge, hope, expectation, postulate) that in Aristotle's view stood at its cradle depends in the last account on the implementation of the Aristotelian model of citizenship. In Cornelius Castoriadis's vocabulary, the autonomy of society (the ability to change things) and the autonomy of its members (the ability to select things that need to be changed) are each other's indispensable conditions. They can be attained only together; and together they fade and die out. Only together can they be recognized and pursued; and neither of the two would survive were the other to be denied or abandoned.

### The modern state as institutionalized critique

The premodern state neither knew of, nor practised citizenship. That did not ward off rebellions against injustice or the promotion of models of postulated justice through critique and rejection of the state of affairs considered unjust. But only some cases of suffering, as Barrington Moore Jr found out, were likely to be censured by the sufferers as 'unjust' and so prone to trigger rebellion. In fact, it was only 'surplus suffering', suffering more painful than the pain suffered in the most recent, still vividly remembered past, that tended to be labelled 'unjust'. Feudal serfs rebelled in the name of the return to *status quo ante*, in the name of the restoration of *Rechtsgewohnenheiten*, of the customary volume of demands on their labour and produce, however harsh those demands might have been and however painful they felt. The customary measure of pain was not a cause for rebellion. It had to be suffered meekly and placidly, since it was not considered to be a human creation, and for that reason appeared beyond human power.

Through ascribing to the human species the ability to immaculately conceive, ever anew, its own condition and to be the sole manager of its own existence, modernity threw open the gates to dissent and resistance against all and any kinds of condition found uncomfortable and experienced as painful. No suffering could, in principle, escape condemnation simply because of supposed inhuman or suprahuman origins or foundations. None of the conditions considered tolerable was from now on to be protected against the possibility (certainty?) of being redefined in the future as unjustified suffering (and there was nothing to stop such a redefinition from being claimed). Setting the rectification/compensation in motion was just a matter of making the case sufficiently persuasive to attract the required resources. As more and more varieties of human suffering were 'disenchanted' (that is, reclassified as manmade), the threshold of endurance and of tolerance to discomfort kept being lowered. Modernity was, after all, a promise of universal happiness and elimination of all unnecessary suffering. It was also a resolve to reclassify all suffering as unnecessary.

When seventy years ago, in *Das Unbehagen der Kultur* (*Civilization and its Discontents*, 1929), Sigmund Freud penned the portrait of modernity self-styled as civilization (that is, as a mode of living together that puts a more humane gloss on human fate), he selected freedom from pain and from other forms of unhappiness like fear or ugliness as the most prominent features of civilized existence. Freedom from suffering, and from fear of suffering, was hoped to favour the courage to experiment and to face the risks that the job of self-assertion requires – and thereby facilitate and safeguard the freedom of individual self-constitution. Self-management of human species was to make every member of the species the manager of her or his fate. Since sovereignty of action lay in the state, it was the task of the legislating and enforcing powers of the state to accomplish that feat. As Jacques Ellul put it, – 'who, according to the average modern man, should reorganize society so that it would finally become what it should be? The state, always the state.'[6] From its inception, the modern state found itself burdened by a daunting, indeed overwhelming challenge. There was no other force in sight, human or inhuman, which could be blamed for human suffering or for its too irresolute and sluggish cure: 'ultimately all problems are political, and solvable only along political lines.' In Ernst Cassirer's words, modern political leaders were cast in the role of 'the medicine men who promised to cure all social evils'.[7]

## The price of emancipation

The snag was that the task laid at the doorstep of the state as the sovereign agency and the ultimate embodiment of self-sustained and self-managing humanity was perhaps too heavy a burden to carry, but the self-reliance and self-responsibility suggested by the individual freedom from constraint proved to be even less bearable. That latter discovery prompted most insightful observers to conclude that 'if man were simply to follow his natural instincts he would not strive for freedom; he would rather choose dependence . . . [F]reedom is so often regarded much more as a burden than a privilege';[8] or that since growing aloneness is an unavoidable companion of all individuation, the accompaniment of individual liberation tends to be 'a feeling of powerlessness and anxiety' and so 'impulses arise to give up one's individuality, to overcome the feeling of aloneness and powerlessness by completely submerging oneself in the world outside.'[9]

Throughout most of the twentieth century the spectre haunted Europe of the all-powerful state ready to seize the opportunity offered by the massive 'escape from freedom' and gladly offering that 'submerging in the worlds outside' which was a sweet dream rather than a nightmare of the lonely, abandoned and frightened individuals. Political reflection on the roads which the nation-states were following, perhaps having already passed the point of no return, was in the case of observers like Hannah Arendt full of sombre premonitions of the 'totalitarian tendency' surfacing ever again with each successive response of the state to new problems. Of 'new problems' there was never a shortage, while still more were expected to crop up in the turbulent world of interstate wars and social battles inside the state. As Cassirer observed, 'in politics we are always living on volcanic soil. We must be prepared for abrupt convulsions and eruptions.'[10] Others, such as Otto Schmitt, welcomed the *Totale Staat* as an all but millennial event – the Second Coming of the lost or recklessly abandoned sacred order of the caring and sharing, but also all-embracing, all-regulating and all-devouring community.

*Evaluations* might have spread over the whole spectrum extending from unpolluted joy to the darkest of despairs, but *expectations* were amazingly similar. George Orwell's and Aldous Huxley's dystopian pictures of the future, often represented as diametrically opposed, differed indeed in every detail – but one: in both, an organ wielding supreme power was placed firmly and for all time beyond the reach of its subjects but penetrated every nook and cranny of their lives. It supervised every step its subjects took or could take and ruthlessly punished all who stepped out of line (that is, if previous drilling did not nip in the bud the very possibility of such

imprudent behaviour). Once the shocks of Bolshevik and Nazi totalitarianism were fully absorbed and digested, Jeremy Bentham's
Panopticon (with its ubiquitous and pernickety surveillance, and its
sharp division between the surveillors and the surveilled), redis-
covered and recycled by Michel Foucault, was welcomed by enlightened opinion as the long sought, eminently accurate model of the
contemporary state and of the tendency innate in all modern power.

The omniscient, omnipresent and omnipotent state from which
the final enslavement (or, for some thinkers, liberation) of the
modern individual was bound to arrive was seen as overdetermined.
The cause of overdetermination was the convergence of two separate, yet complementary tendencies: the subjects' resentment of the
necessity to choose, and the power-greedy politicians' zeal to reduce
their choice to the minimum or prohibit it altogether. Theodor W.
Adorno, in tune with the spirit of the time, profusely elaborated on
both tendencies and their ultimate encounter.[11] With 'individual narcissism' simultaneously beefed up and frustrated, the disappointed
individuals seek compensation and find it in 'collective narcissism
[that] restores to them as individuals some of the self-esteem the
same collective strips from them and that they hope to fully recover
through their delusive identification with it'. On the other hand,
though, 'the religious theme of corruption of the human species
since Adam's fall appears in a new guise, radically secularized already in Hobbes, distorted in the service of evil itself. Because it is
supposedly impossible for people to establish a just order the
existing unjust order is commended to them. What Thomas Mann
in speaking against Spengler called the "defeatism of humanity" has
expanded universally.' The individuals resented responsibilities they
found well-nigh impossible to handle; the state rulers were eager to
oblige and take individual responsibilities away, together with their
subjects' freedom.

Few thinkers of the past century (and their number shrank as the
century advanced in years) gave much credit to the chances of democracy portrayed by Aristotle as the union of the autonomous polity
with its autonomous citizens. Some bewailed the passing of the Enlightenment dreams; some others shed few tears at the funeral of
what they saw from the start as an abortive and doomed illusion, a
bastard offspring of misguided hopes. But almost none foretold for
democracy a long, let alone cloudless, future. Sharp differences of
opinion were underlain by a shared foundation: broad agreement as
to the prospect of the state's expanding powers and its subjects'
shrinking powers. Observers agreed that the collapse of the demo-

cratic illusion may have been preordained by individuals' endemic incapacity for self-assertion (particularly self-guided, autonomous self-assertion of the kind that democracy requires), but that it was the state and its power-obsessed rulers that would ultimately deliver the *coup de grâce*.

## Big Brother's new avatar

To fathom the distance that separates the present generation and its fears from the generation whose fears Adorno, Arendt, Cassirer, Fromm, Huxley or Orwell articulated, we could do worse than take a closer look at the public spectacle called *Big Brother* that took all broadcasting corporations, and their viewers, by storm. Overnight, it became the *talk of the town*. One can be excused for guessing that its astonishing career would not have happened had the kind of life portrayed by *Big Brother* (or the French show *Loft Story*, or the Anglo-American quiz *The Weakest Link*) not already been the most absorbing, perhaps the only *game in town*.

Sometime in 1999, while watching a group of people kept for a month enclosed in a glass dome in the Arizona desert, John de Mol of Hilversum had, by his own admission, 'a big flash' of inspiration.[12] He invented *Big Brother*. His brain child was shown initially on a small private channel 'Veronica', only to become an instant success, the idea being snatched immediately by the biggest broadcasting corporations and being copied since then by twenty-seven countries (the number is still growing, and fast), making its inventor the second richest man in Holland. The success of *Big Brother* was phenomenal even by the standards of the hype-guided ratings boosting common in broadcasting practice. Of the French version of *Big Brother* (called the *Loft Story*), Ignazio Ramonet wrote that 'never before in the history of the French media' was there an event that 'similarly inflamed, fascinated, shocked, agitated, troubled, overstimulated and irritated the country'[13] and that it overshadowed such contemporaneous, normally superpopular events as the Cannes film festival and the football Cup Final. In Britain, an estimated 10 million 18–25 year olds were to vote for or against *Big Brother* competitors. That needs to be compared with 1.5 million people of the same age category expected to vote in the British general election.[14]

John de Mol's perspicacity was indeed remarkable: he had spotted an untapped demand – something that the hundreds of millions of men and women of twenty-seven countries glued to their TV screens must have needed badly and waited for impatiently. Something that, also in a flash, they would welcome for making sense of their life experience, but first and foremost for legitimizing a way of life that made them feel uneasy and for removing the stigma from the kind of life which they suspected they should feel ashamed of. The 5.4 billion dollars for which de Mol's company, Entertainment, was to be ultimately sold to the Spanish Telefonica was a fair measure of the price that those millions were willing to pay for the coveted absolution...

No wonder: the spectacle of *Big Brother* bears an uncanny resemblance to the all-too-familiar experience of the spectators. In that show, twelve men and women of unknown pasts and divergent futures pass a few weeks in each others' company, faced with the task of weaving the mode of their togetherness from scratch and with no promise of durability. They know in advance that they are all meant to disappear from the company, one by one, and that their task is precisely to make the others disappear first...If they fail to do the job, they will be kicked out by the self-same others whom they spared or did not manage to force out in time.

Throughout that life-and-death competition 'as shown on TV', the rest of the world stays invisible; neither the players nor the witnesses of the game know exactly where the food and toys come from and who has decided what the next test will be. 'Big Brother' is a generic name for that rest of the world – and it is demonstrated again and again how whimsical and unpredictable that world is, scurrying from one surprise to another and keeping cards close to its chest. This is – so the spectators may feel – what they have felt or suspected all along, but did not know how to articulate and make into a sensible story. Now they know. And they are consoled: they know now (or at least have been vividly shown) that what they thought to be the outcome of their own – personal and unique – fault or bad luck is the way the world is made and works...

In hot pursuit of *Big Brother* came *The Weakest Link*: another turn-of-the-century television hit, this one invented in Britain and soon after imported, for a huge sum, by the United States. *The Weakest Link* repeats *Big Brother*'s message, but it also says loud and clear what *Big Brother* only whispered: teams exist in order to serve the self-promotion of their cleverest members, and have no value apart from that service. There are six people at the start of *The Weakest Link* spectacle, but all know that only one person will survive to the end, pocketing all the money earned by the other 'team members' who leave the show, one by one, empty-handed. After every round of questions they need to answer individually, 'team members' throw out one of their team-mates, having proclaimed him (or her) to be 'the weakest link' – on the grounds of having added too little money to the account destined to become the private gain of the last (unknown as yet) survivor. Each of the outvoted and excluded is put in front of the camera and asked to confess publicly the private weaknesses responsible for his (or her) failure. Overtly or implicitly, the wisdom and the justice of the story developing in front of TV viewers are confirmed: it is a tough world where the defeated suffer defeat because they have asked for trouble and where the failures have only themselves to blame and no right to demand compensation, or even as much as compassion, on account of their misfortune.

More than anything else, the two most popular television shows are public rehearsals of the *disposability* of humans. They carry an indulgence and a warning rolled into one story. No one is indispensable, no one has the right to his or her share in the fruits of the joint effort just because she or he has added at some point to their growth, let alone because of being, simply, a member of the team. Life is a hard game for hard people. Each game starts from scratch, past merits do not count, you are worth only as much as the results of your most recent duel. Each player at every moment is for herself or himself, and to progress, not to mention to reach the top, one must first cooperate in excluding the many who block the way, only to outwit in the end those with whom one cooperated. If you are not tougher and less scrupulous than all the others, you will be done by them – swiftly and without remorse. It is the fittest (read: the least scrupulous) who survive.

The family of games that capture the imaginations of millions and keep them stuck to the screens (there is no end to the games' 'new and improved' versions in hot pursuit of the amazing success of the original, the latest addition, as I write, having been the American *Survivor*, aptly subtitled 'Trust no one') has come to be known under the generic name of 'Big Brother'. This used to be a painfully familiar, household name to the generations growing up in the dark shadows cast by the watchtowers of the 'Century of Camps'. Immortalized by Orwell, it stood for ruthless and unscrupulous power that fixes the routes everyone else must follow, prescribes the fashion in which they are to be followed and destroys everyone who dares to refuse or does not manage to fulfil the command to the commanding power's full satisfaction. Orwell's Big Brother wished everyone to behave according to his wishes. He knew exactly what he wanted them to do and wouldn't suffer disobedience, however minute, lightly. Orwell's Big Brother was the manager of his subjects' lives, from cradle to coffin. Big Brother was also known to demand gratitude and love from his victims; Big Brother ruled over a kingdom of duplicity and double-talk. In that kingdom, slavery meant freedom, pain meant cure and oppression meant emancipation.

If that was what Big Brother stood for when George Orwell painted his portrait, 'Big Brother' as a name for the discussed family of television shows is a misnomer (it should rather have been called 'New Big Brother', as in Tony Blair's 'New Labour'). If it is not seen as such, then that is only for the fact that the present generation has all but forgotten the old meaning of the term, and so the term has become nothing but an empty verbal shell suitable to be filled with other experiential content. That shell was once used to gather and accommodate the fears haunting Orwell's contemporaries, and the memory of that function determines its present uses. It is still used for collecting and storing fears. Only now the fears are different.

The Big Brother of the TV shows has no face. He does not need one anyway, since he now, unlike in his previous avatar, does not demand love or for that matter any devotion or loyalty. This Big Brother is an eminently useful fellow (he is, after all, 'the rest of the world' and there would be no world without the rest), but he does his job on condition that his wards abstain from all interference with his works and accept his moves without being curious, let alone inquisitive, about their motives. On that easy to accept and not particularly cumbersome condition Big Brother supplies his wards with everything they need to play their own games – a fully equipped stage, beds and bed linen, food and cooking facilities – even the toys and ideas of new games to keep the boredom away and the inmates entertained and happy. He provides the playground and sees to it that it is equipped with the gadgets you need to play. But the rest is up to you. Big Brother is one of those 'don't phone us, we'll phone you' types. There is no point in questioning or protesting against his decisions. Appeals would stay without an answer. First and foremost, however, Big Brother does not care what you do with the toys and the gadgets you've got, how you use them and to what effect. He does not care either whether you win or lose and which one of you ends at the top and which one at the bottom. Big Brother is *impartial*. You cannot call him cruel and so there is no reason to fight him. But if you call him 'just', that may mean only *indifferent*. So there is no reason to charge him with a deficient or misguided justice either.

The rest, let me repeat, is up to you. That rest is a zero-sum game. You'll gain as much as the others lose, not a penny more. And those others' gains will be your losses. There is little point in joining forces and acting in concert, therefore – unless what you have in mind is an admittedly temporary alliance, a step on the ladder that you climb, no longer needed once you've gone one step up. Alliances are good as long as they help you to advance. They become instantly redundant or downright damaging once they don't. From assets they turn into liabilities, and woe to those who overlook the moment when they do.

*Big Brother* is a game of *exclusion*. Excluding others instead of being excluded oneself (that is, excluding others before your turn comes to be excluded) is the name of success. At the start of the game, all competitors are equal. What you have done in the past does not matter. It has left no trace; it did not spoil your chances, but it gave you no advance start either. Each game is, truly and fully, a new beginning. Whatever skills you may have and whatever un-tapped potentials hide inside you waiting to be released, they need to be dug up and used here and now – otherwise they don't count. Everybody here is, for a moment, a complete stranger to everybody else, and so it is from now on that you need to exercise all your wits to win friends and influence people (only to be shortly abandoned once the friendship and the influence have done their job). Everyone around knows as well as you do that in the end only one person (or a couple, as in the French *Loft Story*) will stay on the battlefield and pocket all the spoils. And so everyone is aware that an alliance, if struck, is only 'until further notice' and will not survive the end of gratification.

And then comes the daily ritual of public confession (in the shows the confessional is reduced to a chair in which the penitent sits before the end of the day – with the TV camera deputizing for the absent confessor). Those who have emerged victorious or at least unharmed from the day's battles confess alongside the humbled, the browbeaten or defeated. All report what they felt during the battle and what they feel now at the end of the round. The stories they tell are different, but the messages are monotonously alike: there is no one but yourself (your acumen, cunning, wit, richness of emotions) to be thanked for success, and nothing but the absence or the faults of some or all of those resources to blame for failure.

And there is another message, similarly illuminating; a sobering message, one may say. That Big Brother who sets the scene for all the games of life is a mysterious creature who sometimes, at the moments of his choice, talks to you. But you may not talk back; what would be the point in trying anyway? Big Brother is like the God of the late medieval Nominalist philosophers. Like Him, he is 'capricious, fearsome in His power, unknowable, unpredictable, unconstrained by nature and reason and indifferent to good and evil'.[15] He is, fully and truly, a Big Brother *absconditus*. You know (everyone knows) that 'he is there', but nothing practical follows from that knowledge. When it comes to the nitty-gritty of day-by-day worries, you are still on your own.

## At the receiving end of the New Big Brother's calls

This is why the millions cling, bewitched, to the unravelling saga. No point, indeed, to send to know for whom this particular bell tolls. It tolls for them – for any one of them. The competitors of *Big Brother* or *The Weakest Link* retell again and again their viewers' story. This is how the viewers felt they lived all along, but now they see it vividly and clearly, reduced to bare essentials, shown in a laboratory-like purity that leaves nothing to the imagination and even less to doubt. The shows articulate the logic behind their joys and sorrow – however logical, or otherwise, that logic may be. Above all, the shows put in words and in graphic images the fears that haunted them, but whose nature they were at a loss to pinpoint. The shows do not just explain all that; they explain what is there to be explained... They tell their viewers *what* to think about, and *how* to think about it.

Of course, the story comes to the viewers prepackaged, complete with interpretation, though in images interpretation is more difficult to spot and set apart than in written, read or listened to texts. Besides, even if the interpretation had been noticed and duly separated from the happening itself, it would hardly have baffled or prompted disagreement. After all, the explanation offered by Big Brother shows may be clearer, but it is not novel. It is the kind of explanation of the all-too-familiar ups and downs of the individual's life that one hears over and over again from almost every quarter. The noisy and cacophonous world of ours is bursting with messages – different and often contradictory messages – but the recurrent, relentlessly repetitive motif comes through loud and clear. It was

Peter F. Drucker, the guru of the new neoliberal political and business classes, who first (in 1989) crisply articulated that motif:[16] 'The last western politician of the first rank to believe in salvation by society was Willy Brandt'; 'No one, except perhaps the "liberation theologians" in South America, believes any more in the power of social action to create a perfect society or even to bring society closer to such an ideal... [A]nyone who now proclaims the "Great Society" as Lyndon Baines Johnson did only twenty years ago, would be laughed out of court.' In short, 'the belief in salvation by society is dead', on both sides of the now dismantled ideological barricade, in palaces and in hovels, in 'gated communities' and in urban ghettos. The Big Brother of the 'reality TV' shows (this is how the producers have branded the likes of *Big Brother*, *Loft Story* and *Survivor* spectacles, with the unqualified consent of the viewers) is Drucker's 'New Reality' transcribed for the stage. Big Brother *absconditus* stands for *societas abscondita*.

The world we inhabit and daily re-create is not, of course, a TV Big Brother drama projected on the large screen of society. *Big Brother* is not a photograph, copy or replica of the present-day social reality. But it is its condensed, distilled, purified model; one may say it is a laboratory in which certain tendencies of that social reality, elsewhere hidden, diluted or repressed, are experimented with and put to the test so that their full potential is made visible.

Hannah Arendt pointed out that the concentration camps of totalitarian regimes were

> meant not only to exterminate people and degrade human beings, but also served the ghastly experiment of eliminating, under scientifically controlled conditions, spontaneity itself as an expression of human behaviour and of transforming the human personality into a mere thing... Under normal circumstances this can never be accomplished, because spontaneity can never be entirely eliminated... It is only in the concentration camps that such an experiment is at all possible.[17]

Much the same can be said of the family of Big Brother shows. If the camps served as laboratories in which the limits of the totalitarian tendency endemic to modern society but 'under normal circumstances' tamed and attenuated were tested, Big Brother shows do the same for the 'new modernity' – our modernity. Unlike those experiments, though, the contemporary testing of tendencies is conducted publicly, in the limelight, in front of millions of spectators. After all, what is tested now are the limits of deregulated, privatized and individualized spontaneity; the inner tendency of a thoroughly privatized world.

State governments, to be sure, have neither packed up their belongings nor intend to close their offices. Far from it. Governments are today no less, if not more, busy and active than ever before in modern history. But they are busy in the TV Big Brother's style: letting the subjects play their own games and blame themselves in the event that the results are not up to their dreams. Governments are busy hammering home the 'there is no alternative' message, the 'security is dependency' and the 'state protection is disempowering' messages, and enjoining subjects to be more flexible and to love the risks the flexible (read: erratic and unpredictable) life-setting is fraught with. As Pierre Bourdieu put it, 'all direct and deliberate intervention, at least one that comes from the state, for whatever reason, is discredited in advance...'[18] The ministers who contemplate such intervention, and dare to air their intentions in public, risk being disparaged and condemned as (at best!) unforgivably ignorant of the 'laws of the market' or 'economic interests'. The ministers likely to be praised for their insight, acumen and proper service to national interests are those (much more numerous) among them who – through the regularizing of the state of deregulation – partake of the 'institutionalization of insecurity', making 'of social insecurity the positive principle of collective organization'.[19] A new form of domination is emerging in our times that breaks with the orthodox method of rule-by-engagement and uses deregulation as its major vehicle: 'a mode of domination that is founded on the *institution of insecurity* – domination by precariousness of existence'.[20]

This is the 'reality' characterized, as Ulrich Beck shows in his successive studies, by the 'subjectivisation and individualisation of risks and contradictions produced by institutions and society'.[21] In such a reality 'history shrinks to the (eternal) present, and everything revolves around the axis of one's personal ego and personal life.' The individual may be more than ever before dependent on the play of market forces which she comes nowhere near being aware of, let alone understanding or anticipating, but she will have to pay for her decisions individually taken or not taken. 'How one lives becomes the *biographical solution to systemic contradictions*' – or rather, this is what the hapless individuals are authoritatively told and come to believe to be the case (in fact, a 'biographical solution to systemic contradictions' is an oxymoron; it may be sought, but cannot be found). It is not just the washing-their-hands politicians who dump the systemic contradictions on their subjects' shoulders.

The expert counsellors share in the guilt: they 'dump their contradictions and conflicts at the feet of the individual and leave him or her with the well intentioned invitation to judge all of this critically on the basis of his or her notions'.

The main reason why the experts' advice will not help their clients much, and at any rate not enough, is not the scarcity of individually absorbed knowledge nor weaknesses in the individuals' rational faculties. Even assuming (counterfactually in many, perhaps in most cases) that the expert advice on how to 'take things in the individual's own hands' is sound and that it may, if put into practice, add to the individuals' powers of control over their lives – there still remains the big question of resources without which the advice cannot be taken up, and even less put to a good use.

The subjects of contemporary states are individuals by fate: the factors that constitute their individuality – confinement to individual resources and individual responsibility for the results of life choices – are not themselves matters of choice. We are all today 'individuals *de jure*'. This does not mean, though, that we are all individuals *de facto*. More often than not, control over life is the way in which the story of life is told, rather than the way in which life is lived.

Paradoxically, the call to take life into one's own, individual hands and the pressure to do just that may rebound in *less* individual control over its course. That call and those pressures divert the minds and the deeds of individuals from the collectively set conditions that determine the agenda and the chances of their individual choices and efforts. That call and those pressures play down the significance of common causes and solidary actions and remove the state of society as a whole from the factors considered relevant to life calculations. That call and those pressures insinuate that nothing can be gained from joining ranks and acting in unison; that, moreover, while an individual plight can be moulded and kneaded at will, the way society works has been decided once and for all and is no longer amenable to conscious reform. An individual life is a bunch of alternatives, but there is no alternative to the shape of society in which that life is lived. Above all, 'the private' and 'the public' are set in different worlds, incommunicado to each other. The two spheres are subjected to different and virtually untranslatable logics.

That impression is created and sustained by the forceful individualization of concerns, projects and pursuits, on the one hand, and the fading of the powers of the nation-state, on the other. The present-day political sovereignty of states is but a shadow of the many-faceted political/economic/military/cultural autonomy of states of yesteryear modelled after the pattern of *Totale Staat*. There is little that the sovereign states of today can do, and even less that their governments would risk doing, to stem the pressures of globalized capital, finance and trade (including trade in culture). If pressed by its subjects to reassert their own standards of propriety and justice, most governments would retort that there is nothing they can do in this respect without 'alienating the investors' and so threatening the GNP and the welfare of the nation and all its members. They would say that the rules of the game in which they are compelled to play have been set (and can be revised at will) by forces on which they have minimal, if any, influence. What forces? As anonymous as the names behind which they hide: competition, terms of trade, world markets, global investors. Forces without fixed addresses, extraterritorial unlike the eminently territorial powers of the state, moving freely around the globe unlike the agencies of the state that for better or worse, but once and for all, stay fixed to the ground. Shifty and slippery forces, elusive, evasive, difficult to pinpoint and impossible to catch.

And so, on the one hand, there is receding interest on the part of individuals in their joint/shared affairs. This wilting of interest is aided and abetted by the state only too glad to cede as many of its past responsibilities as possible to private concerns and worries. On the other hand, there is a growing impotence of the state to balance the books inside its frontiers or to impose the standards of protection, of collective insurance, ethical principles and models of justice that would mitigate the insecurity and alleviate the uncertainty that sap individual self-confidence, that necessary condition of any sustained engagement in public affairs. The joint result of the two processes is a widening gap between 'the public' and 'the private', and a gradual yet relentless demise of the art of two-way translation between private problems and public issues, that lifeblood of all politics. Contrary to Aristotle, it seems, the notions of good and evil in their present-day privatized form no longer generate the idea of the 'good society' (or of *social* evil, for that matter); and whatever hope of a supraindividual goodness is conjured up, it would hardly be vested in the state.

## Uncertainty: the prime root of political inhibition

Learning is a powerful, perhaps the mightiest of human weapons – but only in a regular environment, in which certain conduct is as a rule, always or nearly always, rewarded – while certain other conduct is as a rule punished. The human capacity to learn, to memorize and to habitualize a type of conduct that has proved to be successful (that is, brought reward) in the past may be suicidal, however, if the links between actions and results are random, short-lived and change without notice.

Richard Sennett revisited recently the employees of a New York bakery whom he had studied thirty years ago.[22] He found out, with the benefit of hindsight, that the 'routinized time' of which the New York bakers had complained in the past and which they had then detested nevertheless created 'an arena in which workers could assert their own demands, an arena of empowerment'. Routine, Sennett concludes, 'can demean, but it can also protect; routine can decompose labour, but it can also compose a life.' But routine is the last thing likely to be found in the present regime of domination that (to recall Beck) sets the scene for the search for biographical solutions to systemic contradictions. Conditions now change abruptly, defying all powers of reasonable prediction, without following a steady logic or legible pattern. The resulting experience of disjointed time, staggering from this unanticipated episode to that unexpected one, threatens 'the ability of people to form their characters into sustained narratives'. Older workers may remember that in their youth life plans used to be long-term, as were commitments and solidarities, but they wonder whether any reality content has been left in the idea of the 'long term'. They are at a loss when it comes to explaining its meaning to their juniors, who do not share their memories but draw their knowledge of the world from what they see around them. As one of Sennett's conversationalists confessed, 'You can't imagine how stupid I feel when I talk to my kids about commitment. It's an abstract virtue to them; they don't see it anywhere.'

Under the old regime of domination, both partners in the power relation knew well that they were bound to stay in each other's company for a long time to come, since they couldn't 'do it alone'. Commitment was *reciprocal*. In the archetypal 'Fordist factory', that ideal type towards which all institutions of 'solid modernity' strove, Henry Ford depended on his workers for his wealth and power as much as the workers depended on him and his aides for their livelihood. Both sides knew that they would meet again – the next day, and in the months and years to come. This time perspective allowed them to perceive their relations as a 'conflict of interest' (there might be dislike, but no conflict between mere passers-by), and prompted them to set earnestly about mitigating it, making it bearable, and even trying to resolve it to their mutual satisfaction. However antagonistic, unpleasant or irritating the cohabitation might be, the sides would wish to negotiate a mutually acceptable *modus vivendi* once it was certain that the cohabitation would last. Having negotiated such a mode of togetherness, they would trust its longevity. They would obtain thereby a reliably solid frame in which to inscribe and hold their expectations and plans for the future. This gain is the prime motive for engaging in negotiation. It is the prospect of such a gain that makes the partners interested in discussion, dispute, compromise and agreement and prompts them to keep all of them going.

Nowadays, though, the assumption that 'we will meet again' strikes many people as increasingly nebulous. The characters of the life-game come and go and are bound to vanish and be replaced many times over as the game progresses. The scene of action is a-changing, at a pace difficult or impossible for the powers of perception and retention to match. Plots, scenarios and characters change well before the players have managed to finish their lines.

It is not clear what the rules are of the game currently being played. Sometimes the players have good reason to doubt whether there are any rules at all, or whether all the players follow the same set of rules. Alain Peyrefitte traced the spectacular outburst of creative energy in the modern era back to the widespread confidence in oneself and others, both resting on trust in the longevity and undisputed authority of social institutions. 'Pour croître, il faut croire: mais en quoi?'[23] Peyrefitte worries that confidence wilts once the soil in which it has been planted becomes, like the social institutions of our time, infirm and friable. When trust has no firm ground in which to root, the courage needed to take the risk, to assume responsibilities and to enter long-term commitments is dissipated.

In my student years one of the most popular characters in the science of animal behaviour was a fish called a stickleback. Male sticklebacks build nests for the females to lay and store roe. The males guard the nests until the eggs are hatched. An invisible borderline separates the 'home territory' around the nest (that is, the space that the male defends against intruders, attacking all trespassing stickleback males) from 'foreign territory' (that is, all the rest of space, from which the male flees if it comes accidentally across another member of the species). In laboratory experiments two male sticklebacks were put during the spawning season into the water tank too small to keep their respective 'home territories' apart. Confused males, getting contradictory and irreconcilable signals and so unable to choose unambiguously between fight and escape, assumed a 'neither-nor' vertical posture burying heads in sand – obviously a posture completely irrelevant to the quandary, let alone to its resolution. Since my student years the comparative study of animal behaviour has made enormous strides. Sticklebacks may be all but forgotten, but their idiosyncratic conduct has been recognized as a specimen of a much wider, probably universal regularity. Whenever confronted with contradictory, ambivalent, illegible or inconstant, labile signals, animals tend to develop *inhibition* – a sort of behavioural paralysis. The learned, habitualized modes of behaviour are suspended. What follows then is either a behavioural depression manifested in total inaction, or a resort to 'irrational conduct' – moves only tenuously if at all related to the situation causing distress. If the latter option is taken, tension tends to be temporarily relieved through pointless aggression that leaves the causes of distress intact. Similar behavioural alternatives have been observed in the case of signals that are admittedly unambiguous but that portend a danger that cannot be avoided whatever the threatened animal may do (escape and fighting back being both out of the question).

Both situations prevail in human life in the 'liquid stage'[24] of the modern era. Most of the time, signposts and orientation points, far from staying put, seem to be on castors; they change places quicker than the destinations they point to can be reached and hardly ever remain in place long enough to enable the wanderers to memorize the trajectory. More often than not, there are more signs at crossroads suggesting different locations for the sought destination or beckoning to other destinations, unheard of, untried and for that reason tempting. In each case, the result is an anxiety-generating ambivalence. To make the situation even more treacherous and yet more vexing, the few signs that are uncharacteristically clear, uncontested and so judged as reliable suggest roads that many a wanderer is either not resourceful enough to pass or barred from embarking on. Not reaching the destination widely considered as worthy and attractive is a painful experience. Being excluded from the widely undertaken attempts to reach such a destination, or lacking the resources needed to make them, brings an awareness that pain is imminent and yet there is nothing its prospective sufferer can do to stave it off or escape it. This is precisely the kind of predicament that is suspected to preclude rational action and trigger instead either inhibition or random aggression wide off the target.

No wonder that the symptoms of the two characteristic reactions to ambiguity and uncertainty abound, and become ever more salient and ever more widely noted.

On the one hand, interest in 'Politics' with a capital 'P' (that is, in explicitly political movements, political parties and the composition and programmes of governments), and the intensity and strength of political beliefs, not to mention the day-by-day active participation in activities traditionally classified as political, are all evaporating at an accelerating pace. In tune with the mood of the times, 'citizens' are expected to look no further than the next tax cut or pension rise and to have no other interests except shorter hospital queues, fewer beggars on the street, more criminals in jail or faster discovery of the poisonous potential in foodstuffs. Few if any consummate politicians would muster the courage to propose a vision of a 'good society' to electors who, having more than once singed their fingers, are known to prefer a *different now* to a *better future*. Eminent political figures, like Laurent Fabius,[25] in the rare moments when they go as far as proposing 'an idea' (in Fabius's case, a rather banal idea of 'ecodevelopment', that is of development agreeing with an ecological approach – a move necessitated anyway by the internal frictions of the French 'plural left' rather than by the leaders' appetite for grand visions), feel obliged to apologize immediately to the public for talking about something that will take more than a few days to implement: 'J'entend déjà certains commentaires: pourquoi, diable, le ministre français de l'économie et des finances réfléchit-il au longe terme? Ne devrait-il pas se concentrer plutôt sur la gestion immédiate...?'[26]

There seems to be no market for long-term visions of the 'good society'. There are few suppliers, and not many more prospective buyers. Interest in the government of the country and its works, if there is any such interest left, tends to be as short-term as the ministers' crisis-management campaigns. There is little enthusiasm for changing a more distant future as no connection can be seen between the current actions of citizens (or citizens' apathy) and the shape of things to come. Luc Boltanski and Éve Chiapello found that in contemporary workplaces the employees 'no longer make a career, but pass from one project to another, their success in the current project giving them access to the next'.[27] Tony Blair is widely reputed to believe that the purpose of winning the current election is winning the next one.

The other common reaction to powerlessness, aggression, is less an alternative than complementary to inhibition. More often than not the two responses are triggered simultaneously. Withdrawal from the *agora* where political battles are left to small high-tech professional units, since their outcome does not seem to depend on the bravery of little soldiers, is coupled with deploying the spare fighting spirit in places nearer to hand and so apparently easier to tackle. Orwell's 'five minutes of hatred' are no longer orchestrated by a country's rulers: like most other things subjected to the principle of 'subsidiarity', they have been deregulated, privatized and left to local, or better still personal, initiative.

Tabloids time and again fill the vacancy, doing their best to condense, channel and focus the diffuse and scattered frustrations of the politically inhibited: they are glad to oblige and pick up targets on which to release the energy untapped by concerns with 'common causes'. There is no shortage of figures of fear and hatred like paedophiles returning home from a jail term, 'squeegee pests', 'muggers', 'lager louts', the 'workshy', 'false asylum seekers' or 'genuinely economic' migrants. Since fighting any of such figures leaves uncertainty no less daunting than it was before the fight started, and is unlikely to alleviate the gnawing pain of powerlessness for much longer than is taken by successive outbursts of aggression, ever new objects of hatred and new targets of aggression are needed. Tabloids obligingly discover or invent them, and supply them to their anxious readers in a form pre-cooked for instant consumption. But all the tabloids' efforts, however ingenious, would be in vain was there not a deep and plentiful anxiety diverted from its genuine cause and desperately seeking alternative outlets.

Orchestration of aggression seldom taps the whole of the aggressive energy that continuing uncertainty coupled with persistent powerlessness generates. Enough of it is left to spill over and saturate the private, self-operated sectors of the web of social bonds – partnerships, families, neighbourhoods, workplace companionships. All of them tend these days to become sites of violence, often dubbed by the uninvolved as 'gratuitous' by reason of having no evident reason, let alone rational purpose. Family homes become substitute battlegrounds for the games of self-assertion evicted from the public arena. So do the closely watched neighbourhoods from which one hopes to be able to preside over the game of exclusion instead of being its hapless target. So do workplaces, which easily turn from shelters of solidarity and cooperation into sites of cutthroat, catch-as-can competition.

All such means of fighting back the spectre of powerlessness are irrational in the sense of being wide of the mark. They come nowhere near the genuine causes of pain and leave them unscathed. Under the circumstances, however, as long as the root of trouble stays stubbornly out of bounds or is seen that way, they may be interpreted as 'rational' in the sense of a psychological rationalization of the unfulfilled urge for self-assertion and self-esteem. Whatever the verdict, there is no dispute that the substitute outlets for the anxiety generated by the combination of uncertainty and powerlessness deepen and intensify, instead of placating, the anxiety they are meant to combat or dissolve. They tend to fray or tear apart the ties of mutual commitments, this condition *sine qua non* of solidary action, without which the true sources of anxiety can be neither reached nor affected.

Guarding law and order is, however, one of the orthodox functions that the state is still, as before, eager to perform, and so self-propelled and self-steering aggression is not likely to be tolerated. The state would not passively watch its subjects 'taking the law into their own hands'. Family, neighbourhood, street or stadium violence tends to be countered with coercion and repression by state organs; its perpetrators unwittingly invite one more proof of their powerlessness. Somewhat less risk is involved if the aggression is redirected against oneself – one's own body and psyche. As alternative outlets are either blocked or fraught with risks, there are grounds to suppose that the present-day bodily fitness obsession (manifested in dieting, weight-watching, jogging, 'health club' routines and other tiresome and often painful drills in some cases recalling self-inflicted DIY torture) serves, apart from its other functions, the task of such a redirecting of surplus anxiety. It is yet more probable that similar energy diversion explains at least in part the epidemic spread of anorexic and bulimic disturbances, addictive drug use, allergy ailments and other psychosomatic illnesses, as well as the many extant and novel forms of psychic depression.

These are all side-effects of uncertainty, mistaken for cures. The prime casualty of the mistake is political engagement, that constitutive feature of citizenship. And, consequently, of politics in its pristine Aristotelian sense.

## The second secession

The present-day crisis of citizenship and disenchantment with the potential of political engagement are ultimately rooted in the not entirely fanciful impression that agencies of *effective* action, particularly *collective* effective action, and especially *long-term* effective collective action, are missing and that there are no obvious ways of resurrecting them or to conceive them anew. As one would expect in the resulting situation of cognitive dissonance, the discomfort generated by such an impression tends to be alleviated by an added belief that the passing of collective action need not be bewailed since it was, and always will be, at its best irrelevant and at its worst inimical to the advancement of individual well-being and happiness. It can be argued, though, that the apparent credibility of this belief is, to a large extent, the 'sour grapes' effect.

However that may be, it seems that the key to the problems afflicting contemporary political life, and worrying the researchers of that life, needs to be sought and in all probability can be found in departures responsible for the growing impotence of the extant agencies of collective political action.

Summing up the seminal transformations of the eighteenth and the nineteenth centuries, Max Weber concluded that the 'moment of birth' of modern capitalism was the separation of business from the household. Many years later Karl Polanyi would suggest that this separation, coupled with the separation of producers from the means of production already spotted by Karl Marx, set in motion the 'Great Transformation' that we tend to encapsulate in the idea of modern society.

In speaking of 'household', Weber understood more than just the shared kitchen, the bedrooms, the hearth around which the family gathered at meals, and the jointly cultivated family farm or jointly operated family workshop. 'Household' stood in precapitalist times for the complex web of interconnected institutions – neighbourhood, village, township, parish, guilds – into which the family homestead was tightly woven. Within that complex, most of the loose strings of human pursuits tied together. That complex entailed everything necessary to routinely reproduce the pattern of shared life and the orderliness of human interactions. That complex was also the effective collective guardian of ethical standards deemed obligatory to all people involved, of the rights, the duties and the obligations that had to be observed by all: their sole guardian, and for most of its history a sufficient one.

By cutting itself loose from that complex focused on the family household, business enterprise acquired a truly unprecedented freedom. It came to be free from the constraints of ethical obligations and long-term commitments. It became, to an unheard-of extent, norm-free and rule-free territory. Or, rather, it was free to set its own norms and rules, and disregard the norms and rules others would cherish and wish to be binding. It could subordinate its own actions, from conception to completion, to the pursuit of profit and the rational calculation of gains and losses, paying little or no heed to the effects such activities could have on the lives of people directly involved or indirectly affected.

The immediate consequences of that seminal departure are well known. The 'take-off' times of modern capitalism went down in history as an era of blatant, unmitigated greed and unbridled cruelty to the lesser and less fortunate humans, of grimy, rackety and malodorous 'dark satanic mills', of the stench and squalor of the rapidly swelling mean streets, of a widening polarization between the haves and the have-nots, of deepening mass poverty, misery and wretchedness. The unscrupulous exploits of early entrepreneurs, intoxicated with the vast empty space they conjured up away from the cultivated lands of family workshops, craft guilds and parishes, triggered a widespread, almost universal moral outcry. But the complaints of the disinherited and uprooted and the laments of the ethical preachers would have remained voices crying in wilderness were it not for the emergent nation-states that invaded the 'no-man's-land' with a rising resolve to dispute and fold back the rule of its heretofore unchallenged exploiters.

The nineteenth century became an era of constraints, one by one imposed on the no-holds-barred, all-stops-pulled, unscrupulous game of profits. Prohibition of child labour was followed by legal shortening of working hours, safety and hygiene regulations and the endless series of other bills protecting the weaker against the omnipotence of the high and mighty. Above all, the legalization of trade unions and of their fighting strategies gave the victims and the victims-to-be of capitalist progress the right to an effective self-defence. Last but not least, the consistent, even if hotly contested expansion of political rights resulted eventually in a 'beyond left and right' consensus on the necessity of collective insurance against individual misfortune, expressed in the establishment of the welfare state.

We are living now through the process of the 'Great Separation Mark Two'. From an ever more constraining, vexing and obtrusive framework of legal/ethical wardenship exercised by the nation-state, capital managed to escape into a new 'no-man's-land', where few if any rules confine, restrict or hamper the freedom of business initiative. The new space in which the new (global) business moves is by the standards of the last two last centuries fully and truly *extra-*

*territorial*. For all practical intents and purposes, it has become a sort of 'outer space', from which blows can be delivered and hit-and-run raids launched to which all territorially confined plots of earth are vulnerable and which no territorially bound power can resist. That global space lies beyond the reach of all extant institutional guardians of standards of decency and ethical responsibility. History, we may say, repeats itself – though this time on a much grander scale. And so do the human misery and wretchedness that tend to be spawned and grow in the course of the emancipation of business from political and ethical control.

We can learn from Alexis de Tocqueville's study of the decadent years of the *ancien régime* that the actors of the original separation could escape from the net so easily because most of the net's strings were already frayed and frail and the whole net had already been in a state of advanced disrepair. Business would not wish to stay in the net – but that net would not, in any case, be able to hold it. And so the pioneering of a new kind of interfering, prying, meddlesome state authority by French revolutionaries could be seen as deriving from the pressing need to repair the damage perpetrated by the all-too-evident weakness of the old institutions that struggled against the odds and in vain to arrest or at least slow down the relentless disintegration of the social order. This aspect of history, too, seems to repeat itself in the time of the Separation Mark Two. Once more business has emancipated itself from local ties – not from the household this time, but from the nation-state. Once more it has set for itself an 'extraterritorial territory' in which it is virtually free to set its own rules. It seems that the present-day *'ancien régime'*, as represented by the multitude of sovereign nation-states, is increasingly incapable of slowing down, let alone arresting, the escape of business forces from a democratic control now as before locally confined. Worse yet, it also seems that every new act of escape further deepens the impotence of the *'ancien régime* mark two'.

Until its almost complete division into two power blocs that looked askance on any refusal to join (even the few scattered 'uncommitted' countries desperately tried to form a 'non-bloc bloc' of their own), the surface of the earth used to be sliced into the separate and mutually independent territories of the sovereign states. State sovereignty was claimed to be complete and indivisible and struggled to match that ideal, with all similarly sovereign states ready to assist each one of them in the name of sustaining the shared principle.

Such political sovereignty was a demanding matter. It required a capacity to balance the books, an ability to defend one's own boundaries and keep the potentially dangerous neighbours at bay, as well as the power to scramble together and service a complete cultural model providing for every aspect of life in common. For that reason, only relatively few populations could pass the test of statehood. Independence might be a widely coveted and avidly sought prize, but it was accessible only to a selected few. The League of Nations, unlike the present-day United Nations, had but few members.

It all changed, however, once all three (economic, military and cultural) legs of the tripod of powers on which political sovereignty was supposed to rest began to shake, wear out and fall to pieces even in the case of the long-established and relatively resourceful and solidly entrenched states. Few if any nation-states can be said these days to be autonomous, let alone self-sustained and self-sufficient – economically, militarily and culturally. The orthodox severe and stringent tests of statehood are ones that few if any existing states would pass. Economic, military and cultural autarky is no longer required when it comes to claiming and granting political independence. The joint result of all these departures is the progressive political fragmentation (some observers suggest *balkanization*) of the globe. The UN buildings, not planned for such an explosion, burst at the seams.

The proliferation of nation-states goes, however, hand-in-hand with their weakening. Small in size, in their volume of resources, or in both, economically and militarily dependent and culturally impaired states have no clout and far too little bargaining or nuisance power to reach the status of respected and reckoned-with players equal in stature to the principal actors on the global scene. Many, perhaps most seats in the assembly hall of the United Nations, an organization created to set, enforce and police the rules of the global game, are occupied by the spokespeople of the numerous varieties of 'banana republics'; by boarders at the courts of global businesses rather than by self-reliant, resourceful and exacting rule-setters for 'foreign', more correctly nomadic, capital.

## The prospects of global politics

How to explain this puzzle of two processes pointing apparently in opposite directions? Is the present-day proliferation of nominally

sovereign political units a matter of a time lag, a temporary malfunction sooner or later to be rectified? Is this a matter of economic
institutions moving faster, rushing ahead and leaving the slower and
more inert political structures, reluctant to 'modernize', behind, at
least in the initial laps of the marathon race? Are the latter structures likely to rise, albeit more slowly, to the scale of thought and
action already attained by global business and so restore what by
the orthodox criteria we would be willing to recognize as a *systemic
balance*? Perhaps this is what the future has in store. There are,
however, many facts that should caution against jumping to that
conclusion.

These days, *political* sovereignty is not just demanded more
boldly and vociferously than ever before; and not just demanded by
populations that would have hardly claimed it in the past. It is also
more joyously than ever before supported by 'world opinion' and
granted by the powers that count – except when a more resourceful
and potentially noxious neighbour stands in the way. When Slovenia
refused to share its tax income with Belgrade, Helmut Kohl suggested that it should be given independence on the grounds of being
ethnically homogeneous; there was no mention on that occasion of
economic, military or cultural self-sufficiency. That signalled a seminal change in the criteria of political independence in the new globalized world.

To dominate a territory in such a world (unlike in imperialism in
the times of solid modernity) no territorial invasion is required, no
sending in the troops to occupy and to police the conquered territory, setting permanent garrisons and installing administrative
offices. These days all such strategies would seem, by comparison
with the new means available, unbearably unwieldy, cumbersome,
troublesome and above all costly. Today, true might expresses itself
in the ability to avoid such outdated strategies. A calamity to be
avoided more than any other and shunned most earnestly by the
high and mighty is the need to 'engage on the ground' and to take
responsibility for the daily management of local law and order and
daily care for the residents' survival. After all, lands may now be
conquered, subordinated and kept obedient at a much lesser cost.
State 'independence' granted to ever smaller and weaker territorial
units and populations is such a cheaper, and thus 'more rational'
way of spreading and entrenching global rule. Enforcement of free
trade and of abolition of tariffs and excise duties can suffice now to
achieve the kind of domination for which military conquest, managerial takeover and appropriation of territory were once required.

And so state sovereignty becomes easier to obtain, while its scope and contents are progressively impoverished. With economic, military and cultural self-management fast becoming things of the past and surviving increasingly as fictions or empty pretences ('zombie concepts', to use Ulrich Beck's witty term), the state tends to be reduced to the status of an enlarged and ennobled police precinct. The function it is expected to perform is to keep law and order on the ground and so prevent the territory under its rule from turning into a 'no-go area' for nomadic capital. A crucial part of the 'law and order' duty which the state-granted independence is expected to shoulder is to guard the selectivity of osmosis – to set apart those things and people that are let in from those that had better be stopped at the border.

A further function is to see to it that the country offers to those who have been let in, to the travelling salespeople of nomadic capital, a comfortable, hospitable and attractive environment in which they would be glad, if only until further notice, to pitch tents. Such an effect is likely to be attained if taxes are cut and cut again, if the regulation of labour conditions is reduced to a bare minimum, if labour-defending organizations are pacified or muzzled, and above all if no restrictions are observed on the free in-and-out movement of that capital. All in all, the *conditio sine qua non* of keeping the 'global investors' happy and inducing them to seek profits in this country rather than another is to make the condition of native producers and consumers as precarious as possible. *Precarité*, as Pierre Bourdieu has repeatedly pointed out,[28] is the most reliable insurance against effective resistance or rebellion against all powers that be; and also, in our times, against the globalizing pressures.

To sum up: globalization in its present form demands that orthodox-style state sovereignty be severely curtailed. Conversely, the emptying of state sovereignty of its orthodox prerogatives is for the global capital players the most foolproof and most coveted warrant of their unchallenged global domination. In view of such interdependence one wonders whether the present-day political fragmentation – that made all political (let alone democratically supervised) action on a par with the global scope of economic forces non-viable, non-feasible, if not inconceivable – is indeed an effect of a 'time lag' (a temporary malfunction of a system momentarily thrown out of joint, an aberration bound to be cured in the long run), as has been suggested. Is it not rather an endemic and lasting feature of an emergent global system unlike all other social systems we have known? Are not the mutual out-of-jointness of elements, the con-

tinuous disequilibration, the unending series of imbalances and dis-
ruptions resulting in a massive production of uncertainty on every
level of social organization, the very qualities that make the 'new
global disorder' (to deploy Kenneth Jowitt's felicitous phrase) into a
*system*? This is an open question with no straight answer, and
bound to remain such as long as it is but a *theoretical* question. The
answer, whatever it may prove to be, can be only supplied by *political practice*.

Since under a regime of global interdependence the chances of
effective actions and satisfactory outcomes of action are fickle and
erratic, and above all resistant to all fixing, mobility becomes a most
precious and sought-after resource. If chances cannot be 'fixed to
the place' and made to last, one needs to go *where* the chances
appear and *when* they appear – never hampered by local commitments, free to cut the local ties and pack up at short notice, leave
the chattels behind and travel light. Capacity to move has become
the major, perhaps the paramount stratifying factor of the emergent
global hierarchy. No wonder that this capacity tends to be allocated
highly unevenly and has become a focus of contention and a principal stake in competitive struggle. The main factor of stratification is
instrumental in the new polarization of opportunities and life standards, powers of self-assertion and amounts of personal freedom.

Despite appearances (insinuated and made credible by the statis-
tics of air travel, car sales, or the saturation of mobile telephone
networks, that tend as a rule to report the 'totals' or the 'averages'
and so to conceal rather than reveal the social effects of the
'growth'), mobility remains a scarce resource. As recently collated
figures show,[29] long-distance travel is mostly the privilege of the
residents of Western and Southern Europe and North America,
while the richest 20 per cent among them travel about 3.5 times
further than the poorest 20 per cent. All in all, 98 per cent of the
world population never move to another place to settle, while even
in affluent Britain 50 per cent of the population still live within five
miles of the place where they were born. And as the value and
attraction of mobility grow, so do the pains and the deprivations the
promotion of mobility causes.

The blatant inequality of access to mobility is not just the expectable, since 'natural', effect of income differentiation, casting the
costs of transport beyond the reach of the poor. Differentiation of
mobility chances is one of the few strategies avidly and consistently
pursued by the governments of more affluent areas in their dealings
with the population of less affluent ones. That differentiation is

meticulously managed and laboriously defended. The dismantling of all hurdles barring the free movement of capital and its carriers is complemented by the erection of new and ever higher and more off-putting barriers against the multitude wishing to follow suit and go where opportunities beckon. Travelling for profit is encouraged; travelling for survival is condemned, to the joy of the smugglers of 'illegal immigrants' and in spite of occasional, quickly forgotten fits of horror and indignation caused by the sight of 'economic mi-grants' suffocated or drowned in the vain attempt to reach the land of bread and drinking water. The globalized world is a hospitable and friendly place for tourists, but inhospitable and hostile to vaga-bonds. The latter are barred from following the pattern that the first have set. But that pattern was not meant for them in the first place. Besides, it would not bring the benefits for which it has been eulo-gized by its advocates and beneficiaries were it fit for a mass following instead of being a privilege of the exclusive and well-protected few.

No wonder, therefore, that the continuing globalization of human dependency prompts ambiguous, often contradictory reactions. Globalization has no shortage of enthusiastic preachers, epic pro-phets and lyrical poets. It has also its jeremiahs. Reactions are many and diversified, but they all fall into two broad categories.

The first category overlaps roughly with the communitarian ten-dency fast gathering force. Since the nation-state has evidently failed to protect its subjects from the rising tide of uncertainty, perhaps some sort of salvation can be found in retrenchment. With diversity and multivocality obviously harbouring the awesome dangers of *precarité*, perhaps the uniformity of sameness will prove more con-ductive to the safety that is so badly missed? Perhaps the brother-hood/sisterhood of nation may restore the vanished confidence, delivering the security which the citizens' republic so abominably fails to supply? If solidarity between the different is so difficult to obtain (and not particularly eagerly sought either), perhaps one can retreat to the solidarity of primordial ties, preceding rather than following the political process with its awkward negotiation, com-promises and uncertain results? Perhaps one can skip the political process altogether, and so get rid of, rather than resolve, the increas-ingly baffling problem of collective responsibility for, and the social production of justice?

Communitarianism (or should it be, more to the point, called 'tribalism'?) is essentially a dream of a Salem that has managed to free itself from witches and the fear of witches. It cannot help but be targeted against the infidels, the heretics and the lukewarm inside the ranks as much as, or more than, against the enemy outside. A disturbingly thin and easy to efface line separates the lofty vision of a communitarian bliss from the practice of ethnic cleansing and ghettoization. Communitarianism is eminently capable of causing new pains while struggling to cure the old ones.

But in addition, communitarianism is unlikely to mitigate, let alone to eradicate, the pains it promises to cure, though it accumulates its emotional capital and creams off political profits on the strength of that promise. A deep flaw of communitarianism resides in its endemic inadequacy to the task it was conceived to resolve – in as far as that task consists in eradicating the causes of the misery which prompted its constituency to seek remedy in the first place, and so made them wish 'to do something about globalization'. Rather than bridling the globalization forces and staving off the dire consequences of their free rein, the political fragmentation, profusion of hostilities and breakdown of solidarity which communitarianism is capable of generating (perhaps bound to generate) would only pave the way to a yet more absolute, unchallenged domination of the forces it meant to tame and keep at a distance.

Responses of the second category boil down to positing the task of subjecting economic forces once more to the democratic (ethical, political and cultural) control they have managed to escape, breaking up and playing havoc with human solidarity as a result. Of that task one may say many things, but not that it is likely to be easy to perform.

Let me repeat an *effective response to globalization can only be global.* And the fate of such a global response depends on the emergence and rooting in of a global (as distinct from 'international', or more correctly interstate) political arena. It is such an arena that is today, most conspicuously, lacking. The existing global players are singularly unwilling to set it up. Their overt or implicit adversaries, trained in the old yet increasingly ineffective art of diplomacy, seem to lack the needed ability and indispensable resources to do the job. New forces are needed to re-establish and reinvigorate an *agora* adequate to the globalization era – and they may assert themselves only through by-passing *both* kinds of players. This seems to be the only certainty, all the rest being the matter of our shared inventiveness, political trial-and-error practice, and the resolve to see it through to the end. It may seem an abominably inconcrete, non-specific programme for action – but it helps to remember that few if any thinkers could envisage in the midst of the first 'Great

Separation' the form which the damage-repairing operation would ultimately take. What they were sure of was that some operation of that kind was the paramount imperative of their time.

And of that we can entertain no doubt either. What, indeed, is at stake? Woody Allen, with his rare knack for flawlessly spotting the trials and tribulations as well as fads and foibles tormenting/incapacitating his contemporaries, offered a plausible answer to this question (in a prospectus of imaginary 'adult summer courses' for which his fellow Americans would be most happy to register[30]). The description of the course in Astronomy as composed by Woody Allen informs us that 'the Sun, which is made of gas, can explode at any moment, sending the entire planet system hurtling to destruction; students are advised what the average citizen can do in such a case.' Without its political counterbalance, the globalizing process is likely to grow ever more reminiscent of Woody Allen's Sun, while the chances of preventing the planet 'hurtling to destruction' do not seem much greater than those of the average citizen's options in the case of that Sun's explosion... Without an effective political counterbalance, the globalizing process looks like posing solely the sort of dilemma which Woody Allen also masterfully, even if tongue-in-cheek, captured: 'More than at any other time in history, mankind faces a crossroads. One path leads to despair and utter hopelessness. The other, to total extinction. Let us pray we have the wisdom to choose correctly...'

Let me note that despair and hopelessness are reflections of the toughness and resistance of the object one would wish to transform – but also of the weakness of the instruments one is able to deploy in order to transform it. The object may go on resisting as long as the instruments remain weak and so sorely inadequate to the task. It follows from our reasoning so far that effective action seems to stay stubbornly beyond the pale of human capacity because of the acute uncertainty that permeates our individual and shared condition. The uncontrolled spinning on of the globalizing process and existential uncertainty feed and reinforce each other. They form a genuine vicious circle – a new rendition of the Gordian knot that badly needs cutting. The century just ended tied that knot. Finding the way of cutting it will need to occupy the attention of the century that has just started.

# 3

# Living and Dying in the Planetary Frontier-land

The events of 11 September 2001 have many meanings. They will be appropriated and reprocessed by many discourses and construed as turning points in quite a few historical sequences. It is tempting to suggest, though, that the most seminal and longest lasting significance of the events will ultimately prove to be that of a *symbolic end to the era of space*.

A symbolic, rather than the historically correct end of the era – since what happened on 11 September 2001 has only brought to the surface, dramatically displayed and forced into public attention subterranean developments that had been going on for quite a long time and took a few decades at least to mature. The jets stolen on their routes from Boston, like a pebble thrown into a container filled with an oversaturated solution, caused the substances that had already, unnoticed, radically altered the assumed chemical composition of the compound to crystallize abruptly and so to become suddenly visible to the naked eye. And the events of 11 September were also symbolic in another sense: the terrorist assault on the best-known landmarks of the globally best-known city, committed in front of the most numerous TV cameras the modern media can gather in one place, easily won the stature of a globally legible signifier which other events, however dramatic and gory, could not dream of. It showed, again dramatically and spectacularly, how *global* events can truly be. It gave flesh to the heretofore abstract idea of global interdependence and the wholeness of the globe. For all those reasons, it fits the role of the symbolic end to the era of space better than any other event in recent memory.

The era of space started with the Chinese and Hadrian's walls of ancient empires, continued with the moats, drawbridges and turrets of medieval cities and culminated in the Maginot and Siegfried lines of modern states, to end up with the Atlantic and Berlin walls of supranational military blocs. Throughout that era, territory was the most coveted of resources, the plum prize in any power struggle, the mark of distinction between victors and defeated. One could tell who had emerged victorious from a battle by finding out who was still (alive) on the battlefield when the fight fizzled out. But, above all, territory was throughout that era the prime guarantee of security: it was in terms of the length and the depth of the controlled territory that issues of security were pondered and tackled. The era of space was the time of the 'deep hinterland', *Lebensraum, cordons sanitaires* – and the Englishmen's homes that were their castles. Power was territorial, and so was the privacy and freedom from that power's interference. 'Chez soi' was a place with borders that could be made tight and impermeable; trespassing could be effectively barred and entry could be strictly regulated and controlled. Land was a shelter and a hideout: a place to which one could escape and inside which one could lock oneself up, 'go underground' and feel safe. The powers-that-be from which one wished to escape and hide stopped at the borders.

This is all over now, and has been over for a considerable time, and there was no dearth of signals (as one can easily gather from the antiquated flavour of the last paragraph's stories) – but that it is indeed definitely over became dazzlingly evident only on 11 September. The events of 11 September made it obvious that no one, however resourceful, distant and aloof, can any longer cut themselves off from the rest of the world.

It has also become clear that the annihilation of the protective capacity of space is a double-edged sword: no one can hide from blows, and nowhere is so far away that blows can not be plotted and delivered from that distance. Places no longer protect, however strongly they are armed and fortified. Strength and weakness, threat and security have now become, essentially, *extraterritorial* (and diffuse) *issues that evade territorial* (and focused) *solutions.*

The sources of the present-day global insecurity are located in what Manuel Castells dubbed the 'space of flows' and cannot be accessed, let alone effectively tackled, as long as the measures undertaken to cure or mitigate that insecurity are confined to but one or a selected few of the places it affects. Until 11 September, though, the search for solutions to globally gestated threats tended to be substituted by (vain and ineffective) attempts to find localized and personalized exemptions from danger (think, for instance, of the huge demand for family nuclear shelters in the time of the 'mutual assured destruction' Cold War strategy, or of the unstoppable growth in the popularity of 'gated communities' at a time of rising urban violence and crime). The inaccessibility of the global roots of insecurity as long as dealing with them is attempted from inside a locally confined territory, and using only locally available means, has long caused a 'safety overload': a shifting of insecurity-prompted concerns and worries to the action-field of safety. Safety is the only aspect of the certainty/security/safety triad that can be acted upon (whether effectively or not is another matter) in the narrow frame of a single place. Above all, safety-promoting action is the only kind that can be *seen* as a proof that something is being done.

A terrorist attack 11 September style was plausible and on the cards for a long time, due to the global insecurity massively generated inside the uncolonized, politically uncontrolled, thoroughly deregulated extraterritorial 'space of flows' – but it remained an abstract threat pondered solely by scholars fond of taking a bird's-eye view of global affairs. The materialization of that threat in the form it eventually took swiftly reforged the scholars' forebodings into commonsensical truths – having brought the untouchable within touch, the invisible within sight, and the distant within the neighbourhood. It thereby allowed the threat to be translated from the language of *global insecurity*, difficult to master and awkward to use – a semantically impoverished language with few if any syntactic rules – into the all-too-familiar, daily deployed and easily understood language of *personal safety*. In the longer run that translation may assist in the comprehension of the link between the two issues, all too often separately considered, and even enable the reverse translation (of local safety concerns into global security issues). For the time being, though, one thing that seems to have settled in the current *doxa* is the new condition of the *mutual assured vulnerability* of all politically separated parts of the globe.

What has become more evident than ever before is that the degree of vulnerability can no longer be measured by the size of the arsenals of high-tech weapons once developed with (by now old-fashioned) *territorial wars* in mind. As Eric le Boucher summed up the new wisdom that was forced upon us on 11 September: 'the world cannot divide itself into two separate parts – one rich and secure behind its modern anti-missile system, the other left ... to its wars and "archaisms".[1] After 11 September, it has become clear that the 'far-away countries can no longer be left to their anarchy' – that is, if the rich and allegedly secure want to stay rich and indeed be secure.

## Global frontier-land

The new experience can be best summed up in the following thesis: *the global space has assumed the character of a frontier-land.*

In a frontier-land, agility and cunning count for more than a stack of guns. In frontier-lands, fences and stockades announce intentions rather than mark realities. In a frontier-land, efforts to give conflicts a territorial dimension, to pin divisions to the ground, seldom bring results. Suspected from the start to be ultimately ineffective, those efforts tend to be half-hearted anyway: wooden stakes signal a lack of the self-assurance that stone walls embody and manifest. In frontier-land warfare, trenches are seldom dug. The adversaries are known to be constantly on the move – their might and nuisance-making power lie in the speed, inconspicuousness and secrecy of their moves. For all practical intents and purposes, the adversaries are *extraterritorial*. Capturing the territory they occupied yesterday does not mean today's victory, let alone a 'termination of hostilities'. Most certainly, it does not assure a secure tomorrow.

In a frontier-land, alliances and the frontlines that separate them from the enemy are, like the adversaries, in flux. Troops readily change their allegiances, while the dividing line between non-belligerents and those in active service is tenuous and easily shifted. As coalitions go, there are no stable marriages – only admittedly temporary cohabitations of convenience. Trust is the last thing to offer, loyalty the last to expect. To paraphrase Anthony Giddens's memorable concept, one could speak here of 'confluent alliance' and 'confluent enmity'. The first starts in expectation of gain or more convenience, and falls apart or is broken off once satisfaction fades away. The second – even if burdened with a long history of animosity – tends nevertheless to be willingly and keenly suspended (for a time at least) so long as cooperation with the enemy promises more benefits than a showdown.

Starting the war against the Taliban, Donald H. Rumsfeld, the US Secretary of Defense, warned that the war 'will not be waged by a grand alliance united to defeat an axis of hostile powers. Instead, it will involve floating coalitions of countries, which may change and evolve.'[2] His deputy, Paul Wolfowitz, seconded such a strategy vindicating a return to frontier-land conditions (or rather helping to reshape the global space after the frontier-land pattern) when he anticipated 'shifting coalitions', predicting that in the coming war 'some nations might help with certain operations, and others could be called upon in a different capacity.' As he summed up the new military wisdom, 'to be effective, we have to be flexible. We have to be adaptable.'[3] And flexible the operation that followed was indeed – though, inevitably, flexibility cut both ways, and it was soon proved to mean something considerably less straightforward than what Rumsfeld or Wolfowitz meant it to mean.

The American air offensive against the Taliban began under the slogan *'with* Pakistanis against the terrorist' and with grooming Pakistan for the role of the crucial ally. But as the air attacks began to drag on with little to show for the money and effort spent and the trail of destruction left behind, the alternative of paving the way for a ground assault by the vehemently anti-Pakistan Uzbeks and Tadjiks of the 'Northern Alliance' became increasingly seductive. The temptation proved to be irresistible – and the application of a changed strategy ended up with the new masters of the Taliban-cleansed Afghanistan proclaiming war 'against terrorists and *against* Pakistanis'... Preparing for the war, the US Secretary of State with the help of the British Prime Minister courted the friendly and not-so-friendly Arab governments into the war coalition. The first stage of the war wound up with a massacre perpetrated by the victorious gangs of the former 'Northern Alliance' on the Arab volunteers in Afghanistan and the demand to cleanse the country of 'foreigners', whether friendly or hostile in their genuine or putative intentions.

When I write these words, the saga of shifting coalitions is far from reaching its denouement. The temporary new rulers of the country devastated by several decades of internecine wars and several weeks of carpet-bombing are not the coalition thought to emerge at the end of the anti-Taliban campaign. United for the time being by the prospects of ample perks of office and a fresh memory of the awesome power of the Pentagon's reprisals for disobedience, they nevertheless stay as before the kind of bedfellows unlikely to share a bed for long. They probably mark time in expectation of American military targets shifting, as they certainly will, elsewhere – which is what in all likelihood will happen sooner rather than later. Once a bureaucratic institution acquires the capacity to perform a certain kind of task successfully, it is bound to seek actively for new occasions for that task to be performed again. When operating in a

frontier-land, the chances are that it will seek and discover many
more targets for the spectacularly efficient air-force that would
allow it to do just that. And as Gary Younge, the perceptive columnist of the *Guardian*, observed, 'defining a terrorist...is entirely
dependent on the balance of forces at any time. Those the Americans once financed they now seek to execute.'[4] The likely overall
effect of the Afghan war will be less security and more bloodshed in
the global frontier-land.

Under frontier-land conditions, any war against *terrorists* can be
won, given enough flying weapons and enough money to goad and/
or bribe 'floating' and 'flexible' allies into the role of foot soldiers.
But the war against *terrorism* is unwinnable (not winnable conclu-
sively) as long as the global space retains its 'frontier-land' character.
Keeping coalitions 'floating' or 'shifting' is itself one of the paramount factors contributing to the perpetuation of this frontier-land
nature of the global space. The strategy of temporary coalitions of
transient interests, the concomitant avoidance of firmly institutionalized structures empowered to elicit permanent obedience to universal rules, the resistance against the establishment of long-term,
mutually binding and authoritatively supervised commitments – all
stand between the present-day frontier-land and any prospect of
replacing it with a global, politically serviced and controlled order.
There is simply no prospect of gain in building and cementing global
legal and political structures if, thanks to the superior weapons and
apparently inexhaustible resources under command, each successive
objective can be reached without them more swiftly and at much
lower cost. 'Committee wars' are, by comparison, much slower to
take off and much more awkward to conduct. And global authorities, once entrenched, may sooner or later pile up obstacles against
the unilateral determination of targets and the selection of the most
expedient ways of hitting them; they will constrain the freedom of
attackers, or at least render their choices costlier to make than thus
far. Democracy and the rule of law look once move like an odious
and redundent burden.

It is indeed easy to understand why the 'flexible coalition' strategy
coupled with an emphatic rejection of any long-lasting and universally binding structures may be tempting for the powers that, relying
on their competitive superiority, hope to benefit from the resulting
uncertainty, and would not wish to share the anticipated gains
with the less resourceful and fortunate. The point is, though, that
the strategy can serve more than one master – and once applied, sets
the conditions facilitating its wide use by all sorts of unintended,

anticipated and undesirable actors. The 'shifting alliances' of the old-style frontier-land were equally useful to cattle barons and lonely gunslingers with a prize on their heads.

Indeed, the perpetuation of global disorder suits the purposes of the terrorists as well as it serves the world domination of those who wage war against them. One of the principal reasons why the war against terrorism is unwinnable is the fact that both sides have vested interests in the perpetuation of frontier-land conditions. On this one point, both sides see eye to eye, even if they speak in different voices. There is, one may say, an ungentlemanly agreement which neither side of the 'war against terrorism' show any intention of breaking. Both sides militate against the imposition of constraints on the newly gained extraterritoriality of the skies or the freedom to ignore or push aside the 'laws of nations' whenever such laws feel inconvenient for the purpose at hand. This one coalition – the coalition against an equitable, universally binding and democratically controlled global order – seems to be the sole one that staunchly resists 'flexibility' and shows no inclination to 'float'.

A couple or so centuries ago, when the premodern *ancien régime* (of societies sliced into poorly coordinated, often separatist localities, and of the law fragmented into an aggregate of privileges and deprivations) fell apart, blazing the trail for a state and anti-state terrorisms and making society a dangerous place, a vision of a new, supralocal, nation-state level of social integration emerged. That vision triggered and kept on course nation-building and state-building efforts. Whether the practical effects of those efforts matched the visionary ideal or not, and in how many details, is another matter. What did matter in the long run was the fact that there was *a vision*, and an urgency aroused by that vision to invade and conquer the emergent frontier-land in order to tame it, domesticate it and otherwise make it safe for human habitation (that hard and by no means uniformly successful effort was to be called in retrospect the 'civilizing process'). We may say that nation-state politics *preceded* and *guided* the establishment of the nation-state: in a sense, politics created its own object.

No comparable vision has emerged so far in our times, when the fluid-modern rendition of the *ancien régime* (in the shape of the planet sliced into sovereign nation-states with no universal law binding them all) is falling apart, blazing the trail for global state and non-state terrorisms. There is no 'politics of global order' in sight that boasts a vision wider than that of an average police precinct. In the absence of such a wider vision, the sole strategy of imposing the rule of law and order is that of rounding up, incarcerating and otherwise disempowering the agents whose pretensions to exploit the license made possible by the frontier-land setting has been declared illegitimate by those unhampered in their own presumptions. Most certainly, little thought and even less political will have thus far been dedicated to the possible shape of democratic control over the forces currently emancipated from the extant institutions of legal and ethical control and free to deliver blows of their choice to the targets of their choice...

As Clausewitz put it, war is but a continuation of politics by other means. Of the war declared by the United States and Britain on terrorism, Jean Baudrillard said that it was but a continuation of the *absence of politics* by other means.[5] In the absence of global politics and global political authority, violent clashes are only to be expected. And there will be always someone eager to decry the act of violence as terrorist, that is an illegitimate, criminal and punishable act. The expressions 'terrorism' and 'war on terrorism' will remain hotly, essentially contested concepts, and the actions they prompt will remain as inconclusive as they are self-perpetuating and mutually reinvigorating.

## Reconnaissance battles

In a fluid milieu where old routines are quickly washed away and the new ones are hardly ever allotted enough time to acquire a shape (let alone to solidify), groping in the darkness pierced by but a few random shafts of light (a plight ennobled in the currently fashionable sociological rhetoric with the name of 'reflexivity') is the sole available way of acting. All action cannot but be experimental – not in the orthodox sense of the 'experiment' (that is, of a carefully designed test meant to prove or disprove the existence of a predicted/hypothesized/guessed regularity), but in the sense of a random search for one lucky move among many that are ill-conceived and mistaken. Action proceeds through trials, errors, new trials and new errors – until one of the attempts brings a result that could, under the circumstances, pass for satisfactory.

In the absence of routine and tested, apodictically commanded or authoritatively endorsed recipes for success, actions need to be, and tend to be, excessively abundant. Most of the moves are anticipated and feared to be unsuccessful, and the sole service they may reasonably be expected to render is to be eliminated from future calculations as part of the mind-boggling multitude of possibilities. A profusion of trials does not guarantee success, but it sustains the hope that among the many failed and wasted attempts one at least will be on target. George Bernard Shaw, an exquisite professional of the stage but an enthusiastic amateur of photography, is reputed to have insisted that like the cod that needs to spawn thousands of eggs for one new fish to reach maturity, the photographer must take thousands of photographs if he wishes to produce one satisfactory print. Many, perhaps most actions undertaken in the underdefined, underdetermined, underregulated global frontier-land seem to follow, by design or by default, the advice Shaw bequeathed to photographers. Prominent instances of such actions are reconnaissance battles – arguably the most common category of warfare (and violence in general) in our global frontier-land.

In military practice, 'reconnaissance battles' (or reconnaissance-through-battle) have one purpose: to sift the grain of the hopefully possible from the chaff of the impossible or hopeless. Reconnaissance battles *precede* the setting of war objectives and the design of war strategy. They are meant to supply the hard facts needed for the selection of feasible goals and the range of realistic options from which future military actions may be selected.

In the case of reconnaissance battles, units are not sent into action in order to capture enemy territory, but to explore the enemy's determination and endurance, the resources the enemy can command and the speed with which such resources may be brought to the battlefield. The units are ordered to lay bare the enemy's strong points and weaknesses and the shrewdness and miscalculations of the enemy commanders. Analysing the course of a reconnaissance battle, staff officers hope to make intelligent guesses concerning the enemy's power of resistance and capacity for a counterattack, and so suggest realistic war plans.

Reconnaissance battles bear a striking resemblance to 'focus groups', the modern politicians' favourite means of anticipatory intelligence-gathering before deciding on the next move: testing the electorate's possible reactions to steps considered, but not yet taken, before irreparable damage is caused by an ill-advised or wrongly calculated step which is revealed to be unpopular and resented. Indeed, a good deal of current military thinking and the armament policies inspired by that thinking takes the form of 'simulated reconnaissance battles', conducted inside staff conference rooms or during military exercises on experimental ranges instead of on the temporarily unavailable battlefields.

Reconnaissance battles are the principal category of violence in an underregulated environment. The current case of 'underregulation' is the result of the progressive collapse of the structures of authority that previously and until recently were deemed intractable and bound to be suffered meekly however oppressive they might have been felt; or of the appearance of new sites of action where the question of legitimate authority has never been asked, let alone answered. The collapse of old authority structures affects all levels of social integration, but it is particularly conspicuous and consequential at two levels: the global, and the life political. Both levels have acquired a heretofore unprecedented importance amidst the totality of factors shaping the conditions under which lives are nowadays conducted, and both lack traditions that could be invoked and relied upon whenever new and untested, but hopefully correct and success-promising, patterns of action are sought.

Much neighbourhood and family violence is an application of the reconnaissance-battle strategy to life politics. Forms of coercion practised daily in family life, once deemed unavoidable and suffered in silence, have lost or been denied legitimacy (often disguised under the 'it is natural' or 'there is no alternative' verdict) after the powers ready to police them retreated, so that the bluff of the status quo's assumed intractability could be (and so promptly has been) called. New forms of 'pure relationships' (of cohabitation and partnership devoid of established sets of rights and obligations and decoupled from all long-term commitment) exist solely through a continuous and endemically inconclusive experimentation, of which a succession of reconnaissance battles is an indispensable ingredient. With the surrender by the powers-that-be of their past nation-building ambitions, retreat from the *cuius regio, eius religio* rule and the abandonment or bankruptcy of cultural crusades and all other forms of the anthropophagic (devouring) and anthropoemic (disgorging) strategies, deployed for the sake of such and similar purposes, the ethnic and denominational interfaces became another ground for reconnaissance battles. In the course of the dismantling of the panoptical model of social order, with patriarchal families as the elementary cells of the social tissue and the male 'heads of the family' performing the disciplining function parallel to that of the foreman on the factory floor or the sergeant in the barracks, gender relationships have become yet another territory on which reconnaissance battles are daily waged.

On the planetary plane, the political void that has replaced a world tightly structured (after the pattern of Gothic cathedrals rather than classical palaces) by the tensions arising from the mutual containment and reciprocal balancing of two power superblocs currently provides another natural area for reconnaissance battles. A political void is a constant invitation to a bargain-by-force. Neither the outcome of the global game nor its rules are predetermined and there are no global political institutions capable of systematically limiting the range of the players' choices and forcing or persuading them to respect the limits. The responses to the terrorist assault of 11 September have exposed yet further the essential lawlessness of the global frontier-land and the irresistible seductiveness of catch-as-catch-can tactics.

To quote the summary of the Afghan war experience by the *Guardian*'s Madeleine Bunting:

> What the events of the past few days have starkly revealed is that the US had only one interest in this war in Afghanistan, capturing Bin Laden and destroying al-Quaida; that imperative outstripped all considerations of Afghanistan's future. So the timing of the attack was decided by US military preparedness rather than any coherent political strategy for the region, and the US war aim determined the crucial switch in tactics around November 4 when the US decided to throw its weight behind the unsavoury Northern Alliance by bombing the Taliban frontlines.[6]

William Pfaff of the *International Herald Tribune* saw such a sudden U-turn coming, being an inevitable consequence of the US attitude to the world's problems: first, 'Afghanistan has been substituted for terrorism, because Afghanistan is accessible to military power, and terrorism is not'; and then, inevitably, 'official Washington [started] rapidly losing interest in political solutions. There is an increasing disposition toward brute force, and the use of whatever allies are at hand, even if that threatens to leave Afghanistan in chaos, and the war on terrorism stranded.'[7] George F. Will, though from an opposite standpoint, endorsed that verdict on the logic of American strategy: 'In spite of the secretary of state's coalition fetish, the administration understands the role of robust unilateralism. And neither lawyers citing "international law" nor diplomats invoking "world opinion" will prevent America from acting...preemptively in self-defence.'[8] Note that both 'international law' and 'world opinion' appear in inverted commas.

It has been said that the Taliban, the targets of the most recent war on terrorism, were invented by the British, managed by the Americans, financed by Saudi Arabia and put in place by Pakistan.

The trouble with such a verdict is that it can only be pronounced with the benefit of retrospective wisdom. At the moment of writing, the Taliban have been bombed out of existence and the vacant position of Afghanistan's nominal rulers has been filled by West-sponsored and anointed tribal chiefs. In the course of time, though, one will perhaps say of them much the same as one says now of the Taliban, with but minor modifications, once they have filled the place vacated by the assorted terrorists presently defeated.

The condition of lawlessness, eagerly exploited in all reconnaissance battles, is self-perpetuated with every successive attempt, undertaken by whatever side, to turn it to that side's advantage. Each act of violence leads to retaliatory actions that invite responses in kind. As the balance of power and the range of opportunities shift, yesterday animosities are discarded or suspended for the sake of manning newly emerged frontlines. Enemies turn overnight into allies and allies into enemies, as new ad hoc coalitions cut across old ad hoc coalitions and plum prizes are hoped to be gained by a timely changing of sides. And so the waging of reconnaissance battles in the hope of fathoming the opportunities offered by continuous instability becomes an increasingly tempting strategy, gladly resorted to, with a similar zeal and acumen, by those concerned with preserving their privileges and those bent on gaining them alike. Gregory Bateson's 'schismogenetic chains' need no external boosting to perpetuate themselves: they expand and self-replicate, drawing all the procreative energy they need from their own inner logic. As the cycle of offence-to-be-avenged-by-vendetta-to-be-avenged unravels, both sides (to use Knud Løgstrup's terminology) lose their ability for sovereign, self-generated action and become ever more constrained in their next moves. Offences crying for vengeance self-propagate: 'There is no proportionality between what occasioned the affront and the reaction to it', because sides have 'two high an opinion [of themselves] to tolerate the thought of... having acted wrongly, and so offence is called for to deflect attention from [their own] misstep.'[9]

This Gordian knot cannot be untangled; it can be only cut – just as the interminable recycling of vendettas in Euripides' Hellas was cut by Sophocles' rule of law. The cycle of violent reconnaissance battles may grind to a halt only if and when there is nothing left to reconnaisse: if and when universally binding and enforceable rules of conduct that allow no unilateral opting out and disallow the inverted commas when international laws and world opinion are invoked are put in place. When raising an outcry about the violation of human rights stops being a matter of (short-lived) political and military convenience. When, for instance, the principle of women's equality exploited to add ethical splendour to the assault on Afghanistan is applied to the discrimination against women in Kuwait or Saudi Arabia.

## Asymmetrical wars

The term 'asymmetrical war' entered the current vocabulary together with other linguistic novelties – the concept of 'stateless wars' and the more non-committal notion of the 'wars of the fourth generation'.[10] The present-day asymmetrical wars are also stateless. It happens that one or another side in an asymmetrical war is formally commissioned and commanded by a state government, but such a circumstance is thought to be assigned a secondary importance by the fact that the 'asymmetrical enemies' join forces and cooperate in a further weakening of the sovereign powers of nation-states. Some of the combatants may do it by design, some others by default – but all promote supremacy of the extraterritorial, global forces. Judged by the effects of their actions and their impact on planetary politics, all participants in asymmetrical wars are ultimately 'transnational'. They are also transnational in the way they behave: they are mobile, uncommitted to any place, easily shift their targets and recognize no boundaries nor the sanctity of any locally promulgated laws.

There is much that the adversaries entangled in asymmetrical wars share, and the attributes they share are their quite essential, by no means accidental, features. In view of that parallelism of attitudes, similarity of conduct and the convergence of consequences, in what sense can their hostilities be named 'asymmetrical'?

One of the possible meanings of 'asymmetry' may refer to the fact that the weapons and the murderous potential of the enemies engaged in an asymmetrical war are as a rule disproportionate; were the adversaries to meet face to face on a battlefield in an orthodox combat, the confrontation would be swiftly ended, its outcome having been a foregone conclusion from the start. This is one of the reasons why as a rule one of the adversaries tries hard to avoid a direct showdown with the enemy forces and prefers guerrilla-style hit-and-run tactics, hoping that for once a paucity of arms will prove an advantage: the absence of heavy equipment and so a superior facility to disappear, hide and effectively escape confrontation might compensate for the appalling inferiority of weapons. Paradoxically, the weaker side's reluctance to have a face-to-face trial of strength happens to be a highly convenient circumstance for the other, better equipped side, because of the latter's profound (and thoroughly expectable under the liquid-modern conditions that radically alter the pragmatics of domination) resentment against bearing the consequences of victory in the form of responsibility for the day in, day out administration of the conquered lands (the Pentagon stubbornly refused to allow the engagement of ground troops in Afghanistan unless an 'exit scenario' was ready before the army units were sent in). And so on both sides of the mobile and diffuse frontline, though for different reasons, orthodox 'combat' is strongly resisted and at all costs eschewed. The sharp differences in the potency of their weapons and the deployed tactics notwithstanding, *both* sides display a unanimous preference for 'hit and run' strikes, best of all unannounced strikes, but in all cases such strikes as can be, and are, swiftly executed and do not demand that the performers remain on the battleground once the strike has been delivered. For the perpetrator operating away from home territory, one of the most tempting attractions of 'hit and run' tactics is the prospect of washing their hands of the consequences and shifting the task of repairing the damage on to the enemy that has suffered the strike, or yesterday's 'flexible coalition' partners.

The genuine asymmetry of 'terrorism wars' derives however from the different – nay opposite – influence that globalized conditions exert on the plight and the range of choice available to the adversaries. In the era of globalization, mobility and its accessible speed become the principal factors of the new – global – stratification. It is the velocity of transmission at a distance (of information and of action) that puts the global elite (extraterritorial thanks to the distance-defying swiftness of their movement) at the top of power hierarchy. On the other hand, it is the status of *glebae adscripti* – of being 'bound to the earth' – and the constraints imposed on changing places, coupled with the impotence to arrest or even slow down the motility of the power elite, that cast the global underdog at the bottom of that hierarchy. It is this radical difference of status that prompts terrorists and those who wage war against them to act at cross-purposes. This is perhaps the sole trait that offers an empirical grounding to the otherwise 'essentially contested' and indiscriminately used concept of 'terrorism' and allows a distinction to be made between terrorist acts *sensu stricto* and the kinds of punitive strikes by state-commanded forces that fit equally well the definition of terrorism as the 'calculated use, for political or religious purposes, of violence, threat of violence, intimidation, coercion and fear'.[11]

Terrorists (terrorists *sensu stricto*, that is) are prompted to demonstrate the incompleteness of their own immobilization and so prove the vulnerability of the elite despite its superior mobility. One of the purposes of terrorist acts is to show that the verdict of confinement has its loopholes, that confinement is ineffective as an instrument of disempowerment, that blows can be delivered far beyond the limits of confinement – and that, despite the advantages drawn from the speed they command and their freedom to float, the powerful adversaries (who still need to come to ground, time and again, if only to refuel, as well as needing offices to run their businesses and homes in which to enjoy their gains) have their Achilles' heel where they can be hit and wounded – not mortally perhaps, but painfully (and humiliatingly!) all the same. The global elite cannot be slowed down, let alone immobilized – but at least the bluff of the immunity allegedly offered by speed and mobility can be called, or a sham ingeniously contrived so that the self-confidence of the powerful will be eroded and they will no longer be allowed to trust in their invulnerability.

In its response to the terrorists, the elite aims, asymmetrically to the terrorists' intentions, to restate and reinforce the immobilization of their adversary. It tends therefore to emphasize in its strategy the territoriality of the enemy, recasting the issue of world terrorism as a problem of 'rogue states' and reducing the task of fighting terrorism to the incarceration of the targeted terrorists as physical, spatial bodies.

From that asymmetry follows another: the asymmetry of weapons. Each side's weapons are subordinated to the aims of war; these aims being contradictory, one would expect the weapons to bypass rather than confront each other. Unlike the arms known from the hostilities of the 'mutual assured destruction' era, that assigned supreme significance to the conquest and defence of territory, the kinds of equipment developed for and used in the 'mutual assured insecurity' type of war, a war that favours 'hit-and-run strategy' and evasion of face-to-face combat, have to be asymmetrical just like the statuses of their users and the aims of the campaigns they launch. Nowadays, weapons are made to the measure of randomly focused, brief and admittedly inconclusive reconnaissance actions. Indeed, however painful and shocking the blows delivered by the terrorists may be, they can hardly undermine the foundation of their adversaries' global domination against which their opposition is mounted. Conversely, terrorism can hardly be uprooted by the force of the weapons deployed in the counterattacks. 'Hit-and-run' intentions all too often produce 'run-and-miss' practice.

The orthodox, territorial wars aimed at expanding one's own possession of land at the expense of that of the neighbours are by no means extinct; if anything, they are made more likely than before due to the competition for the new stakes offered by the globalizing process. True, the prizes made available, promised or anticipated in the blatantly underdefined and underinstitutionalized world of liquid modernity make it tempting to wage terrorist-style reconnaissance battles in the hope of securing a better share of spoils. If territory is at stake, however, testing the neighbours' stamina and defensive capacity is but a secondary consideration, the prime concern being to attract attention to the cause from the global game's major players, so that they may be more willing (or rather feel obliged) to assist the attackers in obtaining the adversary's submission (as the Kosovo Albanians, for instance, spectacularly succeeded in doing, and the Palestinians, Basques or Kurds have tried hard, but thus far failed to achieve). Because of superficial similarities, territorial wars can be easily mistaken for another specimen of the 'reconnaissance battle' category. The fact that terrorist methods are used and battles with all the 'reconnaissance' marks are waged in the conduct of such orthodox – territorial – wars does not however place them in the category of asymmetrical wars. Disputing a territory, both sides are obliged, willy-nilly and each according to its resources, to resort to similar kinds of weapons and strategies.

Properly asymmetrical wars are a concomitant of the globalizing process. They are cut to the measure of global space, conducted on the global stage and explicitly discard territorial ambitions. Not the territory, but the principle of territoriality and its abolition are at stake – though, whether by commission or by omission, all sides help to entrench the new extraterritoriality of the human condition.

### War as a vocation

The decline of territorial wars coincided with the decline of mass conscript armies. These two fateful departures were closely related in their turn to the passage from the solid to the liquid stage of modernity and the dismantling of the panoptical form of domination; and to follow the causal chain further down – to the end of the 'era of space' and the emergence of the 'era of speed', marked by the devaluation of space and (to deploy Paul Virilio's suggestions) bringing the velocity of tele-vision and tele-action in the 'speed-space' to their ultimate, speed-of-light limits.

Conscript armies have been replaced with professional and highly specialized army units, whose main function (at least in theory) is to destroy and put out of action similarly space-confined targets – units of the enemy's professional army and the new 'sinews of war' of the liquid modernity era, that is the intelligence gathering and process-ing centres, broadcasting stations or fuel and armaments depots. Armies become leaner, nimbler, faster moving. They tend to be groomed for action in dispersion, in small groups or individually, more reminiscent of swarms than the marching columns of yore. The ratio of technical equipment to human power needed to service and operate them is changing radically in favour of the first, and an ever greater portion of the skills once lodged in soldiers' memories and trained habits is transferred to the electronic appliances of targeting, and increasingly also of tactical and strategic decision-making. (One recalls the joke about the automated factory of the future: it will employ only two living beings, a man and a dog. The man will be there to feed and stroke the dog, the dog will be there to prevent the man from touching any of the machinery. As profes-sional armies go, such a future seems not that far away.)

The new fashion of conducting military action aims at excluding, possibly altogether, face-to-face confrontation with the enemy. Hit-and-run tactics are hoped, among other things, to put paid to the traditional banes of invading forces, like threats of fraternization with the natives and a gradual softening of the morale of the con-scripts of the conquering army, which once had to be fought back with the help of intense surveillance and continuous ideological in-doctrination of the troops. The new tactics of striking and killing at a distance, coupled with the shift of the task of target-selection on to inhuman (unfeeling and morally blind) parts of the war machine, has also stretched to unprecedented lengths the technique of 'adia-phorization' of military action, stripping action-on-command from ethical evaluation and moral inhibitions.

The soldier's task, like that of any other professional, is just 'a job to be done'. The propriety of performance is measured, as in the rest of the professions, in terms free from moral import. The sole ethical rules allowed to intervene in the evaluation of professional perform-ance are those of strictly following the logic of hierarchical com-mand, and completing the task set for the action at the least cost and in a manner approximating as closely as possible to the commanders' briefing. Hit-and-run tactics and electronic mediation between human actors and their human targets have jointly accomplished what for the bureaucracies of Max Weber's time remained, obstinately and infuriatingly, only an inaccessible horizon of the 'ideal type'.

The new obsolescence of territorial occupation, redundancy of mass conscript armies and professionalization of the armed forces from top to bottom have allowed wars to adjust to liquid-modern conditions in general and to the operating mode that fits the nature of the 'speed-space' in particular. Going to war in the times of conscript armies called for a protracted period of laborious ideological preparation. Patriotic emotions and feelings of threat had to be lifted to a high pitch at which personal survival instincts are either dimmed and disempowered, or dissolved in the cause of collective salvation. Those about to be called to arms had first to be made ready to die for the country. How far we have moved away from such stark necessities has been vividly shown recently by the promptness with which the readiness to sacrifice life for the cause has been condemned and classified as a symptom of religious fanaticism, cultural backwardness or barbarism – by the countries that for many centuries represented martyrdom-for-a-cause as the proof of saintliness and entitlement to beatification, that less than a century ago adorned their capitals with Cenotaphs around which they gather annually to pay homage to the heroes who fell so that the nation could live, and all along used the cult of fallen soldiers to gain and defend their collective identities.

The advent of professional armies deinstrumentalized patriotic fervour. The collective frenzy now redundant for military purposes can be safely poured out and unloaded during football matches, Eurovision song contests and the Olympic Games; it has been promptly harnessed to the service (and profit) of the entertainment industry. Whatever remains of it is time and again recycled ('spun') to beef up support for one or another of the competing political teams, is sometimes appealed to (with but meagre effect) to boost demand for domestic foods or films – but is seldom if ever resorted to, or needs to be, to make going to war feasible. This allows war actions to be started quickly, overnight if need be, whenever the supreme commander of the armed forces considers such actions desirable and likely to be successful – and in the effect renders the proliferation of wars more rather than less probable. The Vietnam War was perhaps the last fought by American conscripts. Sending to war expeditionary forces composed only of professionals does not involve political risks comparable to those taken by Johnson or Nixon and is unlikely to trigger the kind of popular resentment that caused the protracted post-Vietnam trauma. Besides, that trauma was in large part due to the military defeat, not the dirtiness and immorality of the carpet-bombing of villages and the pouring of napalm on villagers – and the new smart bombs and stealth bombers, coupled with the elimination of combat, guarantee that war may be ineffective, but is defeat-proof. Today, President Bush can declare in one breath that the country 'is at war' and that, in the country, 'business is as usual'.

Subjected to professional conditions of service, the soldiers have gained the status of employees, with all the attendant safeguards of job conditions and rights to compensation in case the contractual standards are not met. Thanks to the high level of skills and know-how that the servicing of high-tech equipment demands, and the intense wear-and-tear of mental and emotional forces caused by the risks involved, soldiers belong to the relatively privileged sector of the labour market that offers better-than-average job security and job satisfaction. But perhaps the most striking effect of the new form of warfare is that during military actions it is the soldiers who enjoy the greatest personal safety. It is the risks to their lives and bodies that are reduced to the minimum. 'In a war won at the push of a button, bravery does not count,' commented reporters from the *Observer*[12] – and it is neither needed nor called for, let me add. During the Afghan campaign seven soldiers lost their lives, only one as a result of enemy action: the others fell victim to 'accidents at work', the usual risk of the most peaceful of professions (this compares with six journalists who were killed by the enemy since, unlike the soldiers, they had to be where the action was and not where it was remotely controlled).

Contemporary military professionals are no longer brave, swashbuckling matadors; they are more like the coolly professional, down-to-earth operators in a state-of-the-art abattoir. In this kind of war, it is solely the casualties among military personnel who truly count and are counted. And it is the soldiers' welfare that is meant when 'saving lives' is proclaimed to be the commanders', and their political bosses', prime concern. The other casualties of the war are 'collateral'. Pressed by Leslie Stahl of CBS about half a million children who died because of the US's continuous military blockade of Iraq, Madeleine Albright, then US ambassador to the United Nations, is said to have answered that 'this was a difficult choice to take', but 'we think that the price was worth paying'.[13] Which

American dignitary would dare to say the same of half a million dead American soldiers? Civilian casualties of war are counted only reluctantly, and more often than not they are uncountable: after all, people killed by direct hits, destroyed by 'daisy-cutters' or in the course of 'carpet-bombings' are but a small fraction of the victims. Towns are shattered and villages are erased, panic is sown, crops and workshops are burnt, and thousands or millions of people are overnight transformed into homeless refugees.

In the military calculations presented in a publicly digestible form by PR or political (the distinction is often difficult to make) spokespeople, all this is perhaps an unpleasant, but all the same unavoidable side-effect of action aimed after all against 'enemy forces', not 'innocent civilians'. In the times of territorial conquest and conscript armies, when the whole of the 'enemy nation' were actual or potential enemy soldiers, the entire population of the 'enemy country' was seen (with good logical, if not moral, reasons) as a 'legitimate target'. Once war becomes a matter of professionals, the targets that are no longer 'legitimate' become collateral damages, difficult to justify, let alone to defend in morally acceptable terms.

The ethical devastation caused by such a shift in classification is enormous, and not easy to grasp in full. 'Side casualties' are more like the uncomfortable side-effects of a potent medical drug: difficult to avoid, necessary to put up with for the sake of the therapy. 'Collateral casualties' lose their lives because the damage done to them counts less in the total balance of the action's effects. They are disposable, 'a price worth paying', and not because of what they have done or are expected to do, but because they happened to stand in the way of the bombers or lived, shopped or strolled, imprudently, in the vicinity of the professional armies' playground. Were it possible to bar the TV cameras access to that playground, the 'collateral damage' could be left out of the calculations (and the action reports) altogether.

The ejection of war and the 'killing business' in general from the focus of ethical debate in which they stood for most of human history, and even more significantly the removal of the actions leading to the murderous effects of war from control by the moral constraints and ethical convictions of the actors, are perhaps the most seminal of the attributes of the new professional army. They set the scene for new kinds of horrors, quite distinct from those born on the battlefields. Thus far, there is no sign of a new Geneva Convention intended to confine and limit the human devastation the new horrors portend.

## Living together in a full world

Habent sua fata libelli... books have their own destiny. The fate of Kant's little book, *Ideen zu einer allgemeine Geschichte in weltbür-gerlicher Absicht*, is as thought-provoking and illuminating as it has been peculiar. Conceived in Kant's tranquil Königsberg seclusion in 1784, it quietly gathered dust, for two centuries, in academic libraries – read only, mostly as a historical curiosity and without much excitement, by a few dedicated archivists of ideas. And after two centuries of exile to the footnotes and bibliographies of scholarly monographs, it all of a sudden burst into the very centre of 'contemporary history'. These days, it is a hard task to find a learned study of our most recent history that would not quote Kant's Universal History as a supreme authority and source of inspiration for all debate of world citizenship – itself an issue that has suddenly found itself at the centre of public attention.

The *fatum* of this particular *libellae* may seem strange and baffling, but it holds in fact little mystery. Its secret is simple: it took the world two hundred years to reach the limits of a tendency that had guided it since the beginning of modern times – but which Kant, having put it to a philosophical test, found in advance contrary to 'was die Natur zur höchsten Absicht hat' 'Nature's supreme design'. Kant observed that the planet we inhabit is a sphere – and thought through the consequences of that admittedly banal fact. And the consequences he explored were that we all stay and move on the surface of that sphere, have nowhere else to go and hence are bound to live forever in each other's neighbourhood and company. And so 'die volkommene bürgerliche Vereinigung in der Menchengattung', a 'perfect unification of the human species through common citizenship', is the destiny Nature has chosen for us – the ultimate horizon of our universal history that, prompted and guided by reason and the instinct of self-preservation, we are bound to pursue and in the fullness of time reach. This is what Kant found out – but it took the world two more centuries to find out how right he was.

Sooner or later, Kant warned, there will be no empty space left into which those of us who have found the already populated places too cramped or too uncongenial for comfort could venture. And so Nature commands us to view (reciprocal) hospitality as the supreme precept which we need – and eventually will have to – embrace in order to seek an end to the long chain of trials and errors, of the catastrophes the errors caused and of the ruins left in the wake of the catastrophes. As Jacques Derrida would observe two hundred year later, Kant's propositions would easily expose present-day buzz-words like 'culture of hospitality' or 'ethics of hospitality' as mere tautologies: 'L'hospitalité, c'est la culture même et ce n'est pas une éthique parmi d'autres... *L'éthique est hospitalité.*'[14] Indeed, if ethics, as Kant wished, is a work of reason, then hospitality is – must be or sooner or later become, ethically guided humankind's first rule of conduct.

The world, though, took little notice; it seems that the world prefers to honour its philosophers by memorial plaques rather than by listening to them, let alone by following their advice. Philosophers might have been the main scribes of the Enlightenment lyrical drama, but the post-Enlightenment epic tragedy all but neglected their script. Busy with equating nations and states, states with sovereignty, and sovereignty with tightly controlled borders, the world seemed to pursue a horizon quite different from the one Kant had drawn. For two hundred years the world was occupied with making the control of human movements the sole prerogative of state powers, with erecting barriers to all other, uncontrolled human movements, and manning the barriers with vigilant and heavily armed guards. Passports, visas, custom and immigration controls were among the major inventions of the art of modern government.

The advent of the modern state coincided with the emergence of the 'stateless person', the *sans papiers*, and the idea of *unwertes Leben*, the latter-day reincarnation[15] of the ancient institution of *homo sacer*, that is the ultimate embodiment of the sovereign right to exempt and to exclude such human beings as have been cast beyond the limits of human and divine laws; to make them into beings that can be destroyed without punishment – and whose destruction is devoid of all ethical or religious significance.

The full burden of the modern classifying, including–excluding zeal was throughout the initial phase of modern history somewhat less exasperating, having been partly relieved by the other modern enterprise: opening an unprecedentedly vast expanse of 'virgin land' that could be used as a dumping ground for those unwanted, and act as a promised land for those who fell by the wayside from the vehicle of progress. No land of course was really 'virgin' at the time Kant's *Allgemeine Geschichte* was sent to the printers; but plenty of lands had already been *made* virgin and many more were to be classified as 'virgin' in the coming decades thanks to the enormous and still rapidly rising power differential between the fast industrializing centre and the lagging periphery. That power of the metropolis was so overwhelming that it could declare the extant human habitation of the 'primitive', 'backward' and 'savage' lands null and void, and summarily recast the population of such lands as a collective 'homo sacer' of the metropolis – thereby offering all the rest a licence to kill. Somewhat later, the technique of summary exclusion from the human race, developed during the conquest of distant lands, was to be ricocheted on Europe; as Aimé Cesairé pointed out in 1955,[16] what the Christian bourgeois (of Europe and its extensions) could not really forgive Hitler was not the crime of genocide, but the crime of having applied to Europe the colonialist actions that had been borne up till then by the Arabs, the coolies of India and the Negroes...

Colonization allowed Kant's premonitions to gather dust. However, it also made them look, when finally dusted off, like a prophecy of apocalypse instead of the cheerful utopia Kant intended them to be. Kant's vision looks that way now because, due to a misleading abundance of 'no-man's-land', nothing needed to be done and so nothing was done in those two centuries to prepare humanity for the revelation of the ultimate fullness of the world.

To get rid of the domestic European *homini sacri*, the lands decreed as virgin provided the Devil's Islands, Botany Bays and other similar dumping grounds to European governments envious of the Russian empire's rule over the infinite permafrost expanses of Siberia. For Europeans fearing the outcasts' lot, the 'virginized lands' offered a promising alternative – a hideout and a chance to 'start a new life'. Irish villagers sought there salvation from potato-blight famine at home, German, Swedish and Polish peasants ran there from overcrowded villages and decaying townships with no jobs and no prospects, Jews sought safety there from Russian pogroms. The untitled offspring of titled families travelled to the 'frontiers of civilization' hoping to restore their power and wealth in military service, colonial administration or business ventures, having first built a new world – a world needing to replace the indolent and somnolent native nobility with brand new elites, and so suited to providing the incomers with brand new career tracks. For many years, modernity, that intrinsically expansive and transgressive civilization, had no reason to worry: the civilization made of the urge to expansion and transgression had seemingly infinite space in which to expand and could look forward to endless new barriers waiting to be transgressed. On the map of the modern world there was profusion of blank spots marked (provisionally, of course!) 'ubi leones', 'here there be lions', and waiting to be spattered with new towns and criss-crossed with new road networks. Those distant blank spots were safety valves letting out the steam and protecting the metropolis from overheating. There were a lot of places for the adventurous to seek adventure, for the gamblers to try their luck and for the defeated to attempt to reverse bad fortune. The world was anything but full.

Well – it is now. No more Statues of Liberty promising to huddle the downtrodden and abandoned masses. No more escape tracks and hideouts for anyone but a few misfits and criminals. But (this being, arguably, the most striking effect of the world's newly revealed fullness) no longer a safe and cosy *chez soi* either, as the events of the 11 September have proved dramatically and beyond reasonable doubt.

That manifestation of the changed existential condition took us unawares – as the change itself took us unprepared. The sacrosanct division between *dedans* and *dehors*, inside and outside, that charted the realm of existential security and set the itinerary for future transcendence has been all but obliterated. *Il n'y a pas de 'dehors'* any more ... we are all 'in', with nothing left outside. Or, rather, what used to be 'outside' entered the 'inside' – without knocking; and settled there – without asking permission. The bluff of local solutions to planetary problems has been called, the sham of territorial isolation has been exposed.

Frontier-lands of all times have been known as, simultaneously, factories of displacement and recycling plants for the displaced. Nothing else can be expected from their new, global variety – except of course the new, planetary scale of the production and recycling problems. Let me repeat: there are no local solutions to global problems – although it is precisely local solutions that are avidly, though in vain, sought by the extant political institutions, the sole political institutions that we have collectively invented thus far and the only one we have. And no wonder, since all such institutions are local, and their sovereign power of feasible (or for that matter legitimate) action is locally circumscribed.

## Refugees in a full world

For the two hundred years of modern history, refugees, voluntary and involuntary migrants, 'displaced persons' *tout court*, were naturally assumed to be the host country's affair and handled as such. Few if any of the nation-states that filled the modern map of the world were as local as their sovereign prerogatives. Sometimes willingly, other times reluctantly, all of them had to accept the presence of aliens inside the appropriated territory, and all had to admit the successive waves of immigrants escaping or chased away from the realms of other sovereign nation-state powers. Once inside, the settled or fresh aliens fell under the exclusive and undivided jurisdiction of the host country. That country was free to deploy the updated, modernized versions of the two strategies which have been described in *Tristes Tropiques* by Claude Lévi-Strauss as the alternative ways of dealing with the presence of strangers.

The available choice was between the anthropophagic and the anthropoemic solutions to the strangers' problem. The first solution boiled down to 'eating the strangers up'. Either literally, in flesh – as, in the cannibalism allegedly practised by certain ancient tribes; or in a more sublime, modern metaphorical remake, spiritually – as in the power-assisted assimilation practised almost universally by nation-states so that the strangers are ingested into the national body and cease to exist as strangers. The second solution meant 'disgorging the strangers' instead of devouring them: rounding them up and expelling them (just what Oriana Fallaci suggested we should do with people who adore other gods and display baffling toilet habits) either from the realm of the state's power or from the world of the living.

Let us note however that pursuing either of the two solutions made sense only on the twin assumptions: of a clean-cut territorial division between the 'inside' and the 'outside', and of the completeness and indivisibility of the sovereignty of the strategy-selecting power inside its realm. Neither of the two assumptions commands much credibility today, in our liquid-modern global world; and so the chances of deploying either of the two orthodox strategies are, to say the least, slim.

With the tested ways of acting no longer available, we seem to be left without a good strategy to handle newcomers. At a time when no cultural model can authoritatively and effectively claim superiority over competing models, and when nation-building and patriotic mobilization have ceased to be the principal instruments of social integration and state self-assertion, cultural assimilation is no longer an option. Since deportations and expulsions make dramatic television and are likely to trigger a public outcry and tarnish the international credentials of the perpetrators, governments prefer to steer clear of trouble by locking the doors against all who knock asking for shelter.

The present trend to reduce drastically the right to political asylum, accompanied by the stout refusal of entry to 'economic immigrants', signals no new strategy regarding the refugee phenomenon – only the absence of a strategy, and a wish to avoid a situation in which that absence causes political embarrassment. Under the circumstances, the terrorist assault of 11 September was a gift to politicians. In addition to the usually brandished charges of sponging on the nation's welfare and stealing jobs,[17] refugees now stand accused of playing a 'fifth column' role on behalf of the global terrorist network. At long last, there is a 'rational' and morally unassailable reason to round up, incarcerate and deport people when one does not any longer know how to handle them, and does not want to take the trouble to find out. In the US, and soon after in Britain, under the banner of the 'anti-terrorist campaign', foreigners have been promptly deprived of the essential human rights that until now have withstood all the vicissitudes of history since the Magna Carta and habeas corpus. Foreigners can now be indefinitely detained on charges which they cannot defend themselves against, since they are not being told what they are. As Martin Thomas acidly observes,[18] from now on, in a dramatic reversal of the basic principle of civilized law, the 'proof of a criminal charge is a redundant complication' – at least as far as foreign refugees are concerned.

The doors may be locked, but the problem won't go away, however tight the locks. Locks do nothing to tame or weaken the forces that cause displacement. The locks may help to keep the problem out of sight and out of mind, but not to force it out of existence.

And so, increasingly, refugees find themselves in a cross-fire; more exactly, in a double bind. They are expelled by force or frightened into fleeing their native countries, but they are refused entry to any other. They do not *change* places; they *lose* a place on earth, they are catapulted into a nowhere, into Augé's 'non-lieux' or Garreau's 'nowherevilles', into Michel Foucault's 'Narrenschiffe', into a drifting 'place without a place, that exists by itself, that is closed in on itself and at the same time is given over to the infinity of the sea'[19] – or (as Michel Agier suggests in a forthcoming article in *Ethnography*) into a desert, that by definition *un*inhabited land, a land resentful of humans and seldom visited by them.

Refugees have become, in a caricatured likeness of the new power elite of the globalized world, the epitome of that extraterritoriality where the roots of the present-day *precarité* of the human condition, that foremost of present-day human fears and anxieties, are sunk.

Those fears and anxieties, seeking other outlets in vain, have rubbed off on the popular resentment and fear of refugees. They cannot be defused nor dispersed in a direct confrontation with the other embodiment of extraterritoriality – the global elite drifting beyond the reach of human control, too powerful to be confronted. Refugees, on the other hand, are a sitting target for unloading the surplus anguish.

According to the UN High Commission for Refugees (UNHCR) there are between 13 and 18 million 'victims of enforced displacement' struggling for survival beyond the boundaries of their countries of origin (not counting the millions of 'internal' refugees in Burundi and Sri Lanka, Columbia and Angola, Sudan and Afghanistan, condemned to vagrancy by endless tribal wars). Of those, more than 6 million are in Asia, 7 to 8 million in Africa; there are 3 million Palestinian refugees in the Middle East. This is, to be sure, a conservative estimate. Not all refugees have been recognized (or clamoured to be recognized) as such; only a certain number of the displaced persons have been lucky enough to find themselves on the UNHCR register and under their care. Of those on the UNHCR register, in Africa 83.2 per cent are in camps, and in Asia 95.9 per cent (in Europe, so far only 14.3 per cent of the refugees have been locked in camps).

The camps are artifices made permanent through blocking the exits. The inmates cannot go back 'where they came from' – the countries they left do not want them back, their livelihoods have been destroyed and their homes burned or stolen. But there is no road forward either: no government would gladly see an influx of homeless millions. As to their new 'permanently temporary' location, the refugees are 'in it, but not of it'. They do not truly belong to the country on whose territory their huts are assembled and tents pitched. They are separated from the rest of the host country by the invisible, but thick and impenetrable veil of suspicion and resentment. They are suspended in a spatial void in which time has ground to a halt. They are neither settled nor on the move, they are neither sedentary nor nomads. In the terms in which the humanity of humans is narrated, they are ineffable. They are Jacques Derrida's 'undecidables' made flesh. Among people like us, praised by others and priding ourselves for our skills of self-reflection, they are not only untouchables, but *unthinkables*. In our world of imagined communities, they are the *unimaginables*. And it is by refusing them the right to be imagined that other – genuine or hoping to be genuine – communities seek credibility for their own labours of imagination.

Only a community frequently appearing these days in political discourse but otherwise nowhere to be seen in real life and real time, the *global* community, an inclusive yet not exclusive community, a community matching Kant's vision of 'Vereinigung in der Menschengattung' – a unification of the human species – may lift the present-day refugees out of the 'unplace' into which they have been cast.

The proliferation of refugee camps is as integral a product/manifestation of globalization as is the dense archipelago of stopover *nowherevilles* through which the new globe-trotting elite moves. What they share is extraterritoriality, their not truly belonging-to-the-place, being 'in' but not 'of' the space they physically occupy. For all we know, they may be the bridgeheads of an advancing extraterritoriality, or (in a longer perspective) the laboratories in which the desemantization of place, the disposability of meanings, the plasticity of identities and the new permanence of transience (all constitutive tendencies of the 'liquid' phase of modernity) are experimented with under extreme conditions and tested in a similar way to which the limits of human pliability and submissiveness, and the ways of reaching such limits, were tested in the concentration camps of the 'solid' stage of modern history.

Refugee camps and the *nowherevilles* share the intended, inbuilt, pre-programmed transience. Both installations are conceived and planned as a hole in time as much as in space, a temporary suspension of territorial ascription and the time sequence. But the faces they show to their respective users/inmates differ sharply. The two kinds of extraterritoriality are sedimented, so to speak, at the opposite poles of globalization. The first offers transience as a facility chosen at will, the second makes it permanent and irrevocable, an ineluctable fate: a difference not unlike the one that separates the two outfits of secure permanence – the gated communities of the discriminating rich and the ghettos of the discriminated poor. And the causes of difference are also similar: closely guarded and watched entries and wide open exits on one side of the opposition, and largely indiscriminate entry but tightly sealed exits on the other. It is the locking of the exits in particular that perpetuates the state of transience without replacing it with permanence. In refugee camps time is suspended; it is time, but no history.

Refugee camps boast a new quality: a 'frozen transience', an ongoing, lasting state of temporariness, a duration patched together of moments none of which is lived through as an element of, and a contribution to, perpetuity. For the inmates of a refugee camp, the prospect of long-term sequels and consequences is not part of the experience. The inmates of refugee camps live, literally, from day to day – and the contents of life are unaffected by the knowledge that days combine into months and years. As in the prisons and 'hyper-ghettos' scrutinized by Loïc Wacquant, camped refugees 'learn to live, or rather survive [(sur)vivre] from day to day in the immediacy of the moment, bathing in . . . the despair brewing inside the walls.'[20]

The rope fixing the refugees to their camp is plaited of push and pull.

The powers ruling over the land around the camp do whatever they can to prevent the inmates from leaking out and spilling over the adjacent territory. The outside of the camp is, essentially, off-limits for the camp's insiders. At the very best it is inhospitable, populated with wary and suspicious people eager to note and to hold against the inmates any genuine or putative error and every stumbling or wrong step the refugees, having been chased out of their element, are only too likely to take. In the land where their temporary/permanent tents have been pitched, refugees remain blatantly the 'outsiders', a threat to the security the 'established' draw from their heretofore unquestioned daily routine, a challenge to the heretofore universally shared world-view and a source of dangers not yet confronted, fitting ill into the familiar slots and evading the habitual ways of problem-solving.[21]

The 'established', using their power to define the situation and impose the definition of all those involved, tend to enclose the new-comers in an iron cage of stereotype, 'a highly simplified representation of social realities'. Stereotyping creates 'a black and white design' that leaves 'no room for diversities'. The outsiders are guilty until proved innocent, but since it is the established who combine the roles of prosecutors, examining magistrates and judges and so simultaneously make the charges, pronounce on their truth and sit in judgement, the chances of acquittal are slim, if not nil. As Elias and Scotson found out, the more threatened the established population feels, the more their beliefs are likely to be driven 'towards extremes of illusion and doctrinaire rigidity'. And faced with an influx of refugees, the established population has every reason to feel threatened. In addition to representing the 'great unknown' all strangers embody, the refugees bring home distant noises of war and the stench of gutted homes and scorched towns that cannot but remind the established how easily the cocoon of safe and familiar (safe because familiar) routine may be pierced or crushed.

Venturing from the camp to a nearby township, refugees ex-pose themselves to a kind of uncertainty difficult to bear after the stagnant and frozen, day in day out routine of camp life. But a few steps from the perimeter of the camp, they find themselves in a hostile environment. Their right of entry into 'the outside' is unclear at best and may be challenged by any passer-by. The inside of the camp seems a safe haven by comparison. Only the adventurous would wish to leave it for any considerable time, and fewer still would dare to act on their wishes.

Using the terms derived from Loïc Wacquant's analyses,[22] we may say that the refugee camps mix, blend and gel together the distinctive features of both the 'community ghetto' of the Fordist-Keynesian era and the 'hyperghetto' of our post-Fordist times. If 'community ghettos' were relatively self-sustaining and self-reproducing social totalities, complete with miniature replicas of the wider society's stratification, functional divisions and the institutions required to serve the needs of communal life, 'hyperghettos' are truncated, artificial and blatantly incomplete aggregates unable to survive on their own. Once the elites had moved out of the ghetto and stopped feeding the network of economic ventures sustaining (however precariously) the livelihood of the ghetto population, the agencies of state care and control (the two functions, as a rule, closely intertwined) moved in. The 'hyperghetto' is suspended on strings that originate beyond its boundaries and most certainly beyond its control.

In the refugee camps, Michel Agier found the features of 'community ghettos' intertwined in a tight network of mutual dependency with the attributes of a 'hyperghetto'.[23] We may surmise that such a combination tightens yet more firmly the bond tying the inmates to the camp. The pull of the 'community ghetto' and the push of the 'hyperghetto', however powerful they may each be in their own right, are superimposed and mutually reinforcing. When confronted with the hostility of the outside environment, they jointly generate an overwhelming centripetal force, difficult to resist, making all but redundant the technics of enclosure and isolation developed by the managers and supervisors of Auschwitz or the Gulag. More than any other contrived social microworlds, refugee camps come close to Erving Goffman's ideal type of the 'total institution': they offer, by commission or omission, a 'total life' from which there is no escape.

Having abandoned or been forced out of their former milieu, refugees tend to be stripped of the identities that milieu defined, sustained and reproduced. Socially, they are 'zombies': their old identities survive mostly as ghosts – haunting the nights all the more painfully for being all but invisible in the camp's daylight. Even the most comfortable, prestigious and coveted among old identities turn into handicaps: they cramp the search for new identities better suited to the new milieu, prevent a coming to grips with the new reality, and delay the recognition of the permanence of the new condition. For all practical intents and purposes, the refugees have been cast in the intermediate, 'betwixt and between' stage of Van Gennep's and Victor Turner's three-stage passage,[24] without however this casting having been recognized for what it is, without a time being set for its duration, and above all without an awareness that the return to the condition that preceded the present casting is all but cut out, and without any inkling of the nature of the new setting that may loom ahead.

All communities are imagined. The postulated *global community* is no exception to that rule. But imagination turns into a tangible, potent and integrating force when it is sustained by socially produced and socially maintained institutions of collective self-identification and self-government, as in the case of modern nations wedded for better or worse and till-death-them-do-part to modern sovereign states. As far as the imagined global community is concerned, a similar institutional network (woven of global agencies of democratic control, a globally binding legal system and globally upheld ethical principles) is largely absent. And this, I suggest, is the major cause of what is being called, euphemistically, the 'refugee problem', and the major obstacle to its resolution.

The unity of the human species that Kant postulated may be, as he suggested, resonant with Nature's intention – but it certainly does not seem 'historically determined'. The continuing uncontrollability of the already global network of mutual dependence and 'mutual assured vulnerability' most certainly does not increase the chance of such unity. This only means, however, that at no other time has the keen search for common humanity, and the practice that follows such an assumption, been as urgent and imperative as it is now. In the era of globalization, the cause and the politics of shared humanity face the most fateful steps they will have made in their long history.

# Part II
# Life Politics

# 4

# (Un)Happiness of Uncertain Pleasures

Most of us, most of the time, know how to use the word 'happiness' and its opposite, 'unhappiness'. We also know when to say 'I'm happy' and when 'I'm not'. But most of us would be hard-pressed if asked to spell out the *rule* that has allowed us to apply one of the 'happiness–unhappiness' pair of words to a particular case. We won't find it easy either to articulate clearly and unambiguously what we *mean* when we say 'I am happy' or 'I am unhappy.' More often than not, we would offer an *explanation* rather than the *definition*: we would say what in our view made us (or can make us) happy or unhappy, rather than what sort of experience we had and would like to report and communicate using one of those words.

The experience of being happy or not is akin in this respect to the experience of a colour. We know how to use the word 'red', but don't know how to describe the experience of 'redness'. At best, falling into a poetic mood, we can use metaphors drawn from other sorts of sensations, but that stratagem would not amount to much more than replacing one ineffable by another. The words 'happiness' and 'unhappiness', like the words 'red' or 'green', are fit to serve our interactions, but they fail to communicate in full, let alone to 'transplant', the experience the speaker means to grasp and convey to others in order to share it. Attaching names to a subjectively lived-through experience that have meanings that others may in turn associate with some of their own sensations wouldn't make that experience less 'ineffable' than it is. When I ask someone to hand over a red pencil, I may reasonably hope that the pencil I get will be of the colour that I'd be willing to name as 'red'. But I cannot say whether I, the asker, and the person who has acted on my request see 'redness' 'in the same way' (and what 'way' would it be?). At best I can assume that both I and he see 'red' *differently* from 'green', 'blue' and other colours. Similarly, we can take it for granted that all of us know the *difference* between 'being happy' and 'being unhappy'.

Admittedly, biochemistry and neurology have recently made tremendous strides in the exploration of organic changes associated with changes of experience. Scientists can offer us the exact chemical composition of the substances that are secreted in (his and my) brains when the sensations prompt (me and him) to speak of 'happiness' or 'redness'. Referring to such data, scientists will pass an objective judgement: the processes that occur in (his and my) nervous systems are, when the 'state of happiness' is reported, broadly similar. This discovery may satisfy our intellectual curiosity, but even a most exact knowledge of the composition and the circulation of chemical substances won't help us much when we wish to describe the sensations we are going through. Such 'non-transparency' of the words, the lack of a one-to-one correspondence between the feelings and the words that serve to convey them, jars with the standards of linguistic precision. No wonder that in all times the question has spurred philosophers into action and triggered long and hot, though hardly ever conclusive disputes.

And yet however satisfactory or disappointing the outcomes of such disputes may be, and whether or not we can verbalize the experience we go through to both our own satisfaction and that of our partners-in-conversation, we know very well (more exactly, each of us knows for herself or himself) *when* we feel happy or unhappy, and we know well what we, the speakers (again, each one for herself or himself), *mean* when we say that we are. Nevertheless, there is a more serious difficulty, one that may lead to genuine communicative confusion. That difficulty arises from the *equivocality* of the term 'happiness'. This name may be, has been, and continues to be in common as well as in specialist speech attached to several, and different, states of affairs. It is not immediately clear to which one of its referents the word 'happiness' is intended to point when spoken.

Władysław Tatarkiewicz, a prominent twentieth-century Polish philosopher and the author of a comprehensive inquiry into the idea of happiness, distinguishes four quite different senses in which the word 'happiness' is deployed.[1] His typology will provide the starting point for our discussion, which will however depart in a number of ways from Tatarkiewicz's own semantic suggestions.

There is, first, an 'objective' sense. We resort to it mostly when we speak of another person's condition. When saying 'she is happy', we do not refer directly to her state of mind or emotions (this state is, as has been pointed out already, inaccessible to our unmediated observation). We base our judgement on the general rule (which we believe to be true) that all or most people tend to experience the state we would be inclined to describe as happy when they find themselves in a condition 'like that' and when things 'like that' happen to them. When I say 'she is happy', I refer ostensibly to that other person's subjective experience, but in fact I assert an expectation derived from a certain theory of connection between the state of the world and the state of the spirit. I know what has happened 'in the world' (she has been promoted, passed a difficult exam, won a jackpot, become a celebrity) and I suppose that the happening should have made her experience happiness.

This first sense in which the term 'happiness' is used already assumes another sense of the 'happiness' idea – happiness as *subjective* experience (*Erlebnis* in German, as distinct from another German term, *Erfahrung*, also translated as 'experience' but suggesting something that 'happened to' the person rather than something that person 'lived through'). In that second, but probably the primary sense, the idea of 'happiness' refers to sentiments, emotions, feelings, states of mind. Of happiness in this sense we speak at moments of delight, bliss, rapture – intense joy. At *moments*: 'objective' happiness may last, but emotions are admittedly volatile and fleeting – they do not last long and they tend to vanish as quickly as they appear.

Tatarkiewicz recalls the third meaning of 'happiness', to which ancient and medieval philosophers dedicated most of their attention. In this use a 'happy person' is a person free from both want and excess; a person who has 'found the golden rule', who 'strikes it just right', who has everything he needs and no more, or rather everything that is worth having and nothing in excess that would make it a burden. The Greeks called such happiness εὐδαιμονία; the Romans *beatitudo*. It is easy to note that there was a partisan and essentially contestable theory incorporated in such usage: a supposition that a happy life (at least in the negative sense of the absence of unhappiness) is a well-balanced life, a life that steers clear of the Scylla of impoverishment and the Charybdis of intemperance, a life of harmony and a life confined to the care of goods worthy of desire and effort. Those last characteristics left such a concept of the 'happy life', as it were, open-ended. It was a matter of opinion as to what is worthy and what unworthy of attention in the pursuit of happiness, and what is indispensable or redundant for a happy life. And there is always the possibility of a pleonasm; one has the right to suspect that things whose possession is praised for making life happy are 'worthy' not thanks to their own intrinsic happiness-generating potential, but because they have already been made objects of desire through mental drill, ideological indoctrination, propaganda or an advertising campaign.

The last of the notions of 'happiness' distinguished by Tatarkiewicz also betrays a philosophical connection and is similarly theory-laden. Like the preceding sense, it is not likely to be found often in contemporary usage; and like it, it is bound to provoke controversy if it appears. Tatarkiewicz quotes Goethe at eighty-one years old declaring that he was happy and would like to live his life for the second time. Goethe referred to the *whole of life*, life as *totality*. That totality contained many moments of intense joy, but obviously it was not short of suffering or frustrations either; as a matter of fact, six years earlier Goethe himself admitted that looking back over his very long life he could not find a mere four-week-long stretch of continuous and complete happiness. Obviously, Goethe's quoted verdict concerned balancing the books of life, and for that reason it did not contradict the admission made six years before. There was no contradiction between the two propositions, Tatarkiewicz insists, because the sentence pronounced on the value of life as a whole is not and cannot be based on the calculation of the sum total of happy moments. It can only refer to the proper balance between joys and sorrows, both indispensable for a 'well-tempered' life.

In common speech as in specialist writings, the term 'happiness' happens to be deployed in all four senses. Resorting to admittedly close synonyms, we may say that these are senses conveyed respectively by the concepts of good luck, of pleasure, of satisfaction, and of good life. Each of the four meanings is short of the kind of precision that is called for by the standards set for scientific definitions. What is more, they could be cleanly separated from each other solely through a refined philosophical argument, but hardly in human life experience and the communication intended to share it. In the practice of human communication the four semantic fields all too often, wholly or partly, overlap. Besides, the boundaries that separate them from each other are hardly ever drawn sharply and unambiguously. Finally, they happen to be, again commonly, used

interchangeably. 'Happiness' often changes its meaning in the space
of one story or even one sentence – unnoticed by the speaker and
the listener alike. Whatever else philosophers have achieved and
may yet achieve through their disciplined reasoning and pedantic
argument, clarity in the common, popular, vernacular human thinking about happiness is unlikely to be counted among their gains.
The idea of happiness seems to be irrevocably doomed to remain
ambiguous. It could be compared to a container ready to accommodate substances of many colours and flavours and most varied
degrees of durability or transience.

The same imprecision and ambiguity of the idea of happiness that
worries and irritates philosophers secures however its continuous
utility in life. It is precisely because the verbal container is so
spacious and so hospitable to diverse contents that it may serve as a
meeting point for human images of good life – that is, of a life better
than the kind of life they live, a life they would prefer to the one
they have experienced so far. Thanks to its haziness the idea of
happiness may offer a meeting ground upon which battles tend to
be fought and negotiations conducted between advocates and adversaries of alternative fashions in which an individual life can be
designed, and the modes of life in common tend to be thrashed out
and negotiated. Different models of the desirable life are juxtaposed
and compared, turning thereby into alternatives. A range of choices
is created and expanded – a platform from which a critique of the
'really existing life' is daily launched.

This is, arguably, the main role played by the idea of happiness in
that unique form of being that describes itself as 'human', and
which on the authority of such self-definition sets itself apart from
all other variants of existence. *The human way of being-in-the-
world is a way that contains the idea of happiness.*

Thanks to the presence of this idea, four feats are accomplished in
one go.

First, that presence makes it obvious that reality *needs not be as it
is* and is not the sole reality that can be. It makes any reality
wanting, 'short of . . .', 'not fully up to . . .' The idea of happiness is,
endemically and incurably, an ongoing critique of reality. Happiness,
by the same token, is a call to action, and the reminder that action
matters, and so does inaction.

Second, that presence makes suffering unforgivable, pain an offence, humiliation a crime against humanity. As it grows ever more
ambitious and demanding, the image of happiness re-presents more
and more aspects of the human condition, old and new alike, as

unhappiness – and so it brings them under critical scrutiny. It is the idea of happiness that *makes the instances of unhappy experience insufferable*, calling for repair, clamouring for remedy. And thanks to its all-inclusiveness, this idea is a standing invitation to complaint, dissent, opposition and rebellion against the status quo; and to demands for its correction.

Third, the presence of the idea of happiness transports causes of action from the already determined past into the yet undecided future. The state of happiness that prompts action is forever outstanding, *ahead of the world as it is*. And so is, thanks to the happiness idea, the 'genuinely human' way of being-in-the-world, never tested in full, always yet-to-be-discovered-and-found and forever sought and struggled for. Such a peculiar cause of action as does not (is impotent to) determine the outcome makes the future into the condition it is known to be: underdetermined, open to experiment, unpredictable.

Fourth, it *unites* humanity in spite of, or rather through, its *diversity*. Happiness is what all humans want – even if they seek what they want in various locations and embark on voyages of discovery following different routes. It is not known after all nor can it be known for sure who holds its secret. This makes other human forms of life, other variants of humanity 'interesting': worth listening and talking to. It renders conversation potentially enriching ('we can learn from each other'), and keeps the ever rehearsed act of 'coming together' permanently full of hope. It prompts and keeps alive the wish to make the unfamiliar familiar, to make the distant close, the alien one's own. It makes the borderline between 'us' and 'them', that most ferociously guarded of frontiers, also the most crowded of sites, cursed/blessed with the heaviest of traffic.

Happiness (one would rather say 'the dream of happiness'; but then happiness is always a dream and can't be otherwise) is the soil in which the seeds of common humanity are sown, sprout and flourish.

## Senecan meditations, or happiness as eternal life

Lucius Annaeus Seneca's dialogue *De Vita Beata* ('On happy life') is a chain of permutations of one pervasive, recurrent theme: the distinction between the true, and a putative, false or deceitful happiness. False happiness is the most treacherous enemy of the real thing. Had it been known to him, Seneca could have quoted Gre-

sham's Law and said that presumptive happiness is like the counter-
feit or inferior coins that chase the genuine and valuable ones from
circulation. Not so simple, though, is the relation between *happiness*
and *pleasure*. True happiness always gives pleasure to the happy
man, but not all pleasures make a man happy. To realise that this is
the case, to know that pleasure may lead the seeker of happiness
further from, not closer to his target, wisdom is however needed.
That kind of wisdom is not a free gift of nature. It is not given to
everybody and cannot be attained without effort. Seneca composed
his dialogue with the aim of imparting that wisdom to his readers.

All humans want happiness, and all embark on the road to happiness; or, rather, we all embark on a road that we *hope* will lead us
to happiness (it is because of such hope that we have chosen and
followed the road we've chosen). But walking the road to happiness,
Seneca warns, is quite unlike walking the road to a city, a shrine, or
another popular spot many wish to visit. When you wish to reach
happiness, you cannot rely on the advice of people you meet on the
way, since those among them who can tell the right way from a
wrong one are few and far between. Moreover, you should defy
your natural inclination or acquired habit and keep away from the
most crowded paths (were the city your destination, not happiness,
the busier the road the more certain you'd be that you were on the
right track). Given the great numbers of those who err, other people's example may be your ruin. In the question of happiness,
numbers carry no authority. Relying on majority opinion won't help
you in your search. The odds are that listening to the majority view
will divert you from the goal. The herd is the last place where the
pattern of happy life could be found.

But you still need help, and so the question is from where may the
help be expected? Whom to consult? Luckily, nature has endowed
us all with *reason*, though not many among us *know* how to wield
that weapon and fewer yet are *willing* to use it. Most would prefer
to hide in the crowd, where wielding the sword of reason is not
required, and may be downright disallowed and swiftly punished –
so sparing themselves the tiresome need to learn the difficult art of
swordsmanship. Were we to listen to the voice of reason instead of
drowning it in the hubbub of hue and cry or stampede, we would
hear that, of the common objects of desire, 'there is nothing that the
passage of time does not demolish and remove', but that time
'cannot damage the works which philosophy has consecrated; no
age will wipe them out, no age diminish them'. Life 'is very short
and anxious for those who forget the past, neglect the present, and

fear the future. When they come to the end of it, the poor wretches realise too late that for all this time they have been preoccupied in doing nothing.' They have nothing to show for all their life trials and tribulations. Even if their restless life was met with the crowd's approval and applause, the '[h]onours, monuments, whatever the ambitious have ordered by decrees or raised in public buildings are soon destroyed.' To those who ran after momentary pleasures 'the time of actual enjoyment is short and swift, and made much shorter through their own fault. For they dash from one pleasure to another and cannot stay steady on one desire.'[2]

Pleasures are short-lived. They cannot be otherwise. It is in the nature of pleasure to be volatile, evasive, impossible to hold. As we read in *De Vita Beata*, pleasures start cooling down at their hottest moment. The human capacity for enjoyment is small, it fills up in no time and then the excitement gives way to listlessness and torpor. Happiness, on the contrary, can only be found in duration. It cannot be otherwise, since the ultimate cause of human misery is the incurable brevity of human life, the imminence of the end and the horror of the void that will follow it. What people conjure up in their dreams of happiness is time arrested – a being that is immune to the passage of time, no longer vulnerable to its all-eroding, all-pulverizing, all-annihilating powers. Pleasures cooperate with death: they cut time short. Unlike pleasures, happiness resists death: it strips time of its destructive powers and repairs the devastation that time leaves behind.

And so, in the last account, it is all about *time*. Or more to the point, it is all about passing away – that terribly painful, yet common, unavoidable and gruesomely persistent occurrence in which time first reveals itself to humans. As Schopenhauer put it, '*Time* and *perishability* of all things existing in time that time itself brings about is simply the form under which the will to live ... reveals to itself the vanity of its striving. Time is that by virtue of which everything becomes nothingness in our hands and loses all real value.'[3] And we all know and cannot forget that this is the case. 'The reason man's life is more full of suffering than the animal's is his greater capacity for knowledge.'[4] Knowledge of death, of its inevitability, contributes more than any other factor to the fullness of human suffering. Knowledge of human mortality would suffice to nip in the bud all interest in living were it not for the human capacity to insert in life a meaning it would otherwise lack: 'we take no pleasure in existence except when we are striving after something – in which case distance and difficulties make our goal look as if it would satisfy us.'[5] Seeking pleasures and struggling for happiness are two alternative ways of 'striving after something'. One strategy that is out of the question is doing nothing...

No strategy would cancel the imminence of mortality, the prime cause of its own urgency. As Pascal would admit a millennium and a half after Seneca recorded his thoughts for the illumination of posterity, '[w]hen I consider the brief span of my life absorbed into the eternity which comes before and after...I take fright.'[6] Such fright lies patiently in ambush, always ready to assault, disarm and take prisoner those reckless enough to ruminate as Pascal did. Reason won't offer the defence they desperately need: it was reason, after all, that set fright in ambush in the first place. The search for pleasure and the struggle for happiness set themselves a humbler and thus more realistic objective: to make life, forever poisoned by the knowledge of mortality, endurable nevertheless. In fulfilling that objective they are, by and large, successful.

That fright can hardly be stifled, let alone chased away. Whatever happens, it cannot be defeated once and for all. One must therefore cope somehow with its obstinate presence, trying to make it less obtrusive and less incapacitating. And there are only two ways in which that can be done.

The way that in Pascal's view most people choose is to stop or suspend thinking: 'to be diverted from thinking of what they are, either by some occupation, which takes their mind off it, or by some novel and agreeable passion which keeps them busy, like gambling, hunting, some absorbing show, in short by what is called diversion.'[7]

The other way, which Seneca would advise his readers to take, is to confront the fate point-blank. To think, think intensely – but not of the brevity of one's own corporeal life, but of two types of things certain to outlive and outlast it, and of one's own capacity to add to their number and value. One of such things is virtue – magnificent, noble, majestic, invincible, indefatigable. The other is wisdom – the unique possession that does not shrink but expands the more it is used. Both carry supreme value because they are immortal. They are immune to the tendency to pass away that mars and corrupts all other, however glittering and seductive, values. For that reason they are worth thinking about. More importantly yet, they are worth pursuing and practising. In them, eternity otherwise denied to mortals has finally met its match.

This is what Pascal and Seneca tell their readers. Both bewail the cowardly but also ill-informed and ill-conceived habit of turning one's back on the truth of human fate and fleeing its challenges. Pascal records the state of corruption, derides and condemns it, but holds out little hope of rectification. Seneca suggests a two-step alternative: taking the road of *vita contemplativa* that leads to *vita activa*. Only through that road can *vita activa* be reached: from existential fright to meaningful, worthy existence there are no short-cuts.

When they wrote, neither Seneca nor Pascal could count on many readers. Few people could read, fewer still could afford the price of books, and very few indeed would wish to spend money to buy them and time reading them. Neither the idea of intellectual war-denship, nor the concept of 'the people' as the philosophers' natural wards had yet been invented. A century and a half had to pass after Pascal's death for the intellectual missionary, destined to carry the torch of learning into the darkest corners of the human habitat, to be born. Many more years were needed for the newly born to be issued with a birth certificate and a home address. Seneca and Pascal took part in a conversation that few people wished or were invited to join. And they could hardly visualize printed records of their musings being sold at railway and airport bookstands.

Seneca gave his solitary musings the name of 'dialogues'. What he (and Pascal) thought of and how he thought it, what he wrote down and how he wrote it were made to the measure of a small, selective company likely to be partners in conversation. They thought through conversing with the elected few who could aspire to be blessed with the kind of mind whose nourishment, in Montaigne's description, 'consists in amazement, the hunt, and uncertainty, as Apollo made clear enough to us by his speaking...ambiguously, obscurely and obliquely, not glutting us but keeping us wondering and occupied.'[8]

Happiness in Seneca's and Pascal's recipes was not a programme aimed at or expected to be embraced by the hoi polloi. Seneca called on his readers to live according to nature, shun all things artificial, unnecessary, unduly excessive, foreign and hostile to what nature offered. And yet the way of life he hoped to be followed once the toxic, infectious pollutions had been distilled, strained off and dis-posed of was itself highly unnatural. People uninitiated into the arcane and abstruse secrets of philosophy followed quite different habits in their lives. The 'nature' to which Seneca appealed was nowhere to be found. Seneca's utterly unnatural nature needed to be laboriously construed, day in day out, in a never stopping effort of a kind that few people could afford and fewer still would enjoy and willingly perform. Adopting Seneca's programme called for a rejection of the common and ordinary, massively followed ways. It demanded setting oneself apart from the 'simple folks'. It meant 'splendid isolation', positing oneself above the rest: self-constitution in opposition to the 'madding crowd'. Seneca's programme was to be simultaneously a unilateral declaration of independence and a border-post.

Seneca's happiness, let me recall, equalled freedom from the fear of death. But the surest way to defeat the fear of death is to annul death's finality and to revoke its sentence to eternal non-being. Death wouldn't be feared if being did not end together with corporeal life. Death would be no more than a change of gear were there things in the span of corporeal life destined to survive death and emerge from the disembodiment unharmed and undiminished. Virtue and thought are such things – and this is why Seneca dwells on both.

*Vita contemplativa* and *virtu* do not die. Thoughts are immortal, and so is virtue: both live forever in the memory and in the deeds of their legatees and self-adopted children.

> There are households of the noblest intellects: choose the one into which you wish to be adopted, and you will inherit not only their name but their property too. Nor will this property need to be guarded meanly or grudgingly: the more it is shared out, the greater it will become. These will offer you a path to immortality and raise you to a point from which no one is cast down. This is the only way to prolong mortality – even to convert it into immortality.[9]

Linking happiness to immortality and immortality to the life of thought and virtue constitutes happiness as privilege. Hard-earned privilege, one that can be worked for by only a few, and gained by the most talented, exalted and devout among them. If this is what happiness is about, then 'the rest' of humans, the great majority of humans, are doomed to the life of pleasure, a life dedicated to *panem et circenses*, belly-filling and diversions. Pleasure is not happiness, just as the delights of the body are not immortal. Death is the ultimate and irrevocable end to the life of pleasure. But death is only a switch of gear in the eternity of virtue and thought, and particularly of that virtue which resides in the 'households of the noblest intellects': the virtue of philosophy.

Seneca's formula was singularly devoid of mass appeal and unfit for mass application. And neither of these was intended.

Proselytizing aimed at massive conversion was not its objective. Seneca's happiness was destined to differentiate, not to congregate and unite: to lay a firm foundation for the aristocratic gesture of withdrawal and standing out from the crowd. It was left to Christianity, the openly and self-consciously proselytizing philosophy, to abolish all border controls and entry visas to the happiness defined as eternal life.

## Happiness as everybody's option

In Christianity, unlike in Seneca's stoicism, eternity is not a *privilege* of a few, but the *fate* of all; not a *prize* earned by a handful of the exceptionally meritorious and resourceful but denied to the inept and undeserving multitude, but a non-negotiable *destination* of the worthy and the unworthy alike. As in other cases of *haute couture* patterns passed into mass production and made available at cut prices in run-of-the-mill high-street outlets, the high quality (in this case the happiness-generating capacity) of the mass production version of eternity was not a foregone conclusion and most certainly carried no guarantee. True, *eternity* did not have to be earned and merited; but its *quality* did. Eternity was not a synonym of happiness. Eternity was for all, but happiness, as before, was only for the chosen. As before, happiness was the reserve of the superior. So what was new and different? It was that other than intellectual skills opened the entry to that exclusive reserve. And that eternal happiness was set not against the brief and transient life of pleasure, but against an eternity of damnation and cauldrons of perpetually boiling sulphur.

For a Christian, eternity could be, as in Seneca's version, an unalloyed blessing; but *pace* Seneca, it could also be a most feared curse. As Piero Camporesi points out, '[t]o the Christian, the journey to the house of eternity represented the anxiety of all anxieties.'[10] There were good reasons for anxiety, for an awesome admixture of horror polluting the otherwise reassuring certainty of eternal life. Christian eternity was 'awesome in its uncertainty, suspended between the sucking abyss and the sublime heavens'; worst of all, it was *immutable*, non-negotiable and unalterable. As Saint Bernardo of Chiaravelle reminded the faithful, on the other side of corporeal life 'there will be no time for pity, no time for judgement. Nor should we believe that there will be any mercy towards the impious, in a place where there is no hope even of correction.'[11]

However brief, corporeal life was the only time when happiness might be earned (unbaptised children who died at birth before they had time to repent and to expiate and atone the original – hereditary – sin would go to Hell and stay there forever). The choice between a life dedicated to (working for) happiness and a life spent on pleasures acquired therefore an unprecedented – eternal – gravity. For Seneca, fascination with sensuous pleasure eroded the chance of an eternity that was happiness. For a Christian, it led to an eternity of pain and misery.

Modernity 'demystified' and 'disenchanted' eternal life. It brought Heaven and Hell to earth and confined eschatological worries to the world of *embodied* living, the sole territory which modern (read: self-contained, condemned to self-reliance, abandoned to its own powers and resources) humanity could reasonably hope to control. Having done that, modernity refused however to endorse the guarantee of immortality. Eternal duration became once more a *task* instead of a *gift of nature*. It had to be earned, as in Seneca's time. But the chance of earning it needed to be cast within everybody's reach, and the road to eternity pointed to by Seneca was singularly unfit for the purpose. The method of earning eternity suggested by Seneca remained in modern times as much as it had been in antiquity accessible only to the selected few. Only a handful of mortals could count on being promoted to the rank of immortals by, for instance, being elected to the French Academy... Leaving things where they stood in Seneca's time would have amounted to disinheriting all but a few humans of their right to eternity, with a life dedicated to *panem et circenses* as the virtually inevitable consequence.

Émile Durkheim was well aware of that danger – made all the more prominent at a time of divorce between the church and the state and the forceful 'secularization' of the ideas of 'man and citizen' (read: Frenchman and French citizen). '[I]f, in rationalising morality in moral education, we confine ourselves to eliminating from moral discipline everything that is religious without replacing it, we almost inevitably run the danger of eliminating at the same time all elements that are properly moral.'[12] To ward off that threat, 'we must discover the rational substitutes for those religious notions that have, for so long, served as the vehicle for the most essential moral ideas.'

Durkheim's work may be seen as a consistent, long-term effort to articulate and spell out such 'rational substitutes'. First came the 'rationalization' of Christian *agape*: 'The individual submits to society and this submission is the condition of his liberation.' The individual won't be free without 'the great and intelligent force of society, under whose protection he shelters. By putting himself under the wing of society, he makes himself also dependent upon it. But this is a liberating dependence.'[13] (These words could be quoted from a standard catechism or collection of Christian homilies if only the term 'society' was returned to the verbal form of 'God' that it came to replace.) Second came the resurrection of the equation of value with eternity, of the one-to-one correspondence between the happy life and duration: the connection powerfully argued by Seneca but dissolved in Christianity. 'If your efforts result in nothing lasting, they are hollow, and why should we strive for that which is futile?... Of what value are our individual pleasures, which are so empty and short?' Fortunately, there is *society*, that, being 'infinitely more long-lasting than individuals', may 'permit us to taste satisfactions which are not merely ephemeral'.[14] (Such words, for a change, could be mistaken for quotations drawn from Seneca's dialogues, if – instead of 'society' – wisdom was selected as the source of true happiness, of satisfactions that 'are not merely ephemeral'.)

That latter replacement – the substitution of an everlasting society for the eternal wisdom of philosophers as the focus for the efforts targeted on happiness – threw open to the hoi polloi a new track to immortality, wide and fit for mass traffic. In its new version, an existence longer than life, survival after death, was an opportunity offered to all, however meagre their assets might have been. No longer a privilege for the lucky few, the modern offer of immortality set no preliminary conditions to whoever might wish to take it up. Exams at the entry to the road to immortality were abolished. This new equality came at a price, though, and the price was the surrender of individuality. Society, as Durkheim kept repeating, was a totality greater than the sum of its parts. It was also a totality that secured its duration by making each one of its parts replaceable and disposable. Society survived thanks to the readiness of its members to give up the chances of personal survival for the sake of the perpetuation of the whole. In the eternal duration of their society individual members could participate only anonymously.

Modern wars became the gruesome and gory spectacles in which that modern tragedy of reaching for (individual) happiness through sacrifice for the sake of (collective) immortality was publicly staged for public enlightenment and applause. Modern war has become, as George Mosse put it, 'a holy war on behalf of a holy nation' and in this way 'death itself was transcended.'[15] While mourning fallen brothers or husbands (and thanks to mass conscription the mourners were the nation as a whole, or almost), the bereaved were told that the shared gain outweighed the personal losses many times over. No happiness was greater than basking in the glory of the nation rescued from perdition through the sacrifice of its defenders. 'Modern war memorials', Mosse observed, 'did not so much focus upon one man, as upon figures symbolic of the nation – upon the sacrifice of all its men.' The common soldier was 'treated as part of an anonymous collectivity.' Mosse describes in detail the extraordinary precautions which were taken by modern nation-states to select the corpses for the memorials of Unknown Soldiers with one purpose in mind: to assure the anonymity of the chosen, while emphasizing that the military rank of the fallen did not matter and that the chance of immortality-through-sacrifice was open equally to all, however lowly in life.

The cult of fallen soldiers was an extreme form of the modern rendition of the ancient opposition between happiness and 'mere pleasure', and of the link between the concerns with happiness and things eternal on one hand and the urge to dispel the curse of mortality on the other. It may be seen as the ultimate pattern that all other modern solutions to that double quandary struggled to imitate, though none with complete success. In all its renditions, the modern solution involved dedication to a common cause hoped to survive its warriors, and to survive thanks to the sacrifice of the warriors' own welfare and personal satisfactions.

Happiness-through-sacrifice retained the marks of its aristocratic ancestry. True, it was now a chance everyone could take, but it was not expected to be taken by all. Fallen soldiers, in one respect indistinguishable from the rest of the nation (difference of rank did not matter!), were strikingly unlike the rest. They were *martyrs* (because of what had been done to them), but also *heroes* (thanks to what they did). Taking the road to (albeit oblique) immortality that had been open to all still remained a privilege of the few. But it was now up to each one of the all to whom the road had been opened to enter it and follow it as far as their strength and determination would carry them.

## Happiness: from reward to right

If asked these days to explain other people's actions, most of us would reply, with only brief if any hesitation, that the pursuit of happiness was their motive. Such an answer comes to our lips without prompting and with not much preliminary thought either: we feel no need to step back, reflect, seek proofs, argue. The pursuit of happiness seems to us a natural predilection and a permanent concern of human beings. It seems to be simultaneously the necessary and sufficient cause of the human refusal to stand still, and the major stimulus to make efforts and take the risks entailed in all seeking, experimenting, discovering and inventing of new ways of being. For us and perhaps all our contemporaries it goes without saying that all individuals do whatever they do because they want to be happy, or happier than they have been thus far. If not for that desire, they wouldn't do what they are doing – most certainly they would not do it by their own will and on their own initiative. As a matter of fact, the very idea of 'coercion' as understood by most of us stands for whatever prevents people from doing what they would have done were they allowed to pursue, unconstrained, their happiness.

This folkloristic conviction used to be uncritically reiterated and thereby regularly reconfirmed and reinforced by the most widely popularized and celebrated scientific studies (whose design and pre-designed conclusions it first inspired). The notorious behaviourist experiments took the pursuit of happiness for their no-proof-required, axiomatic starting point. Rather than deduced or induced from the studies findings, the pursuit of happiness was 'demonstrated' to be a motive of action in all and every one of the laboratory projects – through the simple expedient of defining the prospect and the desire of happiness in advance as that 'something' which stimulates and guides (and thus also explains) the objects' choices. If the objects of study had chosen this rather than that option, it must have been (and so it was) because the option they chose gave or promised them more happiness (code name 'gratification'). Happiness is what the objects of study would willingly choose. The choice and the desire of happiness defined each other. They did not require (nor could be given) any other definition.

Our inclination to read the pursuit of happiness into all human action may be so deeply rooted that it needs no added argument to guide our perception of action's manifest or latent motives. The fact that it has achieved the status of *doxa* (an idea we think *with* but not *about*) does call, however, for pause and reflection. Pointing to the pursuit of happiness as the prime mover of human endeavour (indeed, as the meaning of human life) would not always have occurred as matter-of-factly as it does today. Indeed, there are grounds to suppose that the choice of penitence (and, more generally, of suffering), rather than happiness, as the supreme purpose of life and the destination of human mortals marked most conspicuously and most seminally the 'Western tradition' through most of its history. That suffering and not enjoyment is the true and inescapable human fate was taken for granted. What posited a problem and made it a tall order was reconciliation with suffering, not its avoidance, let alone elimination.

John Bowker, who examined the meanings accorded to suffering in the great religions of the world, concluded that 'it is an understanding of a way in which suffering can be made purposeful that has gone deep into Western tradition...'[16] Bowker considers as the 'supreme contribution of Israel' to that tradition the idea that 'suffering can be made redemptive, that it can become the foundation of better things, collectively, if not individually.' In the rabbinical development of the original insight into the redemptive potential of suffering, men came to be 'encouraged to look for suffering, almost as a kind of opportunity for advancement'. Rabbi Akiba famously described suffering as a condition 'much to be loved', while the Babylonian Talmud averred that 'he who gladly bears the sufferings that befall him brings salvation to the world', and thus serves the best purpose to which human life can be dedicated. Through the whole of Christianity's history, reflection on Christ's mission and martyrdom set a pattern for the conviction that 'suffering can be accepted, as he accepted it, as devastatingly real...' – but also as a much needed instrument of 'repentance and salvation of those on whom suffering was inflicted'. Christ's suffering and ultimate (and ultimately redemptive) sacrifice has become for millennia the pattern by which the virtue of mortal life was measured.

The idea of suffering serving a higher purpose (eternal salvation or collective well-being), and hence of suffering's ennobling and elevating capacity, was not the only theme recurrent in the centuries-long Western efforts to domesticate pain and to reconcile the afflicted to its ubiquity. The other virtually uninterrupted thread ran from the 'vanity, vanity, all is vanity' of Ecclesiastes and the Stoics' reflection on the self-defeating tendency of pleasures, through Blaise Pascal's blunt verdict that 'man's greatness comes from knowing he is wretched',[17] and up to Arthur Schopenhauer's blunt assertion of 'the negativity of well-being and happiness, in antithesis to the positivity of pain'. It might have been too tall an order to demand that wretchedness be loved and gratefully embraced. But being the norm of the human predicament, neither could it be sensibly opposed and resisted. Accepting pain was therefore presented as the most rational attitude that could be taken by that 'greatest of creatures' blessed by, and armed with reason, the greatest of weapons.

Not that humans were likely to cease resenting and fleeing pain. Their conduct, as Schopenhauer would suggest, 'resembles the course of a man running down a mountain who would fall over if he tried to stop and can stay on his feet only by running on; or a pole balanced on the tip of the finger'. Humans dare not stop running, and they are unlikely to succeed if they try. Even that impossibility is not necessarily a bad thing, however, given that the satisfaction of needs that humans so hotly desire may 'achieve nothing but a painless condition in which [they] are only given over to boredom': 'want and boredom are indeed the twin poles of human life.' Worse still, boredom is not the only disaster ready to befall those who hope for and strive for the fulfilment of their dreams. Were a state ever to be reached in which 'everything grows of its own accord and turkeys fly around ready-roasted, where lovers find one another without any delay and keep one another without any difficulty', 'some men would die of boredom or hang themselves' – but some others 'would fight and kill one another, and thus they would create for themselves more suffering than nature inflicts on them as it is'.[18]

To cut a long story short: for most of human history happiness *was not* the self-evident purpose of life. If anything, the contrary assumption prevailed. Suffering and pain were seen as permanent companions of life. Wishing them away would be vain, and trying to evict them an act of conceit – counterproductive as well as dangerous. Happiness may arrive only as an indirect effect of a life full of suffering. It may come only as salvation, the supreme and most coveted of rewards, to humans who have accepted the painfulness of living and agreed to bear it.

The concept of happiness as the supreme purpose of life with which no other purposes should be allowed to compete is, if measured by the scale of human history, of quite recent origin. Even more recent is the elevation of happiness from a rare distinction, a sparingly allocated bonus for the righteous, to the universal right of human individuals.

Having scanned the immense expanses of the recorded part of the human past and its much longer unrecorded yet reliably reconstructed section, Jacques Ellul concluded that 'in the course of their history people set a great number of objectives that did not arise from the desire for happiness and did not prompt actions aimed at happiness; when it comes to the problem of survival, of composing social groups, of play and technical operations, of ideology, concern with happiness is scarcely present.'[19] It was only in the eighteenth century that the spectacular career of happiness as the supreme purpose of life took off in earnest. The American Declaration of Independence declared happiness to be the universal right of all humans. *Becoming a right* instead of *being a privilege* was a true watershed in the history of happiness.

Rather than a reward for virtue or good deeds and an outcome of hard work and sacrifice, a crowning of a life of piety and self-immolation (or, alternatively, an unearned gift of Divine grace or a stroke of good fortune), happiness became a condition that all and each human being could *demand* as a birthright. Humans could also *complain* in the event that their demand was unheard or ignored, and *rebel* if granting it was refused or the promised happiness was slow in coming. By the same token, it has become the *duty* of society to make all and every one of its members happy. In Ellul's view, the right to happiness was therefore a genuine 'Trojan horse' inside the liberal society set to promote individual liberty of choice, including the choice of identity.

It would be perhaps more to the point to say that for many decades the underwriting of the right to happiness by the modern state as the plenipotentiary of the self-constituting and self-governing society embroiled that state in a contradiction it was under an obligation to resolve. It tried to resolve it – earnestly, though in vain.

## Waiting for happiness

The promise of universal happiness, and of more happiness as the time goes by, involved the modern state in a kind of social compact. The state promised to *deliver* the goods, the citizens expected to *receive* them. In exchange for the benefits, the citizen promised *loyalty* to the state; in exchange for its services, the state expected the citizens *discipline* to its commands. The expectation of happiness and ever more happiness came to be the main legitimating formula of social integration and the principal motivation of any individual's involvement in joint endeavours and common causes. And it was now up to the state to demonstrate that such involvement was worth it – that it paid.

Industry was to be the principal vehicle carrying humanity to happiness. It was hoped to put an end to want, hunger, misery, poverty. Backed by technology and science, it was to make life easier, less tiring and more secure. It *was* to but it always 'has not done it *yet*'... Now that the independence and self-reliance of humanity had been declared and its self-sufficiency postulated, the fate of humanity lay in the *future*, instead of being determined once and for all by the ancient acts of Divine creation or Adam and Eve's original sin. Once transported into the future, it was bound to stay there forever. Happiness was bound to remain a postulate and an expectation: its fulfilment a promise always some distance ahead of reality. In fact, it was precisely such a location of happiness that made sense of the exquisitely modern distinction between 'forward' and 'backward', rendered the censure and resentment of 'what is' legitimate, and the interest in what still lies 'ahead' intense.

It was that location of happiness that made sense of the recommended self-sacrifice called 'delay of gratification'. The modern spirit, aided and abetted by modern institutions, raised the ancient sages' wisdom to the rank of a universally binding precept: one should beware of sacrificing future joys for the sake of present indulgence, since future joys were bound to be more joyous and enjoyable than anything the present moment could offer. In the new age of rational calculation the surrender of instant satisfactions was therefore represented, and accepted, as a sound investment. The entries in the savings books, not the contents of the shopping trolleys, were the true indices of reason and good life. Let us note and stress however that this kind of investment looked 'sound' only thanks to the widespread trust in the future; and that such trust, in turn, derived from the perception of the future as a site of happiness.

The agreement to delay gratification carried risks. The future, after all, was then, as it is now, inscrutable – and bound to remain such. Once the known has been sacrificed in the name of something as yet unknown, stubbornly opaque, impermeable and altogether resistant to cognition, the risk has become enormous and impossible to assess in full. Its enormity prompted an inexhaustible demand for soothsayers, diviners, conjurers; and for aspiring political leaders claiming infallible knowledge of the laws of history and consequently the ability to control the future.

As long as 'happiness' and the chronically underdefined 'future' merged and blended, uncertainty (acute uncertainty, *incurably* acute uncertainty) was the most awesome of spectres haunting the type of society that was put and held together by the right to happiness, was organized around the pursuit of that right and rested its claim to its members' loyalty on the promised progress towards its fulfilment. This made of the pursuit of happiness an unnerving, sometimes upsetting, often harrowing task. It involved perpetual risk-taking. It involved mortgaging the future, assuming a responsibility of indefinite scope and indefinable dimensions, and facing the prospect of paying the price for assuming it in a currency as yet unearned and of unknown stock-exchange value.

Meeting the demand, promises of happiness made by modern governments involved as a rule the prospect of a radical reduction in risks and mitigation of the torments of choice. Ironically, happiness came to be associated with the emancipation from the uncertainty caused by its pursuit. The omnipotence of self-governing humanity came to be identified with the ability to deploy freedom of choice for the purpose of making all further choices unnecessary, uncalled for or downright undesirable (Leon Battista Alberti defined 'perfection' as a state in which all change can only be a change for the worse). There was a mostly undercover, yet tight and indissoluble link between elevating the pursuit of happiness to the rank of the ultimate purpose of human togetherness, and the totalitarian tendency endemic to the modern state. The two were born together and together they matured, aged and began to decline. It was perhaps this unsavoury conjunction to which Ellul referred when observing that 'it seems as if humans obeyed surreptitiously a sort of death wish, a desire to depart from themselves, a suicidal instinct.'[20]

However, the equation of the future and happiness was not a failure pure and simple. The proof that it was not is that it withstood the contrary evidence for so long, and that it took such a long time for it to be admitted that it was a failure and even longer for it to be proclaimed as such. Bacon, Descartes and a long line of *les philosophes* could confidently proclaim that the pains and sufferings haunting their contemporaries *would* indeed be cured, that human reason *would* provide the therapy, and that consequently universal happiness, that goal and destiny of humankind, *would* 'in the end' be reached.

They had every right to be confident. They drew their optimism, after all, from the experience of a society in which the main, perhaps the sole reason to rebel and to define suffering as unjustifiable, and so unendurable and intolerable, was the violation of customary usages. It was the *habitual* measure of indecency that set the standards by which the decency of life was measured. Prophets of wonders which the unstoppably progressing knowledge and know-how would eventually bring were in full agreement with the learned opinion of their time. That opinion, in turn, was but a sophisticated rendition of common sense. Happiness being equal to freedom from want, want being the lack of satisfaction of needs, and the sum of human needs being given once for all and knowable – then the moment we learn how to procure the volume of goods sufficient to satisfy the needs and get together to act on that knowledge, happiness will become reality, QED. And so the implementation of the right to happiness was but a question of time...

In a nutshell: one could believe in progress as long as progress was understood as a journey towards a given-in-advance destination; a trajectory with a finishing line, against which one could plot, mile by mile, successive steps to be taken. One could believe in progress and be confident about its imminence as long as one could visualize it as a movement with a *telos*. And one could do so yet more confidently thanks to the tangible concreteness of a *telos* identified with universal happiness identified with the satisfaction of the sum total of human needs identified with the sum total of yet-unmet grievances. It was all the easier to believe in progress thanks to the conviction that progress had an *objective* and that this objective was to 'work itself out of the job' – to reach a point where *no more progress will be needed*. That conviction cut progress, encouragingly and reassuringly, to the measure of a human, all-too-human task and human, all-too human capacity.

## Satisfactions in search of needs

This was not, though, how the passionate and stirring, yet ultimately brief romance with progress was destined to fizzle out.

We have indeed, as predicted, grown much less excited by the happiness the future will bring to the human race, and by the progress that will take us there. We don't give much thought to the future as a repository of unheard-of happiness that will put the present joys to shame. No longer are we sure that change is an unambiguous blessing and that 'better' is a synonym of 'future'. It may seem indeed that progress, as prophesied, 'worked itself out of its job'. If all that did happen, though, it happened for a reason quite different from the one anticipated.

How is 'progress' viewed today? Most commonly, as the need to dispose of some old tools and toys and replace them with new ones that are faster to operate and quicker to enjoy, and preferably equipped with gadgets that can do what the old gadgets could not, or can do with less effort what old gadgets could also do, but much more laboriously or less effectively. 'Progress', as Luc Ferry recently pointed out, 'is no longer subordinated, unlike in the optimism of the eighteenth century, to external and superior finalities, human emancipation and well-being. It has become instead a "movement without a cause", escaping all control, proceeding on its own with no destination or purpose – like a gyroscope or a bicycle that has no other choice but to go on moving, or fall.'[21]

Globalization seems to be, at least in part, responsible for progress falling from grace and losing much of its lustre. After all, 'globalization' stands for departures and developments that are essentially unpredictable; for what *happens to us*, not for what *we do*. 'Global forces' operate in 'extraterritorial space', tearing all reins and running unbridled, unreachable and untouchable by the orthodox and so far unreplaced instruments of purposeful action and rational management (notably by the nation-state, the most powerful of such instruments). And so 'progress' no longer appears to be a manifestation of human mastery over human destiny, a crowning example of the human capacity to steer human history in a rationally selected direction and determine its destination. With all the spectacular 'progress' in the speed and volume of human communication and the tools of 'acting at a distance', the means of control seem to have failed to match the powers that need to be controlled, and be less adequate than ever to the task of controlling them. The hope of the progressive limitation and ultimate elimination of risks and of the reduction of unknown variables in human equations finds little if any support in current experience. The future is unlikely ever to become a kingdom of certainty. The future is, fully and truly, *out of control*, and the credible guess is that it is destined to remain out of control – well, at least for a . . . *foreseeable* future.

The way technology moves has the same effect as the way globalization proceeds: it magnifies the uncertainty under which people act and deprives long-term planning efforts of that self-assurance that once made them seductive.

It no longer seems that we are, or are likely to be, the sorcerers our modern predecessors hoped to become and intended to make us. We are, rather, the hapless apprentices who watch in bewilderment and horror as the brooms run amuck. The brooms we once commanded to sweep the floor and keep the room tidy now accept no other prodding than the intoxication of their own whirl. They bear no constraints other than running out of steam. Instead of doing what *we* need, they keep on doing what *they* are best at doing.

Popular wisdom, slow in catching up with the news but boasting a long memory, may go on believing that need is the mother of invention and that where there's a will there's a way (first the will, then a way). Technology once seemed to be made in the likeness of that wisdom, but it certainly does not now. By now the succession has been reversed and it is the invention that turned out to be the mother of needs; where there's a way the will is not slow to follow...Technological answers *precede* the questions instead of following them. Most of the will is turned towards finding the questions to which answers are already available, and making as many people as possible ask those questions and so be willing to pay for the answers. It is the technological novelties that desperately seek applications, desiring to be solutions but at a loss when searching for the problems such solutions may fit. Their producers know only too well that the hard trick their products (read: their merchandisers) face is to ingratiate themselves with their prospective users innocent of any need or desire to possess and deploy them. User instructions now need long and persuasive preambles spelling out what the product may be used *for*.

To quote Jacques Ellul once more, 'Technique tolerates no judgement from without and accepts no limitation...Technique, in sitting in judgement on itself, is clearly freed from this principal obstacle to human action.' 'The technician has no need of justification.'[22] Justification comes as a rule (if it comes at all) *after* the deed has been done. Technology is not pulled forward by needs protesting neglect and clamouring for satisfaction, but pushed from behind by assets clamouring for profitable use and protesting underemployment of resources. Technology develops *because it develops*: all other explanations come dangerously close to ideological adornment or wishful thinking.

It seems hardly conceivable, therefore, that technology may be a process with a finishing line; that it may at some point reach its target and rest, once the sum total of human needs will have been satisfied and 'all problems' will have found their solution. The sum total of problems seen as requiring solution *grows* instead of diminishing as a result of technological progress. Conjuring up ever new problems, never-heard-of problems and previously unimaginable problems is technology's genuine métier, turning gradually, yet relentlessly, into its mission. It does not seem likely then that the future will adjust better than heretofore and balance supply and demand and that the number of unresolved issues and the volume of overall uncertainty will in the course of time diminish.

All this casts the search for happiness in a thoroughly novel context. The hope that human needs may at some point be satisfied in full, so that no room will be left for unhappiness, might have been an illusion at all times, but in our times that hope looks more than ever pitifully naive and blatantly unrealistic. We – the consumers and the suppliers of 'needs-satisfying' goods alike – would rather expect human needs to go on growing unstoppably, and to grow faster than their satisfaction. The once sacrosant boundary between 'true' or legitimate needs and 'false' or reprehensible, 'pseudo' needs (that is, needs of things one could well do without if not for vainglory and the morbid lust for lucre, luxury and ostentation) has been all but effaced. All needs, the present ones that we know and the future ones that we cannot even imagine, are genuine, and the unimaginable ones no less so than the ones currently deeply felt.

'Needs' grow, beefed up by opportunities to consume. 'Needs' are desires prompted by exposure to such opportunities. The self-proclaimed task of advertising is to inform prospective consumers of new products that they could not have desired before since they were not aware of their existence, and would not desire now if they were not tempted and seduced. Most money allocated to publicity budgets is spent on information about products promising to gratify needs that consumers would not otherwise be aware of having. The purpose of advertising is to create new desires and to modify and redirect the existing ones; but the summary effect of exposure to commercials is never to allow such desiring – desiring of things not yet had and sensations not yet experienced – to relent and cool down.

Desire for any one specific product is not expected to last, and to keep it alive for long would be a sheer waste of money. Nothing boosts the desires so unfailingly and promptly as the 'new', 'improved', and best of all the 'new *and* improved' formula. Designers, producers and merchandisers of consumer goods, as Nigel Thrift found, 'now live in a permanent state of emergency, always bordering on the edge of chaos...in a faster and more uncertain world, one in which all advantage is temporary.'[23] Employees 'confront remorseless pressure to be creative'. They are made aware that (here Thrift quotes A. Muoio's sober advice) 'you're only as good as your last great idea' and that reward for your last round of successful innovation is 'even greater pressure to revisit your success, and to unleash yet another round of innovation'.[24]

As crucial as the briefings about the wondrous capacities of new products and the breeding of new desires is the information about what products are 'out', and which of the recently fashionable and desired products are to be seen as 'dead', the site needing to be cleared for new temptations and new 'I need it, and right away' responses.

Sometimes the keenly beefed up desires are prevented from striking roots that are too strong (and so stay for too long) through the simple expedient of removing from production and from the market the goods that served/stimulated them. 'Durable goods' like cars, computers, photo or video cameras, radios, record/cassette/disc/video players, TV sets or telephone products and their uses may go (will be forced to go) out of fashion simply because the necessary supplies, consumables, spare parts and repair services are no longer available. At other times the desire for products may die (be induced to die: killed) well before the products themselves have aged, outlived their usefulness or been refused the means needed to keep them working. The appearance of alternative products, richer in gadgets, different in design, more colourful or more tuneful, make their predecessors look shamefully out-of-date if not downright inept and frustrating. Businesses multiply and thrive tuned to the *change* of desires and dedicated to accelerating the pace of their succession (companies supplying new ring-tones daily for mobile telephones offer a most recent example).

Some other products cannot be manoeuvred out of use in any of those ways – like, for instance, containers to store records and video-cassettes, bric-à-brac to adorn the sitting room, kitchen utensils, minimalist or extravagant styles of furnishing, bright or muted colours of paint or wallpaper. Alternative means are deployed in such cases to make them not just look inadequate to needs, but feel downright off-putting, revolting and repelling. Defamation campaigns are launched aimed at shaming the owners of no longer promoted products out of using and displaying them, while new standards of *comme-il-faut* and *comme-il-ne-faut-pas* are extolled as a matter of self-esteem and pride. Information on 'what is in' is as a rule accompanied by an announcement of 'what is out'.

### Desires shunning satisfaction

The consumer market is constantly at war with tradition, and desires are the principal weapons of that war. Care is taken to prevent habits, even the most vigorously promoted habits, from solidifying into traditions. Shifting of desires, aided and abetted by drifting attention, is the most effective of preventive medicines.

As Max Weber noted, 'that type of attitude and reaction to new situations which we may designate as traditionalism' was 'the most important opponent with which the spirit of capitalism... had to struggle'.[25] The 'traditional worker' does not 'wish to earn more and more money, but simply to live as he is accustomed to live and to earn as much as is necessary for that purpose'. To a 'traditional worker', the 'opportunity of earning more was less attractive than that of working less'. Whenever early capitalists tried to increase the productivity of labour by making the labourers' work more intensive, they 'encountered immensely stubborn resistance'. Workers acted *as if* their needs were indeed stable and resistant to change; as if the needs had an upper limit in addition to the all-too-obvious bottom line of the 'minimum necessary for survival'. 'Happiness' meant meeting the standards they knew, the ones they were accustomed to and felt as normal and decent. Why should they strain themselves and work harder if they already had 'everything they needed'?

Meeting the customary standards was all the 'perfection' the 'traditional workers'' sought, and they could repeat after Alberti that perfection is a state in which *all and any* change can only be a change for the worse. This is not, however, what the logic of entrepreneurship and the competitive market required: the productive capacity of an industrial plant had to be used to the full, and underused capacity in a machine was an unforgivable waste. Work needed to be regulated by the productive capacity of the available technology, and that exceeded the traditionally shaped, and so limited, motivations; to match the capacity of the self-propelling and self-reinforcing productive technology, labour had to be 'performed as if it were an absolute end in itself, a calling'.

We may say that 'the most important opponent' against which *contemporary* capitalism has to struggle is the 'traditional *consumer*': a person who acts as if the goods offered on the market do what they are proclaimed to do: satisfy needs. The 'most important opponent' of the consumer market is a person who abides by the orthodox definition of consumption needs – a person who experiences 'the need' as a state of unpleasant tension, and identifies happiness with removing that tension, with restoring the balance, returning to the state of balance and tranquility reached when whatever was required to satisfy the need has been obtained. The consumer market's 'public enemy number one' is a person to whom consumption is not 'an absolute end in itself' and not a 'calling'. A person for whom the finishing line of the race to happiness is the state of 'I have all I need and I can stop all that fuss and pull all my irons out of the fire.'

When 'the most important opponent' of capitalism was the traditional *worker*, the task consisted in transforming labour into an 'autotelic', 'end in itself' activity – an activity that had no other purpose but its own perpetuation and intensification and served no other objective but itself. Of course, workers also had to consume to replenish the used-up labour capacity. The workers' need to consume was however a nuisance and a bother: a price that the factory bosses had to pay, reluctantly, for what really counted – for keeping the factory running, machines at full swing, productivity rising. Although it could not be avoided altogether, that price should, like all other expenses, be kept to an absolute minimum. The worker the bosses wished to drill should treat productive effort as a calling, but view consumption as a sad necessity. He should detest all excess, self-indulgence, profligacy. Anything above the level absolutely necessary for survival he should see as sinful and/or shameful, detestable, undignified and morally corrupting. If this is what he felt and did, then while the intensity of his labour would go on growing, his 'genuine needs' (as distinct from those not related to bare survival, and therefore 'false') would not. The only consumption that would be ethically acceptable was that called for in order to enable the *working man*'s calling, which was labour and more labour and more labour still, to be obeyed day in day out.

In our time, when 'the most important opponent' is the traditional *consumer*, it is the turn of *consumption* to be transformed into an 'autotelic', 'end in itself' activity, having no other purpose but its own perpetuation and intensification, serving no other objective but itself. No longer would consumption be a means to an end. No longer should it need to justify itself in terms of something other than the act of consuming, let alone to prove its usefulness in keeping the consumer work-fit. Consumption ought to be 'an absolute end in itself' and a 'calling' (a 'calling' is, after all, a compulsive and compelling, addictive and self-propagating urge that neither needs, nor admits of, rational explanation). It is also to be the only calling, a no-competition-allowed calling, an all-inclusive and self-sustained calling, that one calling against which propriety and impropriety, triumphs and defeats, successes and failings, the happiness and unhappiness of life are to be from now on measured and explained.

It is now the turn of *productive work* to become instrumental. No longer a calling – merely the servant of what truly counts; neutral in itself, nothing to be proud or ashamed of, a recurrent intermezzo in a long, never-ending Wagnerian life opera. As Harvie Ferguson puts it, 'production has been stripped of any lingering enchantment. It is *only* the most fundamental of social relations; important but uninteresting.'[26] In order to elicit dedication, work needs to masquerade as consumption and emulate its playfulness, to fill work-time with surprise and adventure, to furnish the workplace with user-friendly toys. Better still the workplace could be abolished altogether, or rather dissolved into life as such, that is into life-dedicated-to-consumption; it could commit a vanishing act while invading the space of leisure – effacing on its way the work–leisure and the production–consumption boundaries. The valour and glamour of work are now measured by standards set for the consumer's experience.

## Neither having nor being

The modern discourse of happiness used to rotate around the opposition between *having* and *being*. It was the choice of 'to have' or, alternatively, of 'to be' that separated the competitive models of happiness and of all related ideals – good life, virtuous life, meaningful life. Possession, and most particularly the possession of material goods, tended to be seen as inimical to the fullness of being. 'Having' should not aspire to dominate 'being'. 'Having' is, and should remain, being's humble servant, since solely from that service does it derive its meaning, having no meaning of its own. 'Having' had to justify itself in terms of that service rendered to 'being' – not the other way round. Being-in-order-to-have, a being dedicated to acquisition, to the accumulation of possessions, would be but another case of the sickly inclination of means to turn into ends, or of the malign and wicked genie let carelessly out of the bottle.

It is tempting to say that the emergence of consumer society signals the swapping of roles traditionally ascribed to 'having' and 'being' and the reversal of the ideal relation between 'having' and 'being' that the ethical philosophers wished social reality to follow; that it resolved the long dispute in a way contrary to the ethical philosophers' intentions, hopes and expectations. It is tempting – but it would be wrong to surrender to such temptation.

'Having' and 'being' might have been in opposition, but they would not oppose each other were it not for sharing a common ground set by the jointly accepted assumptions. 'Having' and 'being' might have followed different life philosophies, but both philosophies provided glosses on similar understandings of the human condition. 'Having' put into focus *things* that one could be with; 'being' focused on the *humans* one could be with. Both, however, cast 'being with' as a long-term, perhaps permanent, condition needing to be cared for and tended to daily and for a long time to come.

Richard Sennett remembers a drawing that he saw as a child: John D. Rockefeller 'as an elephant crushing hapless workers beneath his huge feet, his trunk grasping train engines and oil derricks'.[27] Rockefeller might have had little love or compassion for his workers (their relationship, as Carlyle had already bewailed a hundred years earlier, had been reduced to a 'cash nexus'), but he 'wanted to own oil rigs, buildings, machinery of railroads for the long term'. That attitude of Rockefeller seems particularly striking if compared with the conduct of Bill Gates, the new champion of the premier league of the affluent and influent, who 'seems free of the obsession to hold on to things', demonstrates 'willingness to destroy what he has made' and has 'the ability to let go, if not to give'. Rockefeller was, unambiguously, on the side of 'having'.

What the other alternative, of being on the side of 'being', would be like, we may read in Max Scheler. It would consist, so we are told, in 'joining the other' in a tendency to perfection, being active 'in assisting it, promoting it, blessing it', abandoning oneself 'in order to share and participate in another being as an *ens intentionale*'.[28] No crushing the others under one's feet here, but readiness to assist them, at whatever cost, in the shared search for perfection – such search precluding either of the partners becoming 'parts of one another'.

Apparently, it would be difficult to conceive of a pair of life formulae more at odds with each other. The opposition between 'having' and 'being' could not be sharper and more comprehensive. And yet there was a common element present in both strategies that allowed them to compete, having made them into alternatives and adversaries. That element was *commitment* – engagement and the obligation to make it last. A commitment entered into or undertaken for a long term, indeed for an indefinite time, promised to be and intended to be kept in health and sickness, for better or worse, 'until death us do part'. And it is that element that is now largely, and ever more conspicuously, missing. Commitment, especially a long-term commitment and particularly an unconditional commitment, is fast appearing to be the antithesis of a good – reasonable, happy, pleasurable – life.

And so the bottom has fallen out of the orthodox opposition between 'having' and 'being'. Neither choice seems to be particularly attractive; both repel and tend to be avoided. Each spells dependency – the first one on possessions, the second one on other people; and dependency is the condition to be escaped at all cost, since to survive, let alone to prosper in an uncertain world, one needs to be constantly ready for change – an instant change, no-advance-notice change. One needs to be ready to travel, in physical or social space, and the person who travels light travels the quickest and most comfortably. Long-term commitments and durable bonds tie hands and feet, as the very name 'attachment' suggests. Neither 'having' nor 'being' seems to remain, therefore, a reasonable option...

It is a commonplace to describe our condition as 'living in a *consumer* society'. What is much less common is the recognition that ours is a bizarre consumer society, looking odd and strange if judged by the attitudes and behavioural patterns that consumers were once expected to display and by which 'consumerism' used to be traditionally defined. Perhaps the most baffling is the vanishing of the once all-important drive for the accumulation of possessions.

Objects (human and non-human alike) are not appropriated in order to be *kept* for a long time to come, possibly forever. They are to be had in order to be *used* – possibly on the spot; to be had only as long as, and no longer than, they are used. The definition of usefulness, of being 'fit for use', has also changed. It no longer refers to the object's ongoing *ability* to render the services it offered at the time of purchase, but to the *desire* its owner feels for its services. The object may be in perfect working condition – but if its uses have lost the added value of novelty or if other objects promise services more exciting (if only thanks to being as yet untried), it is 'of no use'. It clutters the space needed for the constantly growing number of new and improved objects, and so it turns into garbage whose only natural place is on the rubbish tip.

It looks as if the consumer economy is at its best when it comes to cutting short the time separating use from disposal, and as if its staple (and most profusely supplied) products are not, appearances notwithstanding, usable objects, but objects no longer fit for use: waste. It may be argued that the habit of measuring 'economic growth' by the volume of new products rather than the volume of waste is mostly a tribute to an unreformed, but sorely outdated, bookkeeping convention. Indeed, what one can be sure of is that the higher a country's standing in the hierarchy of 'economic development', the larger is the mass of waste it produces, even if other indices of well-being may have failed to reach a respectable level. 'Waste' is an essentially modern invention, but the consumer economy has lifted inventiveness in that area to unprecedented heights.

### Happiness of (disposable) bonds

'Surfing' is a newly popular word that aptly captures the new mentality of the new world of uncertainty. Surfing is faster than swimming, and it does not require immersing oneself in that fluid substance through which (but above which in case of a skilful surfer) one moves. In surfing, the contact with substance is never more than skin-deep, and one towel will suffice to rub off from the body the few wet spots. We seem to have moved further away from the dangers most feared and the standards of precaution as described by Jean-Paul Sartre in his famous meditations on the nature of 'the slime'.[29]

Water, let us recall, was to Sartre the natural element of freedom; it did not compromise the swimmer's autonomy. 'If I dive into water, if I plunge into it, if I let myself sink into it, I experience no discomfort, for I do not have any fear whatsoever that I may dissolve in it; I remain a solid in its liquidity.' It is the viscosity, the stickiness of slime that we fear: 'If I sink in the slimy, I feel that I am going to be lost in it.' Slime's possession is poisonous: 'at the very moment when I believe that I possess it, behold by a curious reversal, *it* possesses me.' 'I am no longer master in *arresting* the process of appropriation.' 'I want to let go of the slimy and it sticks to me, it draws me, it sucks at me.' It seems that something happened to our tolerance of the elements to make the experience of swimming in water so close to the experience of being sucked in the slime that (to be on the safe side) we prefer surfing to swimming. But surfaces tend to be too soft to rest on without sinking or too friable to walk on without breaking through. As Ralph Waldo Emerson observed a long time ago, 'in skating over thin ice, our safety is in our speed.' On the other hand, when one needs to move fast, skating over ice, whether thick or thin, is not a bad choice.

All depth (and be warned: the depth begins just below the surface) seems nowadays to be treacherous. The surface is the sole space that promises relative safety; not the absence of danger, to be sure, but at least the hope that the danger can be fled before it strikes. Moving beneath the surface, as well as holding or being held to the ground, is to invite trouble. To describe the new variety of skin-deep (or, more to the point, skin-shallow) relationships, some sociologists speak of 'network sociality'. This term seems to be a misnomer – a misleading metaphor, obscuring rather than clarifying the character of the new mode of 'being with others'. 'Network' brings to mind first and foremost a web of *connections* – but it is a facility of *dis*connection, of switching *off*, that sets apart the new brand of interpersonal relations and most fully grasps their most salient features. 'Sociality' suggests that the aim of connecting is to build social bonds – while the true emphasis today is placed on the easy dismantling of bonds, on bonds as easy to break as they are to put together.

The news that – after a spectacular yet in the end brief rise – the popularity of e-mail communication is on a downward slope (according to the latest poll, only 5 per cent of respondents prefer it as against 14 per cent last year), while the love affair with mobile telephones grows more intense, took some observers by surprise. It could have been anticipated, however, if the nature of present trends had been rightly understood.

E-mailing and talking on a mobile telephone have the same manifest function (establishing contact), but also very different latent functions. The latent function that mobiles have and e-mail sorely misses is that they enable the talkers to opt *out* of the place in which they are bodily immersed at the moment – to be elsewhere, 'extraterritorial' and untied to the physical space they bodily occupy. In addition, however, they offer the talkers the facility to make their unattachment manifest and publicly known where and when it truly counts. The expectation of another ring lays bare the 'until-further-notice' character of the contacts with the physically close; it makes it obvious that face-to-face contacts bear a secondary importance compared to those other, electronically mediated contacts, and that they could, and would, be broken at any moment. Mobiles are handy (they don't need a socket, they can work at any place and time) as an always-ready-to-use means of keeping a distance from an environment too close for comfort; a means to avoid entering commitments and tying bonds that threaten to become 'viscous'. A distant (and so secure, inoffensive) conversationalist at the other end of the line keeps away the potential meddlers nearby. E-mails, on the other hand, serve passing messages only. They cannot perform those other, truly vital functions that mobiles fulfil so splendidly.

E-mails are attended to in private and are of no use when the winning and demonstrating of extraterritoriality is at stake.

Consumerism is not about collecting and accumulating *possessions*. It is, in its essence, about gathering *sensations* (not necessarily *pleasurable* sensations, or at least not necessarily pleasurable *in their own* right; it is the *having* of sensations, and even more the *hoping* for new sensations, that tends to be experienced as pleasure).

Neither 'having' nor 'being' count for much in the current models of a happy life, but *use*. Instant use, 'on the spot' use, use that does not outlast the enjoyment it brings, use that can be stopped the moment the joys grind to a halt. Since all attractions are burdened with the vexing habit of ageing right from the moment of birth (hardly anything else follows the Heideggerian pattern of 'life toward death' more faithfully than goods to be consumed), they tend to be at their most seductive and enjoyable in the short time that follows their appearance. Desirability of attraction tapers to the desirability of the *beginning* of new attraction.

Consumer life is a never-ending sequence of *new beginnings*. The joy of shopping is greater than any joy the purchased product, brought home, may bring. It is the shopping that counts. Superstore and shopping mall are enticing exhibitions of the pleasures to come. Pleasures are at their best, most alluring and most exhilarating when encapsulated, as *anticipations* of joy, in the exhibits on display. Visiting the exhibition is the supreme pleasure, or rather the meta-pleasure: the pleasure of being in a world promising to please, a world tuned to the gatherers of sensations. Buying things (mostly *on impulse*)[30] and carrying shopping bags to the car park is but a small price the visitors pay, willingly, for the audile, visual, olfactory and tactile sensations these 'temples of consumption' offer in immensely greater profusion than any of the exhibits for sale.

As Harvie Ferguson, elaborating on Kierkegaard's *Either/Or*, explains: 'The more pleasure becomes the sole object of conscious endeavour, the more certainly it eludes the grasp of the longing subject...Pleasure is a relation of desire, a movement towards the completion of the self. But the self is infinitely expendable, so the object world continually takes on new attractions. It is a movement which cannot be completed.'[31] In fact, staying on the move is the sole form of 'completion of the self' conceivable.

The model of a 'happy life' – any such model – is difficult to compose and even more difficult to sustain in a fickle, kaleidoscopically changing, incurably uncertain world. Like all other insights into the future mixed with a hope of controlling its course, models of happiness ceased to be long-term. Certainly the term is not sufficiently long to stretch over individual life as a whole.

A large part of the present-day generation of young educated Japanese has styled itself as 'furita'[32] – a mix of English 'free' and
German 'Arbeit'. 'Furita' refuse stable, apparently 'secure' jobs with
an inbuilt 'career track'. The wish to avoid a humiliating snub when
setting one's eyes on such apparently security-providing jobs, as well
as a well-grounded distrust in the longevity of the life stations advertised as 'long term', may combine in assisting the spread of the 'furita' lifestyle. 'Furita' (there are between 1.7 and 3.4 million of them
according to different estimates) prefer a haphazard choice of brief,
casual and improvised ways of earning pocket money. Long-term
investment – either in material goods or in life partners – is shunned.
Yukio, a university graduate, rides a motorbike to deliver packets for
the Bixe Express Pirate Company. He lives in a cramped, sparsely
furnished little room with his girlfriend, also a university graduate,
who changes 'jobs' daily. Asked 'what next?', Yukio answers: 'We
will see. For the time being it is fine. And I like riding a bike.' Yukio
and his mates have a *pleasurable life* – life lived as a string of pleasurable moments. Moments may not add up, they may not 'amount to'
anything in particular, but each of them is enjoyable, and there are
hardly any empty intervals of boredom that separate them.

Yukio and his mates are not after wealth. They don't dream of
getting richer (nor do they believe that they have much chance of
getting richer). They are not fond of possessions – things are worth
as much and no more than the momentary, instant pleasure that can
be squeezed out of them. Since Yukio lacks an owner's instinct and
shuns possessions for fear of being burdened or tied down, he never
needs to 'invest in the future' or, for that matter, to 'delay gratification'. And a bird in the hand is worth two in the bush ... Paradoxically, capitalist market society, thought to have been built originally
on cupidity, lucre, the greed for things to be had and on the desire
for (tangible, solid and accumulable) wealth, ended up denigrating
material possessions and replacing the value of 'having' with that of
living through a pleasurable (yet volatile and fast evaporating) experience.

In the current images of a happy life, turnover figures much more
prominently than steady profits. The world around brings daily
news of fabulous fortunes made overnight – by happy accident, a
stroke of luck or a flash of a serendipitous idea (hardly ever through
protracted hard work and predesigned long-term effort). It tells also
of the fragility and the brevity of success, and of the short lifespan

of recipes for success lauded as trustworthy or even foolproof. This world has changed the meaning of 'enterprising' beyond recognition. In this uncertain world of ours, a genuine 'entrepreneur' would not contemplate building an 'enterprise' from the foundation to the roof, selecting the least perishable of materials. An 'entrepreneur' worthy of that name would calculate instead whether the profit could be pocketed before the credit was called off and the credit-line closed.

Just four to five years ago respected and universally trusted experts in the most up-to-date technology 'claimed that successful websites needed to focus on "the three Cs" – content, community and commerce' – with the emphasis on content. Many a hopeful followed the advice, only to find out, in the course of months rather than years, that 'the three Cs' they may reasonably expect are (according to David Hudson, an influential American net journalist) 'consolidation, cutbacks and collapse'.[33] The story repeats itself, with awesome regularity, in the case of all or almost all business fashions – as a rule appearing all of a sudden and as a rule for a fleeting moment. Miraculous successes, 'springing out of nowhere', are sinking back in no time into the same nowhere from which they sprang, and goldmines are emptied a few months after being accidentally struck. In such a world, climbing mountain peaks, a pastime notorious for requiring arduous training, meticulous choice of equipment and laborious planning, does not make much sense and does not seem worthy of time and effort.

It is a fast world, in which quick digestion promises more pleasure and less frustration than a big stomach and a rising appetite. Pleasure opportunities come in speedy succession and vanish at an accelerating pace. The trick is to catch each one in passing, consume it on the spot and be ready for the next. To a worried man fond of culinary pleasures yet afraid of not matching the current fashion for a slim body and an anti-fat crusade, Chris St George, fitness director of The Third Space in London, gave the following advice: 'Another session in the gym would certainly help...Increasing the frequency and intensity of your training and building muscle will raise your metabolic rate – this means you will burn calories more quickly, enabling you to "live a more normal life" [i.e., not forfeiting the joys of the palate] without putting on excess body fat.'[34]

Indeed, raising the metabolic rate suddenly seems to be the precept of reason once the big banknote of 'whole life' happiness has been exchanged for a bagful of small coins of quick to come and quick to go pleasures.

The prospect of an accelerating succession of pleasures is, literally, mind-boggling. It helps to get the worry about happiness out of the head. It also helps it to be forgotten that the worry was once there. In the vernacular of the liquid-modern world, this amnesia is the meaning of happiness.

# 5

# As Seen on TV

In ten years, says Jacques Attali,[1] more than 2 billion TV screens will be switched on at any one time. I suggest that it is primarily in this massive, ubiquitous and obtrusive presence of TV-transmitted images that the true impact of television on the way we act and think ought to be sought. Television has conquered the earth and its inhabitants. What is the outcome of that must successful of known invasions, though?

Since the beginning of the invasion evaluations of the new medium's impact on human lives and on the fashion in which they are shared oscillated between the Cassandrian and the Panglossian. The Cassandrians saw the medium as a next and gigantic stride on the road to totalitarian rule which society had travelled since the beginning of modern times: a *Wunderwaffe* of Big Brother and his henchmen, an unsurpassed and irresistible weapon of intellectual disablement, brainwashing, indoctrination and the imposition of thoughtless conformity, wielded by those placed in front of the TV cameras against those sitting in front of the TV screens. The Panglossians welcomed the medium as a next and gigantic stride on the road to emancipation which humanity had followed since that great awakening called the Enlightenment: knowledge being power, and the screen being a glass window through which the crown jewels of human wisdom can be contemplated, TV in the Panglossians' portrayal is, or is bound to become, a most powerful weapon of individual freedom of self-construction and self-assertion.

Cassandrians and Panglossians go on picking bones with each other, and their *querelle* is restaged and given new vigour with each successive informatic invention and the supply to the shops of every new or newish medium. But on one point the antagonists saw eye to eye: TV, just like the rest of the new media, is primarily a way of doing what humans, singly or collectively, have striven to do all along – only have had no time, money, tools, or know-how to do it on such a scale or as fast and with effects as great as they wished them to be. As a matter of fact, one can be a Cassandrian or a Panglossian only in as far as one believes that the *ends* are given and only the *means* are missing – and so the significance of any change consists in affecting the facility with which objectives (which are already known) are pursued and attained (by means heretofore unknown or unavailable).

One possibility which seldom appeared in the disputations swayed by the Cassandrian-cum-Panglossian obsessions was that television did not so much change the hands of the players, as the game itself; that in the case of the media, as in so many other cases, it is the means that seek the goals to which they could be applied, or through their sheer presence conjure up new ends without seeking them; that new means tend to set new objectives as well as a new game whose objectives are the most important of stakes: and that the failure to remember that few if any of the consequences of the new departures are anticipated, let alone designed in advance, results in a memory-induced blindness to the true nature of new realities which follow. I suggest that the paramount effect of television has been a slow yet relentless *cancellation* of the objectives which used to give sense to the Cassandrians versus Panglossians *querelle*.

To Marshall McLuhan goes the credit for the first breach in the cognitive frame jointly fixed by the antagonists of that *querelle*. The discovery that the 'media are the message' shifted attention from the contents of scripts, from their perception and retention, from things planned and controlled or controllable in principle, to the irreversible transformation of the ways scripts are scripted and staged, images are perceived and retention operates – things neither planned nor fully controllable. It was as if the drug's ostensible targets had changed places with its side-effects.

That breach was soon widened by Elihu Katz's seminal reversal of the assumed relation between 'reality' and its 'media representation': his discovery that events may exist solely in and through 'being seen on TV'. From there but one step remained to Jean Baudrillard's *simulacrum*[2] – that curious entity which, after the pattern of a psychosomatic ailment, puts paid to the hallowed distinction between reality and pretence, the 'true thing' and its representation, the fact and the *faitiche*,[3] the 'given' and the 'made up'. Simulacrum is *hyperreality*, a presence more real than reality, since it is a kind of reality which no longer allows an 'outside' from which it could be scrutinized, critically assessed and censured.

In a room carpeted wall to wall you never see the floor beneath: when asked, you would be hard put to it to say what the floor beneath was made of – but unless asked, you would hardly ever give the floor another thought. With the sun never setting on more than 2 billion switched-on TV screens, the world seen is the world as-seen-on-TV. There is little point in asking whether what you see on TV is the truth or a lie. There is little point as well in asking whether the presence of television makes the world better or worse. Indeed, what would the benchmark for judgement be like? Where, except in the imagination, is that 'world minus television' that the entry of television could improve or make worse? You cannot imagine your own funeral without you yourself watching it, and the question whether your gaze makes the funeral a better or a worse occasion makes no sense. It becomes ever more difficult to visualize the world other than as a 'photo opportunity' taken up, as a world without TV visualizing it. The world makes itself present to the eye as a succession of recordable images, and whatever is not fit to be recorded as an image does not really belong in it. Holiday-makers arm themselves with camcorders: only when viewing their video-recorded exploits on a TV screen back home can they be truly sure that the holidays did indeed happen.

World with television differs from the bygone world without, and one is naturally prompted, duly following the canons of induction, to conclude that it is the advent of television which made the difference. Since there are reasons to dislike the world 'as seen on TV', there are also proxy reasons to blame the messenger for the substance of that difference. Blaming the messenger for the evils of the message is a time-honoured custom, most messages tend to be carried these days through the TV aerials and cables, and so there are good grounds to anticipate that blaming television for the ills of the world jointly inhabited by TV producers and the spectators of TV shows will go on unabated.

And yet there are equally good, if not better grounds to suppose that the astonishing headway made by the electronic medium would be unthinkable were not the world ready or inclined to prompt and absorb it. These grounds are no worse than were the reasons which allowed Alexandre Ledru-Rollin, one of the principal fomenters of the 1848 Revolution, to shout at the mob flooding the streets of Paris: 'Let me pass, I have to follow them, I am their leader!'

This is not to say that television is 'merely' a carrier of messages and that the substance of the message would not change were the messenger to be replaced. But it does mean that were they different, the messages would stand little chance of being heard; and that the messages likely to be heard can hardly be carried by a different messenger. Whatever TV does to the world we inhabit, there seems to be a 'perfect fit' between the two. If television leads the world, it is because it follows it: if it manages to disseminate new patterns of life, it is because it replicates such patterns in its own mode of being. Our *Lebenswelt* and the world 'as seen on TV' wink and beckon to each other. TV is, indeed, 'user friendly' – and we are the users it is friendly with. However tempting such a pastime might be, to wrangle over what comes first and what second would be an idle pursuit. Should it be said instead that between the world 'as seen on TV' and the *Lebenswelt* in which we frame our life politics and which we create and re-create through conducting it, there is an affinity as well as a circular (or perhaps a helix-like) reinforcement? We are entitled to bewail the shape of either one of these two worlds, but we need to address out complaints to both of them, joined in an infrangible embrace. Wishing to change the way TV operates calls for nothing less than changing the world.

I intend therefore to suspend for the rest of the argument the question of how the guilt ought to be apportioned to each of the two entities locked in mutual feedback, and the related question of the end from which to start if a change for the better is adumbrated. I wish to focus instead on several instances of consonance (or should we speak rather of resonance?) between the *modus operandi* of television and the modality of the world we shape while being shaped by it – and particularly on such among them as seem particularly relevant to the present state and the future of democracy, that is (to use Cornelius Castoriadis's definition) – the autonomous society composed of autonomous individuals.

## Speed versus slowness

In his passionate critique of television and its works, Pierre Bourdieu points out that 'one of the major problems posited by television is the relation between thought and speed.'[4] This is not just a problem of the difficulty of thinking fast, of the time needed to gather thoughts, to reflect and compare the weight of the arguments. More is involved: in a rapid exchange, when there is no time to pause and think twice before uttering a sentence, the 'received ideas' – trivial ideas, the shared-by-all ideas, ideas that do not prompt or need reflection since they are deemed self-evident and, like axioms, require no proof – are inadvertently privileged. It is the questioning of the allegedly 'obvious', the scrutiny of what is usually left unspoken, the bringing to attention of aspects normally left out of consideration or passed by in silence that require time. But no other communicative medium more fully deserves Benjamin Franklin's famed adage, 'Time is money'. Time is the resource television is notoriously short of. As a French journalist quipped, were Émile Zola allowed to make his defence of Dreyfus on television, he would only be given enough time to shout 'J'accuse!'

Television, whether public or private, has no other world to operate in than the world conquered and ruled by market competition. The 'ratings' (or l'Audimat, whose meekly accepted authority Bourdieu berates) are, we may say, the 'garrison left by the conquerors in the conquered city'. The ratings record the show's 'holding power': to get a respectable score, the attention of viewers must be retained for the duration of the show, and the viewers must trust that this indeed will happen once they have selected the show from among the many others on offer. For commercial television, this is a matter of life and death: there would be no one left in the managerial offices and the studios to assess the outcome of experimental tinkering with the omnipotence of the ratings' verdict. But public television is in no better a position to resist: it operates in the same world, in a world in which market-style competition rules supreme, and the governments of the day without exception insist on it being respected and obeyed – ministers would find themselves in dire straits were they to spend 'the taxpayers' money' on performances which the taxpayers neither enjoy nor even wish to. The ratings race is a competition which all television channels must join and in which they must prove their worth. But none would be able to attract viewers unless it reckoned with their capacity and abided by their predilections.

Human attention is the prime stake in the media competition and the coveted good on which the media capitalize – but it is also the scarcest and essentially the least expendable of resources. Since the sum total of attention cannot be increased, vying for attention is a zero-sum game and cannot but be a war of redistribution: messages can gain more attention solely at the expense of other messages. The information on offer far exceeds the human capacity for absorption and retention: according to some assessments, one copy of a daily newspaper may contain as many bits of information as average persons at the time of Renaissance were exposed to in the course of their whole lives. It is little wonder therefore that, as George Steiner pithily commented, cultural products are these days calculated 'for maximal impact and instant obsolescence': to be noticed, they must be sharp and shocking (*more* sharp and shocking than those beside them), but they can count only for a briefest of timespans, being bound to make room for new sharp shocks. Steiner describes the resulting mode of being-in-the-world as *casino culture*: each game is short, games replace each other in quick succession, the stakes of the game change with lightning speed and often devalue before the game is over. And, of course, in every casino there is a variety of games, each earnestly trying to lure prospective players with colourful flashing lights and promises of dazzling jackpots calculated to outshine the other games in the building.

In a casino, and also in a casino-like culture, long-term planning makes little sense. One needs to take each game as it comes. Each game is a self-enclosed episode: losing or winning one of them has no influence on the outcome of others. Time spent in a casino is a series of new beginnings, each one leading rapidly to a finish, and life patched together by casino culture reads as a collection of short stories, not a novel.

Television chimes well with the skills and attitudes trained and cultivated by casino culture, and prompted by a survival instinct it leans over backwards to chime better still. And so the news presenters try to deliver their lines standing up rather than siting at their desks, while the words they speak are accompanied by the beat of rhythmic, metronome-like sounds emphasizing the rapid passage of time. Casualty departments and accident and emergency rooms become the favourite settings of dramas: nowhere else are lives sliced so thinly and the transience of luck and misfortune put so blatantly on display. In countless quizzes it is the fastest finger on the bell, not the deepest thought, that wins the game. Speed of response counts more than the pool of knowledge from which responses are drawn: knowledge which takes more time to dig up than the fleeting moment allotted to players does not count at all: surfing fast, not diving deep, is the name of life-game 'as seen on TV'. The success of a surfer depends on the ability to stay on the surface.

The casino culture of instantaneity and episodicity portends the end of 'politics as we know it'. Ours is a time of fast food, but also of fast thinkers and fast talkers. Abraham Lincoln could keep an audience spellbound during his four-hour long election speeches. His successors won't survive the electoral campaign if they don't excel in the art of sound-bites and cannot produce short, sharp witticism fit for short, sharp headlines. Grigori Yavlinski, who lectured the much suffering Russians about the arcane causes of their endless suffering and the intricate ways out of their troubles, scraped together 5 per cent of votes, while the 50-odd per cent of Russians who offered their votes to Vladimir Putin did not mind at all their favourite's notorious parsimony with words. Two politicians who recently won landslide electoral victories, Putin in Russia and Tony Blair in Britain, wisely abstained from expounding on their political programmes and philosophies: were they to behave differently, they could perhaps alienate some of the voters by opposing their preferences, but they would lose many, many more by demanding a mental effort they would neither wish nor be able to make, risking boredom and fading interest. Knowing from Anthony Giddens's analyses that the absence of guidelines to be trusted is a most vulnerable and painful aspect of life in our increasingly fluid social setting, Blair preferred to dwell on the appeal to trust him, leaving sorely under discussed the policies which the electors were supposed to trust him to promote. The other constant motif of Blair's electoral speeches was that of 'modernization', a term as vacuous by itself as it is useful in implying a gloss of scientific seriousness and expertise on the universal and perpetual human desire to make things better. After electoral victory there was of course no reason to abandon the victorious strategy. Of one of Blair's newspaper conferences Simon Hoggart, the *Guardian* columnist, had the following to say:

> Not for the first time, I was struck by the way a Blair speech is closer to a musical composition than to a mere rhetoric. Like a piece of music, its aim isn't to inform but to create good feelings. It's no more about facts and policies than the Pastoral Symphony is an examination of the common agricultural policy...Nobody ever finished listening to a Blair speech and said, 'Well, I learned something there.' Instead they praise the bravura performance and enjoy the afterglow created by the mood.[5]

To keep in touch with the surfers, no politician can risk venturing beneath the surface. And *doxa*, that unreflected-upon common creed that colours all reflection is the politician's equivalent of the

surfers' surface. Politicians feel safe when they keep their public
discourse at the level of what Nick Lee recently dubbed 'inscrutable
clarity': 'a certainty that passes as such as long as its grounds remain
occulted, as long as it be delivered quickly enough to escape analy-
sis'.[6] The shorter are political speeches of words, the further they
keep from inspiring dangerous thoughts.

But let me repeat: it would be neither reasonable nor fair to lay
the blame for such a radical transformation of the political process
in front of the television screens. Defenders of the ways the mass
media operate may be more right than they think when they reiterate that the media do no more, yet no less either, than to supply
what their customers need. In the 'liquid' stage of the modern era,
mobility, or rather the ability to keep on the move, is the very stuff
of which a new hierarchy of power is built, the paramount stratifying factor – while speed and acceleration are the principal strategies
aimed at slanting that factor in one's favour. If this is the case, then
two intimately linked capacities acquire an unprecedented survival-
and-success value. One is *flexibility*: the ability to change track at
short notice, to adjust instantaneously to changed circumstances,
never being burdened with habits too solidly settled or possessions
too heavy to move around or too close to the heart to leave behind.
The other is *all-roundness*, versatility if not dilettantism: one should
beware of putting all one's eggs in one basket – time dedicated to
making one's expertise deeper (and so, inevitably, more narrowly
focused) may be sorely missed when this particular expertise is no
longer in demand while other skills rise in price. We know from the
students of evolution that in a fast-changing climate it is the 'gener-
alistic', unspecialized and unchoosy species that have the best
chance of survival.

Of Bill Gates, who to most top executives worldwide 'is a heroic
figure', indeed a present-day equivalent of Henry Ford and John D.
Rockefeller rolled into one, Richard Sennett, who has studied him at
close quarters, has the following to say:

> His products are furious in coming forth and as rapid in disappear-
> ing, whereas Rockefeller wanted to own oil rigs, buildings, machinery,
> or railroads for the long term...[He] spoke of positioning himself in
> a network of possibilities rather than paralysing oneself in one par-
> ticular job...[He is willing] to destroy what he has made, given the
> demands of the immediate moment...[He is] someone who has the
> confidence to dwell in disorder, someone who flourishes in the midst
> of dislocation.[7]

We are not all Bill Gates: when passed down to the less endowed and resourceful among us Bill Gates's meat may prove a poison. Gates's mode of life may be victorious strategy for a few: for the rest it is a recipe for trials and tribulations of a perpetually insecure present and a stubbornly uncertain future. This argument won't cut much ice, though, once confronted with life's hard realities. It is Gates's mode of life that holds the day, and as long as this remains the case, Gates's nomadic spirit will continue to be a shining light for those to whom it shows the road to success as much as for all those whom it lures into the wilderness he helped to set up. And as long as it does, sound-bites have no reason to fear for their future.

### Private versus public

Alain Ehrenberg, the French sociologist, has selected a Wednesday in October 1983 as a date of cultural breakthrough (at least in France's history).[8] On that day a certain Viviane, neither a celebrity nor a person for whatever reason in the limelight, just an 'ordinary' French woman like the millions who watched her, appeared in front of television cameras to announce that her husband, Michel, suffers from premature ejaculation and for that reason she never experienced any pleasure with him. This was, indeed, a break-through: a meeting between television, that ultimate embodiment of publicness, and the intimacy of the bedroom, the ultimate symbol of privacy. Viviane's announcement might have shocked the viewers and reverberated for a while across the wide spectrum of the French media – but the thousands of Vivianes and Michels who have followed suit have long since ceased to make waves. 'Talk shows', the public confessions of things privately lived through, have since become the most common, most trivial and most predictable of television pursuits, and also the ones which invariably boast the highest ratings. We live now in a confessional society. We have installed microphones in confessionals and connected them to the public address network, and venting one's intimacies in public has become the duty *sine qua non* of every public figure and the compulsive obsession of all the rest. As Britain's great wit Peter Ustinov put it, 'This is a free country, madam. We have a right to share your privacy in a public place.' Less witty journalists dress as guardians of the public interest defending the 'people's right to know'.

That Wednesday evening was indeed a moment of cultural up-heaval for France (other countries may date a similar onslaught differently); and for several closely connected reasons.

The first reason has already been mentioned: the passages be-tween private and public have been thrown wide open, the line that once separated the two spaces has been effaced and the long, incon-clusive process of its renegotiation has been set in motion. It is not only that the ban traditionally imposed on the public display of emotions has been lifted, but the meticulous scrutiny and the unre-strained display of private sentiments, dreams and obsessions is en-couraged and, in accordance with the behaviourist formula, reinforced by being rewarded with rounds of the audience's applause – the more hectic the more savage and tempestuous the confessed passions were. Day in day out, presenters and anchor persons nudge the invited audience, and by proxy the viewers glued to their TV screens, to 'open up', drop all defences and let themselves go, stop-ping at nothing and shaking off the bygone ideas of decorum and decency. The lesson delivered is that no inner thoughts and feelings are too private to be vented in public.

The second reason to speak of the TV-led (or rather TV-assisted) cultural revolution is the birth and rapid development of a language which allows private sentiments to be publicly shared and com-pared. The 'subjective' used to be a synonym of the ineffable: the difficulty, perhaps even impossibility of articulate expression was very nearly a defining feature of *private* sentiments and the principal obstacle to the transgression of the private/public boundary. As we know from Ludwig Wittgenstein, there is not and cannot be such a thing as a private language, if 'private' stands for the impossibility of being communicated. 'Talk shows' are public courses in a new lan-guage, spanning the divide between the communicable and the inar-ticulable, between private and public. The appearance of such a language does more than enable actors and spectators to tell what they feel. Once such a language has appeared and the subjective living through of things has acquired names, having thereby become objects that can be sought, found, examined and talked about (moved, as Martin Heidegger would say, from the invisible world of *Zuhandenheit* to the all-too-tangible territory of *Vorhandenheit*), the only sentiments and affections that can be recognized for what they are are those that are fit to be communicated: language creates its own public and its own public space.

The third reason is the inherent propensity of talk shows to repres-ent human life, its subject-matter, as an aggregate of individually experienced problems craving for individual resolution and the deployment for that purpose of individually possessed resources. Again, it is well-nigh impossible to say whether this formidable departure would be better described as TV-led or as TV-assisted. What is certain is that whatever 'is seen on TV' is in tune with the experience supplied seven days a week and twenty-four hours a day by the 'real world'. As Ulrich Beck pointedly commented, our lives have now become 'biographical solutions to systemic contradictions'. You may say that finding such a solution is an impossible task, that systemic contradictions cannot be *resolved* through individual life politics – but here you are, and there is no obvious way leading from life politics to being able to confront systemic contradictions point-blank and so to contemplate striking at their roots.

> Experts dump their contradictions and conflicts at the feet of the individual... *History* shrinks *to the (eternal) present*, and everything revolves around the axis of one's personal ego and personal life... [O]*utside turned inside and made private*... [T]he individual will have to 'pay for' the consequences of decisions not taken... [I]n order for one to survive, an *ego-centered world-view* must be developed, which turns the relation of ego and world on its head, so to speak, conceiving of and making them useful for the purpose of shaping an individual biography.[9]

Chat shows help to accomplish that wondrous transformation, to make the world *ego-centred*, to conjure up a magic avatar: the reincarnation of socially produced antinomies and risks as problems definable in individual terms, as problems which have emerged individually and individually need to be confronted and tackled. One has suffered because one was not skilful and knowledgeable enough to stave off suffering; lack of resolve and determination invariably figure at the top of the long list of individual neglects and errors which are blamed for causing the trouble. The issue of a 'wrong kind of society' is taken off the agenda, or rather never allowed to appear on it; and the void thereby left in the argument is made all but invisible by being filled with denunciation and deprecation of individual unfitness and inadequacy. The verdict is made foolproof by the trial being continually rehearsed and the sentence endlessly reiterated.

Around the institution of the chat show, a community is created; it is, however, an oxymoronic community, a community of individuals united only by their self-enclosure and self-containment. What the members of such a bizarre community have in common is that each

one of them suffers in solitude; they all struggle to lift themselves
out of trouble by Baron Münchhausen's feat of pulling themselves up
by their own boot straps, and no one of them counts on making the
job easier by joining forces with others who are going through a
similar agony. The 'individuality' of problems means that their resolution can gain nothing from being shared in any other way but
talking about them and listening to others who do the same. And
'community' means a quantity of individuals who gather under one
roof or in front of their TV sets in order to behave according to that
pattern.

The audience of chat shows, just like the population of the individualized world from which that audience is drawn, does not make
a team. However coordinated their thoughts and moves may be,
members of the audience enter their togetherness as singles and
finish it reinforced in their conviction that singles they are bound to
remain. During the session, their problems have not acquired a new
quality; they have not been translated into public issues. They have
merely been publicly declared to be private problems and publicly
confirmed to be such.

It may be that 'outside was turned inside' and was made private.
It is also true, however, that with inside turned outside, whatever
stays outside has been effectively overshadowed. With 'the private'
covering the public stage wall to wall, no room is left for anything
which cannot or declines to be turned inside, and no entry is
allowed for it on to the public stage until it has been recycled into
the private. In this sense TV is a *sine qua non* condition of 'turning
outside inside', of shifting the task of resolving social problems to
individual biographies. For politics, the impact is shattering.

The substance of democratic politics (that is, of the mode of being
of an autonomous society composed of autonomous individuals) is
the ongoing process of a two-way translation: of private troubles
into public issues, and public interests into individual rights and
duties. It is this two-pronged translation which fell as the first victim
of 'turning outside inside', the act that was made feasible by turning
inside outside: with such a casualty, politics has been effectively
disarmed. It is now the turn of public faults to become 'ineffable'
(that is, unless reprocessed as personal inadequacies). Ethical flaws
of policies can hardly be grasped in any form but as ethical sins of
the politicians – no one proposed an injunction when President Clinton effectively abolished the American welfare state by removing it
from among federal tasks, while the only time that Robin Cook, the
British Foreign Secretary, was inches away from a forced resignation

was when the tabloids disclosed his marital disloyalty, not when he allowed the sale of British-made arms to a government guilty of the massacre of its subjects.

If there is no room for the idea of *wrong* society, there is hardly much chance for the idea of *good* society to be born, let alone make waves. If the perception of socially committed injustice is the embryo from which models of the just society grow, the perception of personal inadequacy may give birth solely to a model of individual fitness, individual cunning and all-round adequacy. The great accomplishment of the media as they assist in remaking the *Lebenswelt* after the likeness of the world 'as seen on TV' is to speed up and facilitate the replacement of politics as a collective endeavour with life politics, the consummately individual pursuit.

## Authority versus idolatry

Politics with a capital 'P' needs leaders with authority. Life politics, on the other hand, needs idols. The difference between the two could not be greater, even if some leaders happen to be idolized while idols sometimes claim authority pointing to the massiveness of their worship.

Politics is many things, but it would hardly be any of them were it not the art of translating individual problems into public issues, and common interests into individual rights and duties. Leaders are experts in such translation. They give public (generic) names to individually suffered worries and so set the ground for a collective handling of problems which could neither be perceived from inside individual experience nor tackled by individuals separately. They also propose what individuals may or need to do to make collective action effective. Leaders sketch and promote visions of a good society or a better society, of social justice or a society fairer than the one known so far, of a decent and humane way of living together or a shared life more humane than the life lived at present. And then they suggest what ought to be done to achieve any or all such improvements.

Life politics, on the other hand, is from beginning to end enclosed in a framework of individuality: the individual body complete with the 'inner self', personal identity claimed and granted, 'the space' one wants as a rule to have 'more' of, and which one struggles to keep free from others' interference. In Anthony Giddens's famous definition, life politics is centred on 'self-identity as such':

In so far as it is focused upon the lifespan, considered as an internally referential system, the reflexive project of self is oriented only to control. It has no morality other than authenticity, a modern version of the old maxim to 'thine own self be true'. Today, however, given the lapse of tradition, the question 'What shall I be?' is inextricably bound up with 'How shall I live?'[10]

Life politics is self-centred and self-referential. Contrary to what Giddens implies, 'authenticity' is not another form of morality, but a denial of the relevance of ethics. Morality is a feature of interpersonal relations, not of one's relation to oneself: stretching oneself towards the Other, 'being *for*' the Other and endowing the Other's needs with causal power over one's own endeavours are the constitutive trait of the moral self and moral conduct; if life politics subordinated to the pursuit of 'authenticity' leads occasionally to similar results, it does it only accidentally, 'doing favours' to the Other being but a derivative of self-concern and coming, if at all, as a second thought. Furthermore, the 'authenticity' itself is not an updated version of 'being true to oneself'. The locating of life politics at the centre of life is intimately related to the collapse of trust in the 'inner truth' of the self. Unlike in the times of the Sartrean *projet de la vie*, what is being practised under the name of 'authenticity' today is not a life long pilgrimage to the 'heart of the true self', but a long and in principle interminable series of tourist escapades in search of more exciting modes of life, prompted by the never placated fear that some attractive and pleasurable models might have been overlooked or foolishly discounted. Not very often, and not necessarily, may the itinerary of the successive experiments be plotted along a straight line.

It is here that idols come in handy. As the demand for models of a good society shrinks, and the few on offer are hard put to it to lure prospective customers, new and improved models of a good life (good *individual* life, individually composed and individually enjoyed) are eagerly sought, the more varied and numerous the better. Unlike the leaders of yore, idols are made to the measure of that new demand. Idols do not show the way – they offer themselves as *examples*: 'this is how I, a lonely individual like all the rest of you, cope with the challenges of life and manage to swim while being buffeted by tides; I have been plagued by the same troubles and worries that haunt you, but I've managed to cope and get the better of adversity; I've had my share of stumblings and falls, but I never threw in the towel and each time I recovered and got my act

*Life Politics*

together. True, you are not like me: no two guys are exactly like each other, everyone is a universe as complete as it is separate and different, and each one of us needs to use own brains, make own decisions and face up to own risks; but we can learn something from each other's wrong and right moves, from mishaps and strokes of luck. I've ended up rich and famous, so perhaps it stands to reason to suppose that I've mastered the difficult art of life better than many others and that it is worth your while to have a closer look at how this has been done. Of course, there are no foolproof recipes and what works well for one guy may fail for another. But the more hints and clues you get, the greater is the chance of picking the one that suits you best.'

Acute interest in the secrets of the celebrities' private lives is not generated by mere love of gossip, and TV cameras peeping into celebrities' private pastimes are not just the high-tech version of the old keyhole. The updating on the celebrities' love affairs, style of dressing and self-presentation, choice of residence and holidays, daily diet and the contents of iceboxes – the stuff that fills prime-time TV and supplies headlines for tabloid front pages – does not merely pander to timeless human curiosity. In a world in which individually conducted life politics elbows out all other political games in town, examples perform the function once attempted by political programmes and platforms, and gossipy reports about celebrities' ways and means increasingly play the vital role which was once performed by political gatherings, manifestoes and pamphlets. They tell the perplexed what to live for and how to go after things worth living for. They are, indeed, the indispensable educational equipment which life politics cannot do without but would not get from any other source.

It is reasonable to go a step further and to suppose that it is the necessity of engaging in life politics, brought about by progressive individualization, that lies at the roots of the astonishing growth of the cult of celebrities: even of the 'idols' phenomenon itself. Crowds of watchers are needed to infuse the example on display with the authority to transmogrify a mere individual adventure into a model worth emulating – and the ubiquitous craving for such models assures a crowded audience. By the sheer power of its numbers, the crowd bestows charisma on the idols: and the charisma of idols makes watchers into a crowd. The worldwide reach of cable and satellite networks of course facilitates the interplay between demand and supply. Whatever the idols may lack in quality is fully compensated for by the sheer quantity of avid spectators.

Idolatry fits the contemporary mode of life in another respect, too: it chimes well with the fragmentariness of individual life courses. In the notoriously 'flexible' world of abrupt and unpredictable change, reasonable life politics requires that the span of life is sliced into episodes which (as if obedient to Hume's warning *post hoc non est propter hoc*) follow, but do not determine each other. The perpetual ability to be 'born again', to 'have another try' or 'start from the beginning', to abandon the old and embrace the new, acquires under present conditions supreme survival value: this is, roughly, the lesson which the politicians keep hammering home whenever they appeal for 'more flexibility'. Already several years ago, as Richard Sennett calculated, a young American with at least two years of college could expect 'to change jobs at least eleven times in the course of working, and change his or her skill base at least three times during those forty years of labour'[11] – and since these words were written the pace of change has not stayed still. One thing young people can be certain of is that the way they will live their lives tomorrow will be unlike the way they live today. A perpetuity of 'new starts' has replaced the perpetuity of a life project pursued with dogged determination. It is *inconsistency* that promises an edge to the fighters for survival and dreamers of success.

The cult of celebrities is made to the measure of that inconsistency. Notoriety has replaced fame, and the dazzling moment of being in the limelight (it is in the nature of limelight to go on and off, while it cannot be kept on too long for fear of overheating) has replaced the steady glow of public esteem. Where not so long ago an instant commercial success was suspect, since it was seen as 'a sign of compromise with the time and the power of money', today, as Pierre Bourdieu suggests, 'the market is increasingly accepted as a source of legitimation.'[12] Unlike the fame of people of yore, celebrity is short-lived, and the brevity of its ascent chimes well with a life lived as a string of new beginnings. Joining the cult of celebrity is unlike enlisting in a cause – it does not require entering into long-term commitments and so does not mortgage the future. Just like all other headline items, idols explode into attention only to fall shortly afterwards into oblivion (though they may be recycled in staged comebacks and on anniversary occasions). Idols, though, have their moments of glory, and in that they stand out from the grey mass of 'ordinary' men and women who are daily offered as examples to ponder and to learn from in countless 'chat shows' specializing in public confessions.

What idolatry loses in durability, it gains in intensity. Idolatry condenses emotions otherwise dispersed and spread over long time

spans. Again, there is a resonance between the momentary condensation of affects and another remarkable feature of contemporary
living: the high value placed on the intensity of experience at the
expense of its durability. The standard by which the value of experience is measured tends to be its excitement-generating capacity, not
its durable traces. In a society which has cancelled the early modern
injunction to delay gratification, even 'immortality' is of little value
unless it is an 'experience' of eternity fit for instant consumption.
Like other seductive cultural offers, it must be fit for 'maximal
impact and instant obsolescence', promptly clearing the site for as-
yet-untried-and-hopefully-more-exciting adventures.

If the orthodox-style authorities are still around, they need to
compete with celebrities-in-the-limelight on terms which seldom
work in their favour, and certainly strip them of the privilege they
once enjoyed. The humdrum, dull and altogether unspectacular
business of traditional politics is ill-suited to striking the eye among
the crowd of competitors, and if it succeeds, it won't be likely to
attract many watchers, let alone keep their attention as long as it
takes to see the business through. TV quizzes reiterate daily the
message that the date of the third wedding of a pop-star or a foot-
baller's hat-trick count for as much as who won the last war or the
year in which women gained electoral rights. As the perceptive
Czech writer, Ivan Klima, put it pithily:

> Footballers, ice-hockey players, tennis players, basketball players, gui-
> tarists, singers, film actors, television presenters and top models. Oc-
> casionally – and only symbolically – they are joined by some writer,
> painter, scholar, Nobel prizewinner (is there anyone who remembers
> their names a year later?), or princess...until she too is forgotten.
> There is nothing quite so transient as entertainment and physical
> beauty, and the idols that symbolize them are equally ephemeral.[13]

Klima concludes that 'more than anything else, the idols of today
symbolize the futility of human strivings and the certainty of extinction without trace.' What he fails to mention, though, is that the
cavalcade of celebrities is far too colourful and too rapidly moving
to allow a moment of reflection on the futility of strivings and on
the certainty of extinction. The silencing or precluding of reflection
is the most important of the many services that the cavalcade of
celebrities renders to most of us, seeking in the speed of change a
remedy against the insecurity of the present and the uncertainty of
the future.

## Event versus policy

François Brune, the author of *Médiatiquement correct. 265 maximes de notre temps*,[14] quotes a slogan used in the last decade by a French media network, RTL: 'Information is like coffee: good when hot and strong.' To live up to this credo, the media recycle the world as a succession of *events*. It does not matter in what order events follow each other: the World Cup might be followed by the death of Diana which might be followed by Bill Clinton's erotic idiosyncrasies which might be followed by the shuttle bombing of Serbia followed by the flood in Mozambique. The order could be easily reversed or reshuffled: the order does not truly matter since no causal connection or logic is implied: on the contrary, the haphazardness and randomness of succession conveys the unwieldy contingency of the world – *quod erat demonstrandum*. What does matter, and matter a lot, is that each event is strong enough to capture the headlines, but that each disappears from the headlines before it gets cold. 'The grid of events has become the sole approach to the world,' Brune observes.[15] The world is on the move, or at least this is what our experience tells every one of us: and so the quick succession of 'points of public interest' creates the impression we all badly need that we are, indeed, *au courant* with the change, that we catch up with the steadily accelerating reality.

This is not, though, the sole importance of the event. 'The event', Brune points out, 'constitutes the citizens as a public.' Let me comment that this is a new kind of public, blatantly unlike the sort of public which John Stuart Mill in unison with other protagonists of modern democracy praised as the stronghold or greenhouse, or both, of popular sovereignty. The public brought into being (and soon dismantled) by the 'event in public view' is a congregation of spectators, not actors. That 'belonging' which is conjured up by the simultaneity of watching and commonality of focus commits nothing except the attention. The members of the congregation of spectators do not need to follow the spectacle by action: most certainly no one asks or expects them to take decisions on what sort of action ought to be undertaken (except the instant polls which pretend to do just that while asking questions of an essentially aesthetic nature – testing the viewers' appreciation of the spectacle). Events serve to demonstrate that the 'public stage' is for viewing and enjoyment, not for acting.

The congregation of viewers is one more 'peg community': a community formed by the act of hanging individual concerns on a common 'peg' – be it a one-day hero or a one-day villain, a big catastrophe or an exceptionally joyous exploit. Like the overcoats in the theatre cloakroom, the concerns are hung on the peg only for the duration of the spectacle, remaining all the time private properties of their rightful owners. Peg communities bear many markings of the 'real stuff' – they offer therefore the *experience* of belonging, of that quality of life which communities are deemed to deliver and for which they are coveted. They, however, lack the traits which define the 'real stuff': durability, a life expectation longer than that of any of its members, and being (in the famous Émile Durkheim expression) 'a whole greater than the sum of its parts'. Since the 'real stuff' is in today's world prominent mostly for its absence or relentless disintegration, 'peg communities' are the second best choice: the *experience* of community, however short-lived it may be, is the sole surrogate of what is desired to be experienced. Since, however, 'peg communities' are by their nature short-lived and have but a feeble grip on their 'members', each one of them leaves in its wake a void which cries out to be filled again. Here again the endemic mortality of events helps: once cut into the thin slices of episodes, life needs many and varied attention-drawing events to cover up the absence of logic and continuity.

We may say that as consumers of events we all suffer from bulimia. We may also say that, for bulimia sufferers, events (or spectacles, the form in which events reach attention once they are processed by the media) are an ideal food. Bulimia sufferers need to get rid fast of the food they ingest in order to make room for more ingestion – it is not the quelling of hunger, but the act of voracious filling up which they crave and which prompts the doctors to define their form of eating as a 'disorder': events/spectacles are tailor-made for the purpose. They are aimed at immediate consumption and similarly speedy excretion, they are expected to be swallowed without chewing, and they are not meant to be digested. They vacate attention as soon as they enter it, well before they stand a chance of being assimilated and turned into a part of the consuming organism. One should perhaps correct the RTL slogan: that coffee which information imitates is not just hot and strong, it is also *instant*.

In all these respects, events stand in implacable opposition to policies. It was policies which used to perform the integrating function now taken over by events/spectacles. It was policies that originated and gave rise to the communities of the like-minded. But they did it differently, and their products differed accordingly.

The possibility of integration-through-policy would be unthinkable without the assumption of a collective ability to control, indeed to shape the future: without the concept of the future that emerges out of consistent and doggedly pursued action, rather than descending out of the blue following the random play of essentially unharnessable and unpredictable forces. If the art of life in 'liquid' modernity is mostly about swimming safely in tidal waves which cannot be tamed, the ambition of 'solid' modernity was to reforge transience into durability, randomness into regularity, contingency into routine and chaos into order. It wanted to make the human world transparent and predictable, and believed that it could be done.

Such assumptions are no longer held; they command little credibility when voiced. As Pierre Bourdieu emphatically stated:

> those who deplore the cynicism which, as they believe, marks men and women of our time should not fail to refer it to the economic and social conditions which favour and reward it... The capacity to project into the future... is the condition of all rational action... For a reasonable ambition to transform the present in reference to a projected future, a minimum hold on the present is required.[16]

The point is, though, that very few of us can nowadays trust that singly or severally, or even collectively, we have enough grip on the present to dare to think, let alone to resolve, to transform the future. But to have a 'policy', and even more to pursue it steadfastly, makes sense only in as far as we believe that the future can be shaped, that there are ways and means to do it, and that agencies powerful enough to tackle the task effectively either exist or can be constructed. There is little evidence to substantiate this belief. The agencies which in the past boasted the ability to change the world for the better (most prominent among them the governments of nation-states, those acknowledged carriers and guardians of the sovereignty of action) reply to the demands of change with the increasingly sacrosant and no longer questioned TINA formula (There Is No Alternative). They call for 'more flexibility' and more obedience to 'market forces', implying that we will all gain from *less* regulation, *less* control, *less* command over the conditions of the life we share. The big question which defies orthodox political action today is not 'what is to be done' but 'who can and will do it' – whatever it is that might need to be done.

In our fast globalizing world, agencies are no match for dependencies. 'Globalization' means today no more (but no less either)
than globality of our dependencies: no locality is free any more to
proceed with its own agenda without reckoning with the elusive and
recondite 'global finance' and 'global markets', while everything
done locally may have global effects, anticipated or not. In other
respects, though, globalization has made little progress. Most certainly, the political institutions inherited from two centuries of
modern democracy have not followed the economy into global
space. The result, as Manuel Castells put it, is a world in which
*power* flows in the uncontrolled and underinstitutionalized *global*
space, while *politics* stays as *local* as before. The first is beyond the
reach of the second. The emergent 'global system' is strikingly and
dangerously one-dimensional, and such systems are notoriously un-
balanced and unequilibrated.

We could console ourselves, following the present-day Panglossians, that after all we live in a time of transformation and any
transformation must have its share of imbalances and 'lags'. We
may aver, even believe, that the mismatch between the globality of
the economy and the territoriality of politics is a temporary phenomenon, an effect of a 'political lag' which is bound to be repaired
soon. This is, indeed, a consoling belief – the snag is that there are
arguments, valid both empirically and analytically, which detract
from its credibility. It could be argued that the globalization of economic power is itself the major cause of the local fragmentation of
politics and of orthodox political agencies; that once emancipated
from the obtrusive control of political institutions, the economic
forces will use all their power (and they do wield enormous power)
to prevent the 'locals' from regaining that control, singly or in collu-
sion. It could even be argued that far from being a temporary malfunction in the course of an ongoing transformation, the present
combination of global economy and local politics is the portent of
things to come: that the globality of economy and the locality of
politics are, in fact, the 'systemic prerequisites' of the new and peculiar, curiously lopsided arrangement of the world affairs.

Whatever is the case, the brute fact is that the continuing (and
widening) gap between economic power and political agencies goes
on spawning that 'précarité' which 'est aujourd'hui partout'. And
another fact is that as long as there are few if any signs of bridging
that gap, the fluidity of life-settings, the fragmentariness and episodicity of life pursuits that follow the flexibility which all that requires, and consequently the anxieties and traumas which saturate

individual lives-of-choices, are unlikely to subside, and will in all probability intensify. It is to those anxieties and traumas that contemporary men and women try to respond in their life politics. And it is to the measure and in the likeness of such strategies that 'the message which is the media' is made. Fears and dreams fed by the daily efforts to find 'biographical solutions to systemic contradictions' and the world 'as seen on TV' wink at each other and lend sense to each other and vouch for each other's credibility. Whoever asks 'what can we do about the media' must ask 'what is to be done about the world in which these media operate'. One question cannot be answered unless a realistic answer to the other question is found.

# 6

# Consuming Life

Montaigne recalls an ancient story of the wildly ambitious King Pyrrhus who would not rest until he had fulfilled his dreams of new and ever new conquests, and Cineas, Pyrrhus's factotum, who advised him to relax and enjoy the rest right away, skipping the pains and hazards of the war.[1] Pascal was sceptical about the practicality of the advice and derided Cineas for his ignorance of human nature.[2] Yes, it is true that 'all unhappiness comes from one thing – the inability of human beings to stay quietly in their rooms'; but it is also true that 'nothing is less endurable than staying at rest, without passions, adventures, diversions and efforts.' 'Seeking rest, people fight the obstacles which stand in their way: but once the obstacles have been overcome, repose becomes unendurable' (as Montaigne himself put it: 'Of all the pleasures we know of, their pursuit is the most pleasurable'[3]). People tend to sincerely believe that what they truly desire is tranquillity – but they delude themselves: what they are truly after is agitation. What they really crave is to chase the hare, not to catch it. The pleasure is in the hunting, not in the prey.

Why must it be like this? Because of our human condition, 'mortal and miserable', and of the sheer impossibility of finding consolation in anything once we look at it closely. The sole comfort available is an absorbing venture that would divert our attention and prevent us from thinking about death and the brevity of life, the genuine reason for our misery. What we enjoy is 'hubbub and bustle', not their ostensible purposes and rewards. 'The hare would not protect us from the sight of our death and misery, but the diversion of hunting a hare would do so.' We seek and find the denouement to the drama of mortality not in the things we gain and the states we attain, but in desiring them and running after them.

Pascal entertained little hope: there is no escape from human fate except in diversions, and our brethren-in-mortality could hardly be blamed for wanting them. 'Their fault is not in seeking commotion, if what they do is out of a wish to be entertained. What is wrong is to seek things in the hope that their possession will bring veritable happiness; only in such a case is one right to accuse them of vanity.'

Had Pascal been born a couple of centuries later, he would perhaps have repeated after Robert Louis Stevenson: 'To travel hopefully is a better thing than to arrive, and the true success is to labour.' In all probability, he would however sharpen up the Scottish writer's point and observe bitterly that to arrive is no joy at all. To stop travelling is a recipe for despondency and despair, Pascal would have said. From human fate there is no salvation, he would conclude: one can only do one's best to forget it.

To that last statement, though, another great explorer of the human (modern, as will become clear later) predicament, Søren Kierkegaard, would take exception. Seeking diversion instead of confronting human fate point-blank is in Kierkegaard's view a sign of a corrupt or perverse life, a pathology of character. And there is nothing inevitable about that perversion: the corruption is, fairly and simply, resistible.

Kierkegaard's archetype of the pathology in question is the figure of Mozart's Don Giovanni. Don Juan's pleasure is not the *possession* of women, but their *seduction*: he has no interest in the women he has already conquered – his pleasure stops at the moment of triumph. Don Juan's sexual appetites are not necessarily greater than the next man's; the point is, though, that the question of how great these appetites are is totally irrelevant to Don Juan's life formula, since his life is about keeping desire alive rather than about its satisfaction.

> Only in this manner can Don Juan become epic, in that he constantly finishes, and constantly begins again from the beginning, for his life is the sum of repellent moments which have no coherence, his life as moment is the sum of the moments, as the sum of the moments is the moment...

One cannot even call Don Juan a deceiver, Kierkegaard comments. Or, for that matter, a seducer:

To be a seducer requires a certain amount of reflection and consciousness, and as soon as this is present, then it is proper to speak of
cunning and intrigues and crafty plans. This consciousness is lacking
in Don Juan. Therefore, he does not seduce. He desires, and this
desire acts seductively. To that extent he seduces. He enjoys the satisfaction of desire; as soon as he has enjoyed it, he seeks a new object,
and so on endlessly... He requires no preparation, no plan, no time;
for he is always prepared. Energy is always in him and also desire,
and only when he desires is he rightly in his element.[4]

Don Juan's life is thinly sliced into separate and unconnected
moments, but it is Don Juan himself who has sliced it this way. He
*made his choice*. It was his decision to float from one amorous
adventure to another, to drift through life rather than sail. No fate
obliged him to be like that. His life could be different: Don Juan
*could* be different. Kierkegaard would not take without raising his
hands against it the fatality to which Pascal melancholically surren-
dered.[5]

Kierkegaard's Don Juan was a monster, an abominable and detestable exception, a cancerous growth on humanity as it could and
should be. Pascal would not agree: Don Juan was rather what ordinary people would dearly wish to be were they given a chance. They
all wish to 'constantly finish and to begin again from the beginning'
and so to forget about that end which is bound to finish it all and
beyond which there will be no more new beginnings. If Don Juan's
seductive power is the way of living mortal life as if it were eternal,
rather than poisoning it with worry about an eternity beyond his
grasp due to the finitude of the future (or, to deploy Max Scheler's
terms,[6] if he has made the choice of turning the shared human fate
into a private destiny, rather than using his destiny as a weapon
against fate) – then this is exactly what all of us tend to grope for,
though very few of us reach Don Juan's exquisite skills and most are
diverted from the life of diversion well before the condition they
dream of has been attained.

It seems that history has settled the disagreement in favour of
Pascal. But neither Pascal nor Kierkegaard – not even Max Scheler –
could anticipate the advent of *consumer* society which would transform distraction, once an individually contrived hideout from fate,
into the socially constructed lot; a society in which 'constantly finishing and beginning again from the beginning' would no longer be
a sign of monstrosity but a way of life available to all and the only
way of life so commonly available.

## Consumers and consumer society

Pascal's and Kierkegaard's contemporaries did, of course, consume, as all people at all times have done and do. Like all living creatures, they had to consume to stay alive, even though being humans and not mere animals they had to consume more than sheer survival would require: being alive in the human way set demands which topped the necessities of 'merely *biological*' existence with more elaborate *social* standards of decency, propriety, 'good life'. Such standards might have been rising over time, but the point is that in the past the sum total of 'consumables' needed to gratify them was at each moment fixed: it had both its lower and its upper limits. The limits were drawn by the tasks expected to be performed: before humans could perform them, they had to be fed, shod and sheltered, and all that in the 'proper manner'. They had a fixed number of 'needs' which they had to 'satisfy' in order to survive. But consumption, being a servant of needs, had to justify itself in terms of something other than itself. Survival (biological and social) was the *purpose* of consumption, and once that purpose was met (once the 'needs' had been 'satisfied') there was no point in consuming more. Falling below the standards of consumption was an ethical reproach for all the rest of society, but climbing above them was equally an ethical, though this time personal, fault. Indulging in the pleasures of the flesh, gluttony and intemperance were long frowned upon if not condemned as mortal sins, while Thorstein Veblen, still at the threshold of the consumer age, bewailed 'conspicuous' or 'ostentatious' consumption serving nothing but vainglory and self-conceit.

The distinctive mark of the consumer society and its consumerist culture is not, however, consumption as such; not even the elevated and fast-rising volume of consumption. What sets the members of consumer society apart from their ancestors is the emancipation of consumption from the past instrumentality that used to draw its limits – the demise of 'norms' and the new plasticity of 'needs', setting consumption free from functional bonds and absolving it of the need to justify itself by reference to anything but its own pleasurability. In the consumer society consumption is its own purpose, and so self-propelling. Orthodox psychology defined 'need' as a state of tension which would eventually disperse and wither away once the need had been gratified. 'The need' which sets the members of consumer society in motion is, on the contrary, the need to keep the tension alive – if anything, getting stronger with every step. Our ancestors could recommend the 'delay of gratification'. Consumer society proclaims the *impossibility* of gratification and measures its progress by ever-rising demand.

To avoid confusion, it would be better to follow that fateful change in the nature of consumption and get rid of the notion of 'need' altogether, accepting that consumer society and consumerism are *not about satisfying needs* – not even the more sublime needs of identification, or self-assurance as to the degree of 'adequacy'. The moving spirit of consumer activity is not a set of articulated, let alone fixed, needs, but *desire* – a much more volatile and ephemeral, evasive and capricious, and essentially non-referential phenomenon; a self-begotten and self-perpetuating motive that calls for no justification or apology either in terms of an objective or a cause. Despite its successive and always short-lived reifications, desire is 'narcissistic': it has itself for its paramount object, and for that reason is bound to stay insatiable however tall the pile of other (physical or psychical) objects marking its past course may grow. The 'survival' at stake is not that of the consumer's body or social identity, but of the desire itself: that desire which makes the consumer – the *consuming desire* of consuming.

## Needing, desiring, wishing

And yet, whatever its obvious advantages over much less pliable, inert or slow moving needs, desire bound the consumer's readiness to shop with more constraints than the suppliers and merchandisers of consumer goods found palatable or indeed bearable. After all, it takes time, effort, and considerable financial outlay to arouse desire, bring it to the required temperature and channel in the right direction – but even that is not enough: as Geoff Williams reminds the would-be purveyors of consumables (in the American journal *Entrepreneur* of August 1999), consumers should not ever be allowed to 'awake' from their 'dreams', and so the promoters of commodities must 'work hard to ensure a consistent message'. Consumers guided by desire must be 'produced', ever anew, and at high cost. Indeed, the production of consumers devours an intolerably large part of the total costs of production, distribution and trade – and a part which the competition tends to stretch ever further rather than cut down.

But, as Harvie Ferguson suggests, consumerism in its present-day form is not (fortunately for the producers and merchandisers of consumer commodities) 'founded upon the regulation (stimulation) of desire, but upon the liberation of wishful fantasies'. The abominably constrictive 'needs' have had their day as the principal motive of consumption, but even the desires which came to replace them would not muster enough power to keep the wheels of consumer society in motion. The notion of desire, Ferguson observes,

> links consumption to self-expression, and to notions of taste and discrimination. The individual expresses himself or herself through their possessions. But for advanced capitalist society, committed to the continuing expansion of production, this is a very limiting psychological framework which ultimately gives way to a quite different psychic 'economy'. The wish replaces desire as the motivating force of consumption.[7]

The history of consumerism is a story of the breaking down and discarding of the successive tough and 'solid' obstacles which limited the free flight of fantasy and, in Freud's vocabulary, trimmed the 'pleasure principle' down to the size dictated by the 'reality principle'. 'Need', deemed by nineteenth-century economists to be the very epitome of 'solidity' – inflexible, permanently circumscribed and finite – was discarded first and replaced for a time with desire, much more 'fluid' and so expandable than need because of its half-illicit liaisons with fickle and plastic dreams of authenticity and the 'inner self' waiting to be expressed. Now, though, desire's turn has come to be discarded. Desire has outlived its usefulness: having brought consumer addiction to its present state, it can no longer keep up the pace. A more powerful, and above all more versatile stimulant is needed to keep the acceleration of consumer demand on a level with the rising volume of consumer offer. 'Wish' is the much-needed replacement: it completes the liberation of the pleasure principle, purging the last residues of any 'reality principle' impediments: the naturally gaseous substance has been finally let out of the container. To quote Ferguson once more:

> where the facilitation of desire was founded upon comparison, vanity, envy and the 'need' for self-approbation, nothing underlies the immediacy of the wish. The purchase is casual, unexpected and spontaneous. It has a dream quality of both expressing and fulfilling a wish, and like all wishes, is insincere and childish.[8]

Wishes like these, on the loose, unfastened and licentious, may confirm Pascal's adumbrations, yet they also seem to signal the defeat of modern ambitions. If Pascal was right, then the modern attempt to lock human desires in a steel casing of set needs went against the grain of human nature, and modern order-building was a war against that nature.

The human aversion to the dull monotony of rest was one part of human nature which the modern builders of rational order wished to be tamed: Don Juan's fondness for 'finishing quickly and beginning from the beginning' was the main adversary confronted by the order-builders. Rational order could not be erected on the moving sands of diffuse, unfocused desire – the voice of reason would be inaudible were the cacophony of passions to reign unabated. Modern capitalism could 'melt the solids', but the modern ambition was to replace the found solids with others that were purpose-built and more solid than anything the irrational meanderings of past history could have left in their wake. Modernity was not an enemy of solids – far from it; but it was not just any solid that was good enough to pass the stern test of reason. The inherited solids, as de Tocqueville observed, were already in a state of advanced putrefaction; they had been assigned to the melting furnaces not because of their solidity, but because they were not solid *enough*. Since the frames of the old routines were falling apart, they had to be urgently replaced with new ones – this time more artfully designed and meticulously constructed, resistant to erosion, intended to stay and keep their shape for a long time to come. From Bentham's Panopticon to Frederick Taylor's scientific management and Henry Ford's assembly belt, efforts never ceased to assemble and consolidate such frames for human conduct as would fully and truly leave the endemically whimsical and erratic passions strictly out of bounds and leave no room for any irrationality, that of human wishes included.

Desires and wishes, particularly of the 'unexpected and spontaneous' kind, used to be eyed by order-builders with suspicion: just as 'nature' portrayed by the popular science of the time suffered no void, the would-be modern routines suffered nothing that failed the test of reason – no dysfunctionality or functional indifference. There was no mileage in whims and caprices; unforced, unsought and unsolicited conduct spelled trouble for 'pattern maintenance'. Any other freedom except the 'recognition of necessity' felt like a thorn in the body of rationality. In such a scheme of things, consumption – just like the rest of life's pleasures – could be only a handmaid of rational routine (a ransom reluctantly paid by the rational order to the ineradicable irrationality of the human condition), or a pastime exiled to the margins of life's main track where it could not interfere with the proper business of life.

### The reality principle and the pleasure principle strike a deal

The 'reality principle', as Sigmund Freud famously declared, was the limit set to the 'pleasure principle' – the boundary over which the seekers of pleasure could trespass only at their own peril. The two principles were at cross-purposes; it did not occur to either the managers of capitalist factories nor the preachers of modern reason that the two enemies could strike a deal and become allies, that pleasure could be miraculously transmogrified into the mainstay of reality and that the search for pleasure could become the major (and sufficient) instrument of pattern maintenance. That, in other words, fluidity could be the ultimate solidity – the most stable of conceivable conditions. And yet this is precisely what the consumer society is about: enlisting the 'pleasure principle' in the service of the 'reality principle'; harnessing the volatile, fastidious and squeamish desires to the chariot of social order, using the friable stuff of spontaneity as the building material for the lasting and solid, tremor-proof foundations of routine. Consumer society has achieved a previously unimaginable feat: it has reconciled the reality and pleasure principles by putting, so to speak, the thief in charge of the treasure chest. Instead of fighting vexing and recalcitrant but presumably invincible irrational human wishes, it has made them into faithful and reliable (hired) guards of rational order.

How did this wondrous transformation come about?

First came the reclassification of human desires; once the irritating though unavoidable costs of production, they have been transferred in the accountancy books to the side of profits. Capitalism discovered that the morbid urge for distraction, that major scourge of profit-making from the exploitation of productive labour, may become the largest and perhaps an inexhaustible source of profit once it is the turn of the consumers, rather than the producers, to be exploited. As George Ritzer points out,

> the focus in contemporary capitalism, at least in the United States, seems to have shifted from the valorization and control processes, indeed from production as a whole, to consumption. The essence of modern capitalism, at least as it is practiced by the core nations, may not be so much maximizing the exploitation of workers as the maximization of consumption.[9]

Far from needing taming and incarcerating, desires should be set free and made to feel free; better still, encouraged to run wild, to ignore all limits and go on the rampage. 'Acting on impulse', that epitome of irrationality in the world of producers, savings books and long-term investments, is destined to become the major factor of rational calculation in the universe of consumers, credit cards and instant gratification.

Then, the fragility and precariousness endemic to the pleasure-and-distraction-seeking life have been reclassified from being the major threats to the stability of social order into being its chief support. Modernity has discovered that the condition of volatility which results in the perpetual insecurity of actors may be made into the most reliable of pattern-maintaining factors. The politics of normative regulation has been replaced by the 'policy of precarization': the flexibility of human conditions pregnant with the insecurity of the present and uncertainty of the future has been found to be the best raw material for the construction of a tough and resilient order; life sliced into episodes with no strings to the past and no bind on the future eliminates the challenge to order more radically than the most elaborate (and exorbitantly costly) institutions of panoptical surveillance and day-in, day-out management. As Pierre Bourdieu points out, 'those who deplore the cynicism which in their opinion marks the men and women of our time should not omit to mention the economic and social conditions which favour or demand, as well as reward it . . .'[10]

Bourdieu coined the term 'flexploitation' for the strategy deployed (whether deliberately or matter-of-factly) by that novel policy of social integration and conflict prevention. Flexploitation no longer promotes rationality of behaviour, nor is it meant to: after all, while the ability to make future projections is the condition *sine qua non* of all rational behaviour, making future projections all but impossible (except in the shortest of terms) is the principal objective, and most conspicuous effect, of the 'policy of precarization'. Whatever the rationality of consumer society may mean, it does not aim to rest – in stark opposition to the society of producers of the 'solid' stage of modernity – on the universalization of rational thought and action, but on a free reign of irrational passions (just as its routine rests on catering for the desire of diversion, its uniformity on the recognition of diversity, and its conformity on its agents' liberation). The rationality of consumer society is built out of the irrationality of its individualized actors.

## Holism made fallacy

Speaking of 'policy', we tacitly assume the presence of 'policy-makers': there must be someone (or something) for whom the happy reunion of the reality and pleasure principles was an objective to be systematically pursued or a strategem consistently deployed, being calculated to suit their interests best. Many studies of consumer facilities and habits bear an uncanny resemblance to detective novels: in the stories told of the birth and ascendancy of consumer society, the plots tend to grind relentlessly to the unmasking of the scheming culprit(s). There is hardly a piece without some singly or severally acting villains – be it a conspiracy of merchandisers, the sly intrigues of their advertising henchmen, or brainwashing orchestrated by media moguls. Explicitly or implicitly, the shoppers/consumers emerge from the story as victims of collective brain damage: gullible and duped victims of crowd hypnosis.

The stories in question are misleading without necessarily being false. They carry a lot of truth (none of the appointed villains is without guilt: if not as an accomplice, then at least as an accessory-after-the-fact) – and yet vital chunks of the truth remain untold and unaccounted for. What is missing in the argument and left out of consideration is a possibility that, far from being deceived and falling into a skilfully laid trap, the members of consumer society try hard, just as all human beings do, to respond sensibly to the conditions of life which may be, but may not be, rational and suitable for rational conduct and render rational strategies effective: that, in other words, under certain conditions irrational behaviour may carry many a trapping of rational strategy and even offer the most immediately obvious rational option among those available.

As we know from Karl Marx, one thing which is not for choosing is the conditions under which the choices are made and which sort out the few realistic and effective choices from the many that are nebulous and abortive. People do make history – but seldom if ever is the history they make 'made to order' and seldom does it resemble the end-state they divined and pursued in their labours. Sociologists have chosen to call that disparity between rationally conceived ends and the kinds of realities that emerge in the course of pursuing them the 'unanticipated consequences' of human action, pointing out that whatever is there in the world people inhabit is a consequence of their deeds yet not the kind of consequence they expected or desired. The conditions which made the consumer society feasible, and the actions of its major protagonists effective, are the unanticipated consequences of the history of modern capitalism over more than two centuries. The sellers of goods and of their images may be earnestly and vigorously cultivating the conditions under which their own and their addressees' actions make sense and bring results, but no one planned these conditions in advance 'in order to' create the setting in which present-day practices would become viable. If anything, the conditions in question belied the projections and dashed the hopes of the most insightful thinkers and people of action of the 'solid modernity' era.

In her eye-opening study of the way in which social scientists compose and share their stories, Barbara Czarniawska considers the reasons why writing a novel of the classic 'realist' type, until recently identified with the novel as such, has nowadays become all but impossible. The realist novel, she says,

> celebrated holism as the only proper perspective on both society and the individual... This kind of narrative presupposed, as a scene on which public action by moral agents could unfold, a stable social order, a clear-cut political economy, and a collective psychology in which personal character and public conduct were assumed to be inseparable. When such assumptions became untenable, some proclaimed 'the end of the novel'.[11]

The holistic assumptions of the intimate link between personal conduct and society at large have however become untenable, and writing a 'realist' novel, which drew a line between the solid world out there and fickle and error-prone humans desperately trying to find their way through the labyrinth by choosing all the right turns and omitting all the wrong ones, has become a daunting, perhaps an impossible task. The holistic assumptions were not the private property of the 'realist' novelists; they shared them with the enlightened opinion of their time (as well as with the common human experience of the 'solid modernity' era), notably with the most reputable psychologists, who in order to learn more about human behaviour used to send hungry rats through the corridors of a maze and recorded the time the rodents needed to learn the quickest way leading through fixed and inflexible passages to the pellet of food permanently placed in one, and always the same, of the many cells of the labyrinthine edifice. The conduct of the laboratory rats, much like that of the characters of *Bildungsromane*, was all about learning, and learning fast, and being rewarded by learning well and punished for neglect or sloth in learning. But to conceive of conduct in such a fashion, the walls of the twisted corridors of the maze had to retain their shape, if not forever than at least long enough for the learning to reach completion; and the norms and institutions of society (those equivalents of the maze passages) which the heroes of

the realist novels had to learn to follow and obey had to be resistant
to change and steady enough to be projected into the undefinable
future.

Indeed, for Émile Durkheim, it was 'an undoubted fact' that

> we need to believe that our actions have consequences which go
> beyond the immediate moment: that they are not completely limited
> to the point in time and space at which they are produced, but that
> their results are, to some degree, of lasting duration and broad in
> scope. Otherwise they would be too insignificant: scarcely more than
> a thread would separate them from the void, and they would not
> have any interest for us. Only actions which have a lasting quality are
> worthy of our volition, only pleasures which endure are worthy of
> our desires.[12]

All people, Durkheim insisted, 'aspire to detach themselves from the
present'. That applies to a child and the savage and to the 'civilized
man' (whether 'of average culture' or 'more developed') alike; they
differ only in how far ahead they look and think – in the length of
that 'future' which stretches beyond the fleeting present that makes
the present worthy of their attention and effort. 'The perspective of
nothingness', Durkheim seems to repeat after Pascal, 'is an intolerable burden to us.' But unlike Pascal, Durkheim believed in tune
with the hopes and intentions of 'solid modernity' that rather than
trying to divert and distract ourselves and drown our fears in fleeting
pleasures, we would tend to escape the dread by 'living in the
future'. Diversion is not a solution: 'what value are our individual
pleasures, which are so empty and short?'; but fortunately, individual pleasures are not the only option; it is our good luck that 'societies are infinitely more long-lived than individuals' and thus 'they
permit us to taste satisfactions which are not merely ephemeral.'

We may all be 'mortal and miserable', but societies are 'infinitely
more long-lived' than any of the mortals: to our transient individual
life they represent eternity. To the mortals, they are bridges into
immortality. We may trust societies as a secure shelter for our life
accomplishments. Investing in the perpetuation of society, we may
participate in things eternal; through society, we can recast our
transcience into duration, and so stop our mortality making us miserable. Those who can say in good conscience, 'in thee, my Society,
have I put my trust', may also hope that the verdict 'unto dust shalt
thou return' can be averted or quashed.

Contemplation of society's immortality may be a highly gratifying
pastime for philosophers. When embraced from the philosophical

perspective, itself defiant to the eroding powers of time, it looks today (and will tomorrow and the day after tomorrow) as 'infinitely more long-lived' (immortal when measured by brief individual exist-ence), as it did in Durkheim's time. But at the dawn of the twentieth century, philosophers could pride themselves on striking a chord in 'human, all too human' experience. They spoke in the name of a society busily composing solid frames in which transient human deeds could be inscribed to last forever and promising to make such frames rock-hard. Durkheim's words were recorded at a time when (in Alain Peyrefitte's words)[13] self-reliance, confidence in the others around, and trust in the longevity of social institutions combined and gelled into the courage to act and the long-term resolve to see the action through. To the ears of his contemporaries, Durkheim's words sounded therefore anything but abstract or far-fetched: they restated the beliefs daily corroborated by everyone's experience.

The triune trust documented by Peyrefitte has by now been broken, and it has become clear to anyone (except perhaps those living in philosophy, the art of conjuring continuity out of discon-tinuity – that 'epistemological premise' of 'continuous time') that none of the three trusts can survive, let alone thrive, on its own. Self-confidence, the audacity to set one's life as a project, and the determination to see that project to completion through thick and thin, is unlikely to appear unless prompted and bolstered by trust in the long-term stability of the world around, of its demands and of the rules that tell, and tell authoritatively, how to go about meeting them. 'The conditions of time in the new capitalism', Richard Sen-nett observes, 'have created a conflict between character and experi-ence, the experience of disjointed time threatening the ability of people to form their characters into sustained narratives.'[14] Such conflict is only to be expected, given that uncertainty, though always a ubiquitous accompaniment of human existence, has nowadays ac-quired novel, previously unexperienced features: it is now 'woven into the everyday practices of a vigorous capitalism. Instability is meant to be normal...'

Were there a long-term logic behind the torn and mangled experi-ence of a world changing with little or no warning, humans would hardly glean it from their daily experience; unlike birds and philoso-phers, they seldom rise above the ground they tread high enough to spy it out. 'Society', firm and whole as it may appear in the social-scientific studies, makes itself present to most of us mediated by occasions which do not necessarily connect into continuous and coherent experience. For most of us, most of the time (except when we fall into philosophical mood), 'society' is a summary name for the people we meet in the place where we earn our living, the partners we live with under one roof, the neighbours with which we share the street, and the ways and means of dealing with all of them which we think will meet with approval and bring proper effects. And the snag is that of none of those constituents of the idea of 'society' can we say now, judging from our experience, that they are 'infinitely more long-lived' than ourselves and that therefore they offer us 'satisfactions that are not merely ephemeral'. *Pace* Durkheim, it is now each of us, individually, that is the 'longest living' of all the bonds and institutions we have met; and the only entity whose life expectation is steadily rising rather than shrinking.

Indeed, there are few if any reference points left which could reasonably be hoped to lend a deeper and longer-lasting significance to the moments we live. If trust is the hinge attaching the mobile (and transient) to the steady (and durable), it would seek a frame in vain. It is myself, my living body or that living body which is me, which seems to be the sole constant ingredient of the admittedly unstable, always until-further-notice composition of the world around. My life may be too short for comfort, but the lifespan of anything else seems disconcertingly brief by comparison. Few if any partnerships are entered into with a belief that they will last 'until death us do part'. Fewer and fewer families can be vouched to outlive its members. Few if any painstakingly acquired skills may be hoped to last for the lifetime of their proud owner. No places of work can be anticipated to sustain the job currently performed, or for that matter to offer any kind of job, until the retirement of its current holder. Few if any neighbourhoods are likely to withstand for long the irrepressible vigour of developers, and if they do they would hardly resist the virus of slow yet relentless dilapidation and demise. Few if any among hard-won possessions are likely to retain their allure for long, surpassed as they tend to be by new, more seductive attractions. Few if any hard-learned styles and habits will go on bringing satisfaction and esteem for long. In this world, putting all one's eggs in one basket is no longer the ultimate imprudence. Baskets as such, however many, should be looked at with suspicion: few people of sane mind would entrust any eggs to any of them.

Whoever chains themselves to an unseaworthy vessel risks going down with it at the next tide. By comparison, surfing seems a safer option. 'Eternity' acquires a sinister flavour, unless it means an uninterrupted string of episodes: the perpetual ability to 'finish quickly and begin from the beginning'. If the assets of long-term security are not available, long-term commitments are liabilities. The future – the realistic future and the desirable future – can be grasped only as a succession of 'nows'. And the only stable, hopefully unbreakable continuity on which the beads of episodes could conceivably be strung together so that they won't scatter and disperse is that of one's own body in its successive avatars.

Niklas Luhmann wrote of modern society that it is 'modern' in as far as it 'marks its newness by relegating the old':

> Whether we like it or not, we are no longer what we were, and we will not be what we are now... [T]he characteristics of today's modernity are not those of yesterday and not those of tomorrow, and in this lies modernity. The problems of contemporary society are not problems in maintaining a heritage, whether in education or elsewhere. Much more important is the constant creation of otherness.[15]

In the *Lebenswelt* around as much as in its only epicentre, the self, continuous discontinuity is the only form continuity may take – the only one to be found and the only one to be sensibly – realistically – coveted. In the game of life, 'society' has moved from the role of a caring albeit exacting warden/keeper into the position of one of the players (not even *primus inter pares*). Once the mainstay of stability and the warrant of assurance, it has now become the prime source of surprise and of a diffuse, frightening because unknowable, danger. It is erratic, as all players are: it keeps its cards close to its chest and likes its moves to take people unawares, time and again catching its partners napping. In the game of life, its constantly changing rules are themselves the major stake. There is next to nothing that the individual players can do to escape surprising moves and their consequences; the only thing individuals can do is to practice one-upmanship, struggle to outsmart the prankster, try their best to stay alert and be ready to change tack when the wind shifts; try never to be left behind or caught napping.

To stay seaworthy seems the only realistic purpose: the one task which the individual may – just may – take responsibility for and responsibly carry on. History, says Ulrich Beck,

> shrinks *to the (eternal) present*; and everything evolves around the axis of one's personal ego and personal life... The proportion of life opportunities which are fundamentally closed to decision-making is decreasing and the proportion of biography which is open and must be constructed biographically is increasing.[16]

The overall result of all this is the 'subjectivization and individualization of risks and contradictions produced by institutions and society'. In short, individuals are doomed to seek 'biographical solutions to systemic contradictions'. An impossible task, to be sure, one that defies logic and one that cannot be undertaken in anything remotely reminiscent of a coherent and systematic way. Since there is no personal strategy which can arrest (let alone prevent) the vagaries of 'life opportunities', or short of arresting them can defuse or outweigh their impact, fragmentation of the big task which one cannot tackle into a plethora of small tasks which one can handle is the only reasonable way to proceed. Let's take one thing at a time, and let's worry about crossing that other bridge, out there in the foggy future, when it emerges from the fog and we know for sure that there is indeed a bridge to cross.

It is here, in this predicament of individuals doomed to compensate for the irrationality of their *Lebenswelt* by resorting to their own wits and acumen (to quote Beck once more, 'experts dump their contradictions and conflicts at the feet of the individual and leave him or her with the well-intentioned invitation to judge all of this critically on the basis of his or her own notions'), that 'consumer society' comes into its own; that life turns into a shopping spree and is neither more nor less consuming than the excitement, adventure and challenge of the shopper's activity are able in principle, and manage in practice, to be.

## Choosing reassurance, reassuring choice

There is a 'mutual fit', an 'elective affinity' between the inanities of the consumer market and the incongruities of the task which the individuals are presumed to perform on their own: their duty to compose individually the continuity which society can no longer assure or no longer intends to promise. Indeed, one is tempted to say that the marriage between the two protagonists has been made in heaven and that no man or woman, certainly not when acting singly or severally as they do, can tear it apart. There is a nearly 'perfect fit' between the characteristics of the commodities the consumer market offers, the fashion in which it offers them, and the kinds of anxieties and expectations which prompt individuals to live their lives as a string of shopping expeditions. Two irrationalities meet, cooperate and jointly self-reproduce through the rationality of sellers' calculations and the rationality of buyers' life strategies.

The consumer market has achieved the uncanny feat of reconciling and blending two mutually contradictory values which are both avidly sought by the members of individualized society: it offers, in one package deal, a badly missed reassurance and the guarantee that is keenly desired yet unavailable elsewhere of goods replacement, even a money-back guarantee, in the event that the presently sought reassurance wears off and a new reassurance needs to be put in its place. The consumer market promises, and delivers, a comforting certainty of the present without the frightening prospect of mortgaging the future. It supplies durability through the transcience of its offerings – a durability which no longer needs to be painstakingly built piece by piece, through perpetual effort and occasional self-sacrifice. It proffers eternity in instalments, each bit coming ready for immediate use and meant to be disposed off without regret or remorse once it is used up.

The consumer market sets the finishing lines close enough to prevent desire from exhausting itself before the goal is reached, but frequently enough for the runners never to worry about the durability of the spoils' value and for desire never to ponder frustration but always be eager to start afresh and never lose its vigour; and as Pascal observed a long time ago, it is the hunting not the hare that people call happiness. Admittedly, temporary identities can only be conjured up from a differentiation from the past: 'today' derives its meaning from cutting itself off from a 'yesterday'. The never-ending process of identification can go on, undisturbed by the vexing thought that identity is the one thing it is conspicuously unable to purvey. And so, on the one hand, the spectre of durability, and indeed of direction, is rising out of the rapidity and swiftness with which diverse transient states succeed each other. On the other hand, there is no worry that the objects of desire might outstay their welcome and that their refusal to vacate the stage for the yet-unscripted plays of the future might spoil the joy of the future chase.

The consumer market offers choice complete with the reassurance that the choice is right: the authority of experts and of the recondite knowledge they are trusted to possess, or the authority of great numbers of satisfied buyers, or the authority of huge demand that exceeds the offer, tend to be as a rule attached to the products on the department stores' shelves. At the same time, the sellers make no secret of the fact that the goods currently on offer will be, inevitably, superseded by some as yet unknown 'new and improved' ones, and for their customers the awareness that this must sooner rather than later happen is not at all off-putting. On the contrary, that know-

ledge is a vital part of the reassurance they seek:
know that no decision is final, that none has i
quences, that each one can be safely taken since li
sions it will bind the decision-maker only 'until fui
us note that since such awareness is shared by the
buyers, no disappointment is ultimate and conclusiv
validate the rationality of the game and the wisdom
The game of 'finishing quickly and beginning from the᠎ ᠎ ᠎ ᠎ is
self-propelling and self-propagating, securely defended against adversary tests and the *experimentum crucis* of ultimate futility.

### Feeding uncertainty, feeding on uncertainty

The game is self-perpetuating for one more reason. It is addictive:
protracted participation in the consumerist game results in an in-
stilled incapacity to seek 'biographical solutions to systemic contradictions' in any other way. To become a consumer means to be
dependent for one's survival, even for the keeping of simple daily
routines, on the consumer market. It means to forget or fail to learn
the skills of coping with life challenges, apart from the skills of
seeking (and, hopefully, finding) the right object, service or counsel
among the marketed commodities (in a New Year version of *Cinderella* staged by Channel Four in 2000, the Prince matter-of-factly
assumes that the magic mountain where Cinderella acquired her
ball-dress must be a shopping mall). The chronic deficit of certainty
may be recompensed by consumers in one way only: by pursuing the
avenues laid out and made passable by marketing and shopping. We
all live in a society of spare (and disposable) parts, and in such a
society the art of repairing malfunctioning objects, characters or
human bonds is all but uncalled for and obsolete.

George Ritzer grasps perfectly the dual attraction of market-medi-
ated consumerism when he discusses the 'action holidays' pre-
scripted and pre-packed by travel agencies – when he observes that
'most inhabitants of a postmodern world might be willing to eat at
the campfire, as long as it is a simulated one on the lawn of the
hotel.'[17] Tourists of the consumer society want their holidays to be
escapes from daily routine – but also to be escapes from the hazards,
confusions and uncertainties endemic to their daily life; the holidays
they would gladly pay for should be predictable, calculable, efficient
and controlled. The holiday companies, just like MacDonald's restaurants, are expected to provide, first of all, shelters of security and

dictability. Adventures should be carefully planned to include a happy end, excitements should be sanitized and pollution-free, the 'far away from everywhere' must be located no more than a car drive's distance from shops and restaurants, the wilderness ought to have exits that are well mapped and signed, wild beasts should be either tamed or locked in secure enclosures, and snakes, if encountered, should have their poisonous teeth removed.

What makes the dreamed-of holidays alluring to the seekers of adventures and strong emotions is the certainty (included in the package and protected by travel insurance) that someone, somewhere, knows exactly what is going on and how it is going to end, so no shock will be 'for real', being 'an experience of' rather than the thing itself. Nothing really disastrous, let alone irrevocable, will occur, and if (God forbid) it does occur due to someone's mistake or neglect, opting out is not just conceivable, but on the whole easy, while the dissatisfied customer can always sue for compensation even if the 'money-back guarantee' was missing from the contract. Cinema goers made *The Blair Witch Project* an astounding box-office success as they flocked to see their innermost fears vividly, and horrifyingly, portrayed: being cut off from the nearest socket for portable computers and from access to the internet, finding that mobile telephones are unusable or absent, suspecting that the game is 'for real', that the ending of the spectacle has not been fixed in advance and that there is no switch-off button – these are the most awesome of the nightmares that haunt the 'incapacitated-by-training' consumers. *The Blair Witch Project* made the ineffable anxiety tangible, gave visible shape to misty apparitions – but, let us note, not just any shape, but one that sets consumer society firmly in the role of the exorcist-in-chief and the last shelter for the perplexed and the ignorant.

As fears go, the consumer market may legitimately contest and refute its responsibility for parenthood. As has been argued before, the anxieties of uncertainty offer a potentially fertile soil for the marketeers to cultivate. But the crops – the *names* of the fears on which the dispersed anxiety would eventually focus – are products of farming and depend on the techniques the farmers deploy and the materials they use. The choice of techniques and materials is, in its turn, dictated by the farmers' understanding of 'best gain'. In addition, no farmer worth his salt would rely on the natural fertility of the soil and even less would he allow the fertility found to be exhausted by drawing from the soil all its nutritional substances in one go. Good farmers (and marketeers are better than most) would take care to ensure that fertility could continually recuperate and grow by the skilful use of fertilizers, whether natural or artificial.

Uncertainty-generated anxiety is the very substance that makes the individualized society fertile for consumerist purposes; it needs therefore be carefully and lovingly cared for, and must on no account be allowed to dry up or evaporate. More often than not, the production of consumers means the production of 'new and improved' fears. The affair of the millennial (hum)bug offers a pattern daily and ubiquitously repeated: no one could say for sure that the bug was a figment of the imagination, and even less could one call the bluff of those who insisted on being in the know even if the surmise that they were bluffing was correct. Most reasonable people would therefore follow Pascal's advice of the 'safe bet'. A multibillion pound industry of computer-system testing and reprogramming would be created in a truly Divine manner, *ab nihilo*, and the act of its creation would be almost universally greeted with a sigh of relief. When the day of reckoning finally comes, the failure of the prophesized catastrophe to materialize will be, again universally or almost, the proof that it was averted thanks to the purveyors of the anti-bug services, and as another clinching test of the omnipotence of marketable expertise. The whole episode would anyway be soon forgotten as other fears came to usurp the headlines, but the memory of that omnipotence would stay, making the ground yet more fertile for the next panic-production.

Let us note that – wisely – consumer markets seldom offer cures or preventive medicines against natural dangers, like earthquakes, hurricanes, floods or avalanches; promises of protection and salvation focus as a rule on dangers artificially created. The latter have a clear advantage over the former, since they allow the fears to be cut to the measure of the available cures, rather than vice versa.

The trained incapacity of the consumers is by far the best of the weapons of consumer goods suppliers. American giants of genetic engineering finance research which 'proves beyond reasonable doubt' that without genetically modified crops the feeding of the world's population will shortly become impossible. What the research reports tend to be silent about is that their pronouncements bear all the marks of self-fulfilling prophecies; or, rather, that what they do is to provide a gloss on their sponsors' practices, while making such practices more palatable through reversing the order of causes and effects. The introduction of 'genetically improved' seeds casts great numbers of farmers out of business and makes the rest incapable of producing their own seeds for next year since the 'improved' grains are as a rule infertile. Once that happens, the assertion that without a constant and rising supply of GM stuff the feeding of humankind won't be possible acquires the authority of an 'empirically proven truth' and can no longer be questioned. The practices of the genetic engineering industry may well serve as a pattern of the paramount function in a consumer society – that is the production of (willing or unwilling, yet cooperative) consumers. George Ritzer's 'McDonaldization' would not work unless it was complemented by 'Monsantization'.

To conclude: the powers and the weaknesses, the glory and the blight of the consumer society – a society in which life is consuming through a continuous succession of discontinuous consumer concerns (and itself consumed in its course) – are rooted in the same condition: the anxieties born of and perpetuated by institutional erosion coupled with enforced individualization. And they are shaped and reproduced by the response led by the consumer market to that condition: the strategy of the rationalization of irrationality, the standardization of difference, and the achievement of stability through an induced precariousness of the human condition.

# 7

# From Bystander to Actor

Stanley Cohen's great merit was to bring together, as two variants of the same phenomenon and the same quandary, the two kinds of wrongdoing that seldom meet in scholarly analyses, though in real life they never stay far away from each other for long and most of the time seek each other's warm and salutary embrace. The first is 'doing evil'; the second, refraining from opposing evil or from preventing it being done.[1]

It has been and remains customary to examine and analyse 'doing evil' – inflicting pain and suffering, or commanding others to do it – under the rubric of 'perpetrators'. It was a foregone conclusion that doing evil is causally related to certain peculiar ('natural' or 'nurtured') characteristics of the evil-doers or equally peculiar settings (again, either 'natural', as in Hobbes's pre-social men's *bellum omnium contra omnes*, or artificially designed with evil intentions or evil, albeit unanticipated, consequences), in which the prospective evil-doers have been placed only partly, if at all, by their choice.

It has also been customary to examine and analyse the absence of resistance and opposition to evil on the part of those who, having caused no pain or suffering by their own actions, saw the evil being done (or knew that evil was being done or was about to be done), under the rubric of 'bystanders'. It was an integral part of the definition of 'bystanders', indeed one of their principal defining features, not to be among the perpetrators. The classic triangle of roles played in the course of evil-doing separated the bystanders from the perpetrators no less radically than it set them apart from the victims.

Distinguishing bystanders from perpetrators may make a lot of legal (or, more generally, institutionally warranted) sense. Indeed, underlying the distinction is the vital difference between actions punishable by *law* and actions (or inaction) unnamed in the legal code and therefore incurring 'merely' *moral* guilt and the opprobrium such guilt invites. Whatever may be wrong in the passive witness or the bystander's stance is different from the wrong that results from the perpetrator's actions, and it is the presence or absence of legal prohibition that makes the difference. Drawing the line between the two reprehensible roles in the evil act, let alone drawing the line unambiguously and in an undisputed fashion, would be a hopeless endeavour from the start if it were the moral condemnation of evil-doing, rather than the penal retribution it does or does not attract, that guided the hand. But even when the common habit is obediently followed of awarding authority to the letter of law rather than to inarticulate and ineffable moral sentiments, a wide and hotly contested area tends to be found between the undisputed *crime* of perpetration and the regrettable, yet excusable and forgivable *misdeed* of 'bystanding'. In that grey area bystanders confront the risk of becoming accessories to the devil and turning into perpetrators. The place and time when the sinister avatar occurs is however exceedingly difficult to pinpoint, let alone to locate in advance, fence off and surround with warning signs.

The habit of analytically separating the crime of commission ascribed to the perpetrators from the sins of omission attributed to bystanders can be challenged and faulted on other counts as well. If perpetrators and bystanders are made to reside in universes of their own, framed by separate and self-sustained scholarly discourses (usually by criminology in the case of perpetrators, and ethics in the case of bystanders) with few if any shared points, the analysts, inevitably, will tend to generate separate conceptual networks and explanatory schemes for each of the two categories. They will tend to constitute perpetrators and bystanders as distinct categories with psychological characteristics and social locations all of their own. Once initiated, the separation will acquire its own momentum and vigour. Inquiries will proceed in two increasingly diverging directions, multiplying the indices of distinctiveness while rendering the discovery and mapping of the ground common to both progressively more difficult.

And yet there is an affinity between 'doing evil' and 'non-resistance to evil' – and it is much closer and more intimate than the scholars engrossed in the exploration of one but neglecting the other would notice and admit. Such an affinity would be plainly visible to an unarmed and untrained eye (if the idea of an innocent eye held any water in our times). Blindness to affinity is induced and contrived. This blindness is a by-product, or side-effect, of the thorough institutionalization of the distinction between socially prescribed strategies, deployed respectively in the treatment of those named by the law and those about whom the laws keep silent. It took a lot of effort to set the two categories apart. It needs even more effort to bring them together again.

Such an effort has been undertaken by Stanley Cohen, and to remarkable effect. Cohen has blazed a trail through the dense thicket of institutional choices and their ideological glosses to lay bare the painstakingly concealed, barely visible common ground on which the perpetrators and the passive witnesses of evil meet. That common ground is, in Cohen's vocabulary, *denial* – a term whose 'conceptual ambiguities', by his own admission, 'are gross', but which despite his efforts he could not adequately replace by any other term. Denial is what makes *both* the perpetration of evil and the refraining from reacting to evil psychologically and sociologically feasible; it is for them both an indispensable condition and a principal instrument.

'Denial' is the answer to such vexing questions as 'what do we do with our knowledge about the suffering of others, and what does this knowledge do to us?' – the questions that arise whenever 'people, organizations, governments or whole societies are presented with information that is too disturbing, threatening or anomalous to be fully absorbed or openly acknowledged. The information is therefore somehow repressed, disavowed, pushed aside or reinterpreted.'[2]

We may say that those who perpetrate evil and those who see evil, hear evil, but do nothing about it, are confronting a classical case of Leon Festinger's 'cognitive dissonance': having to hold simultaneously two contradictory and incompatible views. Both are constantly exposed to the possibility that their actions (or passivity) might be held against them, having been declared iniquitous, execrable and calling for punishment. In the incurably polyphonic world of 'liquid modernity', in which values and truths are anything but absolute and are unlikely to be universally accepted as absolute, the justification of actions committed or inactivity chosen is no more solidly grounded than their condemnation. Perpetrators and bystanders alike feel therefore, poignantly and constantly, the need for emphatic and vociferous denial. That need will never go away and allows no pause or momentary lapse of vigilance. Dismissing, even playing down, the potential threat of devastating charges is

hardly a feasible option unless the accused can count on a superiority over their accusers formidable enough to render the accusations,
if not irrelevant, then (what truly matters) devoid of practical consequences.

There are many forms of the denial of guilt (or pretension of
innocence, which amounts to the same thing), but the arguments
used are astoundingly similar. Denial has a two-tier structure (lack
of knowledge, and lack of opportunity to act on knowledge), which
can easily accommodate all the variety of the most commonly used
arguments. Scrapped of embellishments, all arguments reveal one or
other of the two patterns: 'I did not know' or 'I could not do.' The
first is a straightforward, unthinking, almost offhand response to the
cognitive dissonance: 'I (we) did not know'...that some people
suffered; that the pain was inflicted by others; that such horrifying
things happened at the far end of the chain of actions of which my
action was but one of many links...If the argument from ignorance
loses credibility, the argument from impotence comes to the rescue:
'I could not do'...anything, since the alternative to doing nothing
was too horrible to contemplate; besides, nothing would've changed
whatever I'd done or refrained from doing – the odds against pre-
venting/repairing the evil-doings were overwhelming.

In the era of information highways the arguments from ignorance
are fast losing their credibility. Information about other people's
suffering, conveyed in a most vivid and easily legible form, is instantly available almost everywhere (once access to the worldwide
web of information highways ceased to require even the nearness of
a telephone socket, distance stopped being an excuse). This has two
consequences that posit ethical quandaries of unprecedented gravity.

The first: 'bystanding' is no longer the exceptional plight of the
few. We are all bystanders now – witnesses to the inflicting of pain
and the human suffering it causes.

The second: we all confront (even if we don't feel) the need for
exculpation and self-justification. Few if any do not feel the need to
resort at one time or another to the expedient of guilt denial.

Let us note that in an age of universal accessibility and instantaneity of information, the 'I did not know' type of excuse *adds to the
guilt* rather than brings absolution from sin. It carries a connotation
of 'selfishly, for the sake of my peace of mind, I refused to be
bothered', rather than of 'the truth has been guilefully hidden from
me.' In the age of confessions, when the public sphere is increasingly
used as a showcase for displaying the most private intimacies, *any*
hiding of *any* information is seen as an offence and prompts resent-

ment. By proxy, absorbing the information on offer, attention and retention, 'being in the know', joining the latest talk of the town become a virtue. Lack of interest, indifference to information, ignorance of the latest buzz words and buzz issues, not being *au courant* with the flow of the news are, on the other hand, causes of shame. Almost any talk engaged in these days is talk of the town (or conducted in its style even if it ostensibly has private matters as its subject-matter), and little talk of the town can be ignored in any of this talk. 'I did not know' is, purely and simply, out of tune with the spirit of the time.

What remains, then, as the last-resort excuse is 'I could not do anything' or 'I could do no more than I did.' These days, it becomes indeed the most *popular* excuse of the bystanders, and perhaps the only *viable* strategy of denial at the disposal of bystanders.

The 'there was nothing I could do except what I did do' stratagem dissolves the punishable guilt of evil-doing into the universal and for that reason unpunishable even if regrettable plight of 'bystanding'. In a world of global interdependency the difference between the bystander and a co-perpetrator, an accomplice or accessory to evildoing becomes increasingly tenuous. Responsibility for human misfortune, however distant the misery may be from its witnesses, can hardly be denied; not with any degree of conviction. At no time therefore was the demand for ever new, ever more inventive and refined variants of the 'there was nothing I could do' type of denial of responsibility as great and rising as quickly as it is today.

## Being a bystander in a world of global dependency

The psychologist Petrūska Clarkson offers a straightforward, commonsensical definition of the bystander: 'A bystander is a descriptive name given to a person who does not become actively involved in a situation where someone else requires help.'[3] Examples follow, meant to clarify the meaning further: 'It is bystanding to be witness to, but not to confront, a racist, misogynist or homophobic joke. Letting a friend drive while drunk is bystanding. It is also bystanding... not to confront or to get help to deal with a colleague whom you personally believe to be disabled or impaired, for example, due to stress, burnout or addiction.' Clarkson is also a poet, and so unlike most other psychologists can send warm human blood running through the veins of cold definitions – as in a poem, included in her same book, called 'Killing of Kindness':

> There is an old man near you or a young woman, a child or a baby, a
>     dog, a friend or a place,
> Absorbing the violence, the viciousness, the vileness and the vice and
>     someone is standing by
> Passively looking, merely observing, inwardly cringing, finding good
>     reasons for not engaging,
> Estrangingly ever from feeling the kindness, our human kindness, the
>     sameness of being and pain

Making offensive and humiliating jokes is the joker's decision; driving after one drink too many has been the friend's own choice; the colleague has probably brought the trouble upon herself by her own misconduct or imprudence. The 'bystander' was not responsible for such choices made by others in front of her eyes, and even less for the chain of past choices that have led to the present condition where there is no good choice – not legally, physically, or spiritually; bystanders are 'not *really*' responsible for the horrors they witness. Of that guilt, the bystander is *innocent*. But, Clarkson insists, *innocence is no excuse* for staying put and refusing to move a finger (the bystander's guilt is that other sin: the sin of inaction). And yet, aware that this is exactly how the argument from innocence is commonly deployed, in human practices as much as in their theoretical glosses – as an excuse, self-justification, proof of righteousness – Clarkson risks bold indictment only in the other capacity of the poet . . .

Let us note, though, that the extent of the bystander's responsibility and thus the issue of the bystander's degree of innocence is hardly ever an open-and-shut case. In most instances it remains a moot question, bound to provoke no end of contention. The causal links can be reconstructed in more than one way, and just how small the contribution of one or another factor needs to be for it to be declared truly insignificant or to be considered a difference that makes the difference is a matter of judgement rather than of fact.

There are other doubts, yet more fundamental and yet more resistant to final proofs and ultimate solutions. Would the perpetrators – the 'real culprits' – engage in their evil deeds if they could not count on the indifference and non-interference of all those around? If they did not know for sure or at least have good reasons to believe that the witnesses were not likely to turn into actors? If they could not hope that the disgust and indignation aroused in witnesses by their deeds – however strongly felt – would fail to be reforged into loud protest, let alone active resistance?

To cut a long story short, a strong case can be made for the bystander's guilt – at least a guilt by *omission*. Refraining from action carries a causal load not much lighter than the acting, while the certainty (or high probability) of a general non-resistance by the non-lookers may carry a heavier responsibility for the ill actions and their effects than the mere presence of a number of ill-intentioned villains. Last but by no account least: no *legally* proper and binding verdict of innocence has the power to absolve, let alone to redeem the defendant from *moral* guilt.

Keith Tester elaborates on Karl Jaspers' inventory of types of guilt, in which *moral* guilt (of which culprits with a moral conscience, such as are 'given to repentance', are aware) is set apart from *metaphysical* guilt.[4] The latter, in Jaspers' view, stretches 'beyond morally meaningful duty'. Metaphysical guilt occurs whenever human solidarity has stopped short of its absolute, indeed infinite, limits. Unlike moral guilt, metaphysical guilt does not require proof, or even a suspicion, of a causal link between the action (or inaction) of the supposed culprit and the case of human suffering. In a metaphysical sense, I am guilty whether or not I've contributed, deliberately or inadvertently, to the pain suffered by another human being.

Emmanuel Levinas would perhaps incorporate Jaspers' 'metaphysical guilt' into the category of moral guilt as such. For Jaspers the absence of a causal connection between the culprit's conduct and the sufferer's pain does not have the power to efface guilt, and this is because the postulate of *absolute human solidarity* is the foundation stone of all morality and undetachable from a moral stance. For Levinas, what makes the presence or the absence of a causal connection irrelevant is the postulated *unconditionality of human responsibility for the Other.*

Levinas and Jaspers may cut their categories differently, but the resulting disagreement is mostly terminological. In both cases, the terms are sought to convey the essential distinction between the realm inhabited by *legal subjects* and the universe of the *moral self*. The cause-and-effect link, the principal *differentia specifica* of Jaspers' categorization, is devoid of potency and assigned only secondary significance in Levinas's.

The dethronement of causality and the endowment of interhuman solidarity and responsibility with the power to dismiss all ontological argument might have been the constitutive feature of the moral self – indeed, its transcendental prerequisite – at all times. In the era of globalization, however, the long-standing dispute between ethics and ontology loses much of its past sharpness, together with its subject-matter. In our world of universal interdependency, the realm of the causes and effects of human action and the scope of humanity overlap. Virtually no human action, however locally confined and compressed, can be certain to have no consequence for the lot of the rest of humankind. Nor can the lot of any segment of humanity be self-contained and depend in its entirety on the actions of its members alone.

Commenting on Edward Lorenz's memorable intervention in 1979 under a title that has since become one of the best-known phrases coined in the past century ('Does the flap of a butterfly's wings in Brazil set off a tornado in Texas?'), Roberto Toscano suggests that 'today the fact of global interconnectedness demands, in international relations, ethical standards that go beyond a strict, legalistic concept of responsibility. The butterfuly does not *know* about the consequences of the flapping of wings; but the butterfly cannot *rule out* that consequence. We move from responsibility to a related but more restrictive concept: that of precaution.'[5]

While retaining its eternal function of giving birth and life-sustaining nourishment to the moral self, 'responsibility for the Other', a fully and truly *unconditional* responsibility that now also includes the duty of prevision and precaution, becomes in our times the 'brute fact' of the human condition. Whether or not we recognize and willingly *assume* responsibility for each other, we already *bear* it, and there is little or nothing at all we can do to shake it off our shoulders. Five per cent of the planet's population may emit 40 per cent of the planet's pollutants, and use/waste half or more of the planet's resources, and they may resort to military and financial blackmail to defend tooth and nail their right to go on doing so. They may, for the foreseeable future, use their superior force to make the victims pay the costs of their victimization (were not the Jews under the Nazis obliged to pay the train fares on the way to Auschwitz?). And yet responsibility is theirs – not just in any abstractly philosophical, metaphysical or ethical sense, but in the down-to-earth, mundane, straightforward, causal (ontological, if you wish) meaning of the word.

Our responsibility extends now to 'humanity' as a whole. The question of coexistence (of 'mutual assured survival') has stretched far beyond the problem of good-neighbourly relations and peaceful cohabitation with people on the other side of the state border, to which it was confined for most of human history. It now involves the human population of *the earth* – those already alive and those yet to be born. The factual, if not the recognized and the assumed responsibility has already reached the limits of humanity – but the odds are that it won't stop even there for long. The *full*, whole-hearted acceptance of the humanity of 'savages', 'aborigines', 'tribesmen', 'travellers' and other varieties of half-humans, not-fully-humans and not-really-humans may still remain an 'unfinished project', but the roll-call of the beings yet to be admitted into 'humanity' (that is, as objects of ethical concerns and moral responsibilities) expands as quickly as, perhaps still faster than the list of those already given a residence permit. The growing popularity of the 'declarations of rights of animals *as* living beings' – like the widely read studies of Frans de Waal, Francis Kaplan or Jared Diamond[6] – signal a radical shift in the perception of the ultimate limits of human responsibility.

## Excursus: What can we learn from the story of 'animal rights'?

Jean-Jacques Rousseau argued more than two centuries ago that animals had the same right to moral care as humans since they shared with humans the capacity to feel pain and to suffer. Immanuel Kant denied that animals had a *right* to human care, on the grounds of their lack of intellectual powers. However, he charged humans with a *duty* of care on the grounds that they possessed precisely what animals lacked: the capacity to reason. Animals are useful to the humans, and to be of use they need to be cared and provided for, and above all protected from harm. Giving consideration to animals' needs is therefore the humans' duty to themselves.

After more than two centuries of confinement to the margins of 'civilized opinion', Rousseau's and Kant's messages, sent yet not received in far-away times, have now surged out of the black hole of oblivion to land in the topmost sector of the political agenda. On the way they have blended and congealed into the idea of reciprocity between the animals' rights and the humans' interests. As one would expect of ideas struggling to get a hold on rapidly shifting attitudes, the attributes that are common to humans and animals now tend to be paid more attention and seen as more important than the differences between them. One by one, the boundaries between humans and the rest of living creatures, laboriously fortified in the past and proclaimed to be impassable, are effaced. Kant's verdict is unlikely to withstand the pressure. Culture and morality are no longer seen as the exclusive property of *homo sapiens* and the boundary-mark of humanity. This is not so much a matter of the scientific discovery of facts as of an 'attitudinal shift': a sudden willingness to see what previously went unnoticed, and to dismiss as of secondary or no importance what previously was put right at the centre of the world picture. But what has brought such a shift about?

One could venture a guess (a credible supposition, as a matter of fact) that insisting on the uniqueness of *homo sapiens* lost its function once the need and the urge to differentiate the 'degrees of humanity' (and so also of 'bestiality') of the superior and inferior ('civilized' and 'retarded') members of the human race fizzled out, having lost its pragmatic urgency and political usefulness. The less controversial and the less hotly contested the shared membership of humanity is, the less sacrosanct and less adamantly guarded is the boundary separating humans from non-humans.

The pressing urge to deny or devalue the humanity of some members of the human species was, arguably, the prime motive for seeking, finding or inventing proofs and symptoms of human uniqueness. One may object to this supposition, pointing out that the search was prompted as well, and most vigorously, by the desire to remove all ethical obstacles and moral constraints from the modern intention to gain 'mastery over nature', and to force nature once conquered to fit patterns dictated solely by whatever was deemed to fit the welfare of humankind. This objection, though, may be objected to in turn: the idea of 'mastery over nature' was, after all, born together with the practice of mastery over humans and was from the start bound to lose both urgency and credibility once that practice came to be contested and to fall from grace. Practice prompted the idea and supplied the conceptual net in which the idea could be articulated. Mastery over men was projected, conducted and reported in terms of invasion, conquest, colonization, and the assimilation/expulsion alternative, and it was these terms that infused sense into the project of mastery over nature. Once these terms had been discredited and the practices to which they referred declared criminal, the bottom fell out of the project of mastery over nature. And so, suddenly, the hallowed boundary between (human) culture and (inhuman) nature lost the importance it was assigned and carried for several centuries. One after another, the border guards abandoned the border posts and the border controls began to be phased out.

## On the difficulty of becoming the one who acts

And so we are all bystanders now: knowing that something needs to be done, but also knowing that we have done less than what was needed and not necessarily what needed doing most; and that we are not especially eager to do more or better, and even less keen to abstain from doing what should not be done at all. To make the bystander's plight, distressing as it always is, more harrowing yet, the gap between things *done* and things *to be done* seems to be swelling instead of shrinking. There are more and more goings-on in the world which we sense are crying for vengeance or remedy, but our capacity to act, and particularly the aptitude to act effectively, seems to go into reverse, dwarfed ever more by the enormity of the task. The number of events and situations that we hear of and that cast us in the awkward and reprehensible position of a bystander grows by the day.

Keith Tester puts in a nutshell what is fast becoming the most crucial and vexing quandary in our globalizing world: '[T]he world is, amongst other things, a producer of horror and atrocity yet seemingly there are no resources which might be the basis of the generation of a moral response to many of these instances of suffering.'[7] In other words, Tester asks why there are so many bystanders in this world of ours. How come that our world has turned into a huge, uncharacteristically efficient branch of modern production: an admirably efficient factory of bystanders.

The first answer that comes to mind the moment Tester's question is asked is, of course, the distance between the viewer and the suffering on view. It will not have been Clarkson's 'old man, young woman, child or baby' *near you* that have failed to arouse a moral response and so made Tester, and us with him, pause and ponder the arcane process of the conveyer-belt-like assembly of bystanders. It is instead all those people in pain – poor and miserable men and women of all ages living (or dying) far away from our homes and from the streets we are ever likely to walk. The distance between us and them is enormous – intractable, impassable – by the standards of our ability to walk or travel or the tools we know how to handle and are able to operate. Our experience of their suffering is mediated by television cameras, satellites, cables, screens. A mediated experience enables only a similarly mediated response: digging into our wallets and paying some agency for relieving us temporarily, until the next horrifying images flash on to the screen, from pangs of conscience.

There are images aplenty. They appear in our sitting rooms with awesome regularity. They also sink into oblivion a few days or hours later as if to make room for other images, no less, if not more, shocking and never slow in coming.

Watching terrifying pictures of famine, homelessness, death on a massive scale and utter desperation has turned by now, says Tester, into a new 'tradition' of our mediocratic age. Like all things traditional, they've lost power to shock as they have been made 'unproblematic through the practices of mundane and habitual everyday routine'.[8] This is, as Tester points out, another (expectable) case of Georg Simmel's 'blasé attitude': 'just like the city, television offers so much that our powers of discrimination actually cease to be able to work effectively.' Henning Bech, a most insightful analyst of the contemporary experience of urban living, coined the concept of the 'telecity' to make salient the intimate kinship between the detached responses, or non-responsiveness of the *flâneur* (always *in*, but never *of* the urban crowd) and the TV addict's experience. Established charities and the animators of one-off 'carnivals of pity' complain about the 'compassion fatigue'. This is, though, exactly the kind of reaction they should have expected from the residents of the telecity. The telecity's residents find tiring (boring) anything that lasts beyond a fleeting moment and threatens to outlive the excitement its novelty has triggered. Why should some images of misery be exempt from that rule?

The most obvious answers are not necessarily the best, though. There are at least two other factors that deserve a closer look whenever the riddle (and abomination) is pondered of the notoriously short-lived and flickery, and seldom more than lukewarm, responses to the televised horrors of distant suffering.

One of these factors has been spotted and recorded by Ryszard Kapuściński, a most indefatigable explorer of the paradoxes, antinomies and inanities of our shared global home: the gap between *seeing* and *knowing*.[9] Depending on what is presented to view, the absorption of *images* may thwart rather than prompt and facilitate the assimilation of *knowledge*. It may also bar an *understanding* of what has been noted *and* retained, let alone penetrating its causes.

The suffering 'as seen on TV' is in most cases conveyed through images of the emaciated bodies of the hungry and the pain-twisted faces of the ill. Hunger calls for the supply of food; disease cries for drugs and medical know-how. Both promptly arrive: lorries loaded with surplus food that, to keep prices high and the stockholders' income rising, clutters the warehouses of affluent countries; and the earnest, devoted and noble volunteers of Médecins sans Frontières carrying surplus drugs that clutter, for much the same reason, the warehouses of the pharmaceutical multinationals. Nothing is shown, and no word is spoken, of the *causes* of famine and chronic illness. No inkling of the steady destruction of livelihoods by trade *sans frontières*, of the tearing apart of social safety nets under the pressure of finance *sans frontières*, or of the devastation of soils and communities by monocultures promoted by the merchandisers of genetically engineered seeds in close cooperation with the missionaries of economic reason from the World Bank or the International Monetary Fund. Instead, a persuasive and pervasive suggestion that what has been 'seen on TV' is a self-inflicted disaster visiting distant, exotic and 'very unlike us' tribes who have blundered themselves out of decent human living. And that – thank God (or our prudence) – some fortunate folks with good hearts like us, fortunate because sensible and industrious, are around, ready to salvage the hapless from the blood-curdling consequences of their bad luck and ill-considered conduct brought about by ignorance or sloth. Come the day of Band Aid or Comic Relief, and the celebrities intended to prompt us to switch on, surrounded by seasoned entertainers intended to keep us switched on and computers intended to keep us proud of having switched on, anchor the spectacle of our benevolence and choke with emotions on our behalf while keeping us abreast of the vertiginous progress of our charity. As if by a magic wand, we are transported from the dark and mean hiding places of wrong-doers' accomplices to the all-singing, all-dancing holiday camps of selfless and magnanimous *chevaliers sans reproche*. Our joint responsibility for the human disasters we are invited to help repair is not implied and does not spoil the festival of mutual absolution. Conscience is pricked and placated in one go – in one charitable gesture.

Kapuściński lays bare the gap between seeing and knowing. Yet wider, a truly abysmal gap yawns however between *knowing* and *acting*. Were we to become, despite the adverse odds, aware of the real roots of human misery on display, what (if anything) could we do to eradicate them, let alone prevent them from taking root? Luc Boltanski asks the most pertinent of questions that can and ought to be asked: 'What form can commitment take when those called to act are thousands of miles away from the persons suffering, comfortably installed in front of the television set in the shelter of the family living-room?'[10]

Tester recalls Alfred Weber's anxiety caused by the emergence of a global network of radio broadcasting:[11] 'the world has become a much smaller place – it is scarcely possible honestly to maintain any kind of pretence of ignorance of what is going on' – anywhere, however remote the corner of the globe. But things have moved much further still since Weber's expression of anxiety.

It is not just the *volume* of available (indeed, ubiquitously obtrusive) knowledge that has grown beyond all expectations: the *quality* of the information has radically changed as well. What we know and know of is not just a version of the events we have not seen – a hearsay that we are free to believe or not, a third-person story that we may trust or doubt, accept as true or dispute and with a modicum of effort argue out of conscience. Once images replace words (photo- or video-graphic images, those frozen and preserved pieces of 'reality', its ever more faithful replicas, not just 'analogue', but 'digital' – read undistorted – copies), the processed, mediated nature of information is concealed from view and can no longer be held against the veracity of the message and authorize a truth contest. Virtually or not, we are now *witnesses* to what is going on in those faraway places. We not only *hear about* the pain people suffer, we *'see it with our own eyes'*. As Stanley Milgram's famed experiments have shown, eyes are incomparably more morally sensitive than ears. Even if we are 'comfortably installed in the shelter of our living rooms', we watch, at close quarters, people dying of famine and of other people's cruelty. Our moral selves are daily accosted and molested, prodded, challenged, pressed to respond.

The snag is, though, that as the circulation of knowledge about our and other people's plight gets ever more effective, the same cannot be said of our capacity for ethically inspired acts. The network of our mutual dependence gets tighter with every advance of globalization, but the gap between the reach of the 'unanticipated' (or just ignored or unreckoned with) consequences of our actions and the scope of whatever we can do consciously and deliberately to mitigate such consequences grows wider. The outcomes of our action and inaction reach far beyond the limits of our moral imagination and our readiness to assume responsibility for the weal and woe of the people whose lives have been directly or indirectly affected. This is why, paradoxically, our shared capacity to do harm seems infinitely greater that our shared capacity to do good. As if the tools and technologies of causing (collectively, though unintentionally) misery surge forward, leaving behind the tools and technologies of causing (collectively and deliberately) bliss. The tools of happiness, unlike the vehicles of misery, all seem small in scale, for individual use only, fit solely for servicing private life and individual action. What we can do to alleviate the plight of those affected seems much less potent than what we do, intentionally or by default, to contribute to their misery.

This is *not* to say that globalization promotes callousness and moral indifference. There is no reason to suppose that we have become, or are becoming, less sensitive to human suffering than our ancestors used to be. If anything, the opposite seems to be the case. We are less and less tolerant to pain – and also to the sight of pain suffered by others, humans or animals (if we are assured, that is, that the pain is 'for real'). Many varieties of human misery once meekly accepted as unavoidable and ordinary, indeed an indispensable accompaniment of human life, have been recast as superfluous and gratuitous, unjustified or downright offensive, and above all calling for remedy, revenge, or – short of those – for (pecuniary) compensation.

The problem though is that, unlike in the past, the scale of our awareness of the fate of others and the scope of our ability to influence that fate (whether to damage or repair it) *do not overlap*. Our ancestors were direct witnesses to most consequences of their actions because these consequences seldom, if ever, reached further than their naked eye (and armed hands) could reach. With the new, global network of dependencies and with technology potent enough to allow for equally global effects of actions, that morally comfortable situation is gone. Knowledge and action no longer overlap, and the realm of their encounter shrinks steadily by comparison to the rapidly expanding area of their discordance. They are out of joint more often than they merge. This new situation may be schematically represented by two circles whose surfaces only marginally coincide:

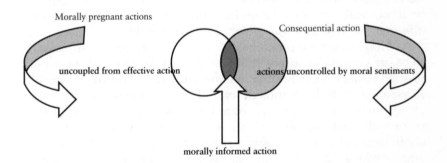

Only a relatively small part of the outcomes and repercussions of our actions or inactions are ethically controlled and guided by moral sentiments; few have had consideration given to their possible effects on other than the direct addressees or participants of the action currently in focus. On the other hand, only relatively few messages about other people's suffering come to us complete with clear information about what we can do to help, and especially to help radically. Much of the morally pregnant knowledge on offer discourages commitment to action since it is far from evident what (if anything) can be done by us to make a real difference. Many, perhaps most of our actions do have an impact on the conditions of others, including distant and unknown others, but only a few of them are from the start accompanied by ethical reflection.

No wonder that it is easy to refuse commitment without much moral torment, and that it is easy to find arguments legitimating the denial of guilt. Admonished to seek (as Ulrich Beck memorably phrased it) *biographical* solutions to *systemic* contradictions, to rely solely on our own, individually owned and individually managed resources, and told/shown daily that everyone else follows or tries hard to follow that admonition, we grow used to the idea that our individual life itinerary is the sole realistic concern and the sole ground on which to focus an action one wishes to be effective instead of time-wasting. It hardly occurs to us that there may be some reason (and hope) in trying to reform the wider conditions under which our biographies (and the biographies of all the rest of our fellow humans) are shaped and biographical solutions are desperately sought. If it were suggested to us to try such reform we would treat the advice with disbelief and we would mistrust the advisers. A refusal of commitment, on the grounds of the assumed idleness and ultimately the impotence of collective action, seems to be a rational step to take, a legitimate conclusion from a sober, 'rational' evaluation of the possible and the feasible.

And yet...However rational the refusal of commitment appears to be, its logical elegance will not always lay the pangs of conscience to rest. Conscience is known to stubbornly disregard the reasons of Reason and to have reasons of which Reason knows not. We do not always switch off the pictures of horror. Time and again we do wish to help the victims, though we seldom go beyond telephoning the credit card number or mailing a cheque to the address of the charity agency displayed on the screen. Sometimes we add our indignant voices to the chorus of condemnation of the invidious perpetrators of atrocity (when named) and the chorus of praise for the victims' helpers (if picked up by the reporters from their self-chosen anonymity). Almost never does the commitment go far enough to strike at the roots of wrongdoing. Were we to wish to take up such a commitment, we would be hard put to it to find out where to start and how to proceed from there.

Commitment is *not* inconceivable; neither is a *long-term* commit-ment, nor a fruitful, *effective*, changing-the-world long-term com-mitment. But powerful forces conspire to bar entry. The absence of a proper insight into the tightly sealed cocoon of interdependence, in which the horrors already seen have gestated and those yet un-known and still to be hatched incubate, is a most difficult hurdle to pass round or kick out of the way. The chain of causal connections is too ramified, twisted and convoluted to be followed by people who are untrained and in a hurry; but in addition many of its links tend to be buried away in secret compartments that are plastered all over with 'entry forbidden' warnings and are impenetrable without security screening and stingily issued passes. The fragments of the chain accessible to view seldom form a cohesive system with clearly marked points of entry and 'install' and 'uninstall' buttons.

Admittedly, the obstacles to effective long-term commitment are numerous and many of them are intractable. It can be argued, though, that the barrier most difficult to negotiate is the one-sidedness of the globalizing process. The progressive interlocking of global dependencies is not paralleled, let alone checked and bal-anced, by similarly global, and potent, instruments of political action. Diffuse and sporadic 'anti-globalization' protests, however brave and dedicated, are a poor match for the concentrated might of the multinationals, cosseted, shielded and kept out of trouble day in, day out, by governments vying for the Michelin stars of hospital-ity and by the heavily armed forces they command. To remove that hurdle, a better insight would not suffice. But at least it would be (to use Churchill's memorable phrase) 'the end of the beginning'.

## Chasing the 'political moment' in the globalized world

By the end of the twentieth century the normative powers of nation-states, and particularly their practical capacity for sovereign normative regulation, have been thoroughly eroded. Business (and particularly big business, the business that truly counts when it comes to the balancing of state books and securing the livelihood of state subjects) has made a successful bid for secession from the realm of state sovereignty. The economic foundations of human sur-vival and well-being are now once more politically 'extraterritorial', just as they used to be two centuries ago, at the threshold of the modern era, when business managed to escape from the tight ethical supervision of the local community into a 'no-man's-land' not yet occupied and administered by the emergent modern state – into a veritable frontier-land where the 'cash nexus' was the sole social bond and cut-throat competition the sole law of the country.

In our times an ethically empty space has emerged once more, and inside it the economic powers are free to follow their own rules or, as the case may be, to ignore rules altogether. This new void has been plotted as a result of the emancipation of economic powers from the legislating/policing powers of the self-same *nation-state* that two centuries ago managed to bridle the economic forces that ran free from *communal* control. This time, however, the secession has not been followed as yet by the emergence of legislative powers capable of imposing ethically pregnant constraints on the newly unbridled economic forces. Economic forces are free to act globally, but there are at best only germs and premonitions of a globally binding legal and juridical system, global democracy or a globally binding, enforceable and obeyed ethical code.

Ethically motivated and informed global action has no adequately global instruments. In the absence of proper levers and vehicles of effective action, we all seem to be – each one of us individually and all the individuals together – cast in the role of bystanders and bound to carry that role for an unbearably long time to come. Periodic outbursts of protest against eviction from political decision-making and compulsory bystanding (the genuine fuse, one may suspect, of the guerrilla-style 'anti-globalization' happenings) seem to be the only, sorely inadequate, alternative to a meek acceptance of the state of affairs. They draw attention, arouse awareness of the risks ahead; sometimes they succeed in forcing the hand of the high and mighty on a few points currently in focus. All in all, however, though full of sound and fury, they signify little real change in the balance of power – however noble their intentions and however great the courage of their actors may be. On the other hand, a steady, long-term commitment to collective action meant to cut at the roots of the human misery gestated in the new global ethical void has all the appearances of a nebulous dream. It is that nebulousness that wraps the Fukuyama-style announcement of the 'end of history' in the mist of credibility.

But only such a commitment – a steady, long term commitment – deserves to be called 'the political moment par excellence', as Luc Boltanski suggests,[12] 'an act that transforms spectator into actor'. Nothing short of such a commitment will do. The other, most frequent responses to the sight of human misery, such as hounding particular culprits of particular misdeeds or lauding particular benefactors of particular victims, bring at best a temporary and local relief. Most commonly, they alleviate the most painful symptoms of the disease only to detract from the urgency of its cure. All too often, however, they offer a much needed and gratefully accepted fig-leaf to the powers-that-be, eager to channel the gathering tide of moral revulsion away from the genuine sources of ethical outrage, and keen to hide the fact of doing nothing to make the outrage less likely to occur. At their worst, as Boltanski warns, they may cause *more* misery – as in the case of 'those in power who exploit past victims to take possession of the future while ignoring present suffering' instead of 'casting eyes on the unfortunate and looking evil in its face without immediately turning away towards imaginary benefactors and persecutors'. Quoting Kouchner and Tricaud, two persons who came to know more deeply than most others the trials and tribulations of confronting point-blank evil-doers at their work and bringing succour to their victims, Boltanski demands that whoever volunteers to break out of the vicious circle of the bystander's plight 'should always stay at the bedside of minorities', but 'without illusions, since the minorities may themselves become oppressive'. It is not only that the exit from the bystander's cell seems to be bolted, but the road outside seems to be full of traps and ambushes.

A commitment which is able to steer clear of all such dangers, and which is of the magnitude necessary to make the effort resolute and consistent (particularly if such a commitment is to be undertaken by a great number of people rather than by a few exceptionally broad-minded, warm-hearted and dedicated individuals with strong ethical convictions) is unlikely to be made as long as confidence in the effectiveness of public speech and in its potency to prompt concerted collective action remains as tenuous and fragile as it tends to be today in our thoroughly individualized society. 'To take the claim that speech is *effective* seriously, we need the support of the complicated political construction of the Polis.'[13] And we may add that it is precisely that construction that is currently in trouble – in a state of disrepair and in urgent need of a long overdue overhaul. Trust in the effectiveness of committed speech, and particularly speech oriented to the kind of established political institutions that can be hoped and reasonably expected to subordinate their actions to ethical reasons and act for the sake of ethical objectives, is no longer there. It needs to be laboriously built and entrenched jointly with the ethically motivated institutions that are now either absent or too weak for the task.

Drawing on Adam Smith's *Theory of Moral Sentiments* and Immanuel Kant's *Critique of Judgement* – two fundamental statements strikingly different in the styles of their arguments yet converging in their conclusions and messages – Boltanski suggests that the sought-after polity can only take the shape of Kant's 'aesthetic community', that is, a community of shared taste built and sustained by the staunch and mutually reconfirming and reinforcing commitment of its members. The road to such a community, again in Boltanski's view, is bound to lead through committed speech, dialogical in its intention, aimed from its start and throughout the ensuing dialogue at the approval of the others to whom it has been addressed: at showing that the topic with which the speech is concerned is *worthy* of approval

This is, admittedly, not a particularly firm foundation on which to build a strong community confident of its own survival. On the contrary, the 'aesthetic community of compassion' seems to be marked by an endemic fragility that needs to be compensated for by the continuous, emotionally charged dedication of its builders, wardens and actors.

All this is but a collection of proverbial 'rules of thumb'. These are hints rather than instructions, broad strategic principles rather than marching orders, reflections of the ways and means of construction rather than a building schedule. No more could be legitimately expected, though, from the concerned and responsible analyst of the present-day human condition. To quote Tester once more,[14] what a responsible sociologist wishing to loyally acquit herself of her responsibility may do is 'to diagnose the present without, however, offering any prognosis' nor an 'explicit ethical code or ideal'. What the committed sociologist needs to do is 'to propose that there might be much more to being human than all of this, but then have the honesty to refuse to say what that more might be'. It is the job of committed speech aimed at turning into community-building action to usher people into the territory that the diagnosis has mapped and to guide the steps to be taken; to provide a *practical* answer to the abstract question.

True, there is no guarantee that the answer will be given, heard when spoken and accepted when heard. But there is no other way to find out but to try to offer a suggestion of an answer and to submit the offer to the considered judgement of fellow humans. It is the duty of the sociologist to spell out frankly the 'underdetermination' of all conceivable solutions to the shared quandary; to present in full the complexity of positing the task and struggling to fulfil it under condition of acute uncertainty. And let us note that the vagueness and ambiguity with which the winding road from bystander to moral actor has been sketched are not unlike the incompletion of another concept (ably discussed by Robert Fine in reference to Hannah Arendt[15]), 'not so much a fault as a prescription for making judgements and taking decisions with the tools we have in hand'. This may be the lot of all committed speech: it cannot but *give hostages to fate*. Or rather give hostages not so much to *fate* as to the *dialogue* – hoping that the number of those now silent, uninterested or busy with other concerns who will eventually take part and add to the dialogue's richness and vigour will grow. There is no other medicine against the silence/indifference syndrome except committed speech.

Only a long, uphill struggle ahead can be promised to people who resent and abhor their plight as bystanders, as well as to people who wish bystanders to acquire the means and to develop the determination needed to lift themselves to the status of moral actors. Both have yet to find the means, as well as the courage and the will necessary to apply them. The goal that such means are to serve and hopefully reach can hardly be expressed better than by Hannah Arendt when she looked back at the evils of a 'century of bystanders'. The task, she noted, was to 'assume responsibility for all crimes committed by human beings, in which no one people are assigned a monopoly of guilt and none considers itself superior, in which good citizens would not shrink in horror at German crimes and declare "thank God, I am not like that", but rather recognise in fear and trembling the incalculable evil which humanity is capable of and fight fearlessly, uncompromisingly, everywhere against it.'[16]

Musing over the legacy of the century that had just ground to its close, Göran Rosenberg suggested that meaningful time divisions do not necessarily agree with the round numbers in the calendar. The nineteenth century, he proposed, marked by now bygone youthful exuberance and self-confidence, started in fact in 1789 and ended in 1914. We may suggest that the twentieth century, marked by the sinister discovery that evil can emerge from the civilizing drill not only unscathed, but also refreshed and reinforced, started in 1914. It is still very much an open question when it is going to end. And it is up to the bystanders struggling to transform themselves into actors to provide the answer to that question; *to be* that answer.

# Conclusion: Utopia with No *Topos*

To measure the life 'as it is' by a life as it *should* be (that is, a life *imagined* to be different from the life *known*, and particularly a life that is better and would be *preferable* to the life known) is a defining, constitutive feature of humanity. Human being-in-the-world means being ahead-of-the-world. The 'human' in 'human being' is what 'sticks out', runs ahead from the rest of being – while 'the world' is that rest which has been left behind. 'The world' stands for limits – the limits that exist, though, in (and through) the process of being broken and transcended.

*Human* life is propelled and kept on course by the urge for transcendence. Transcendence – transgression – is the modality of human being-in-the-world. Barring transgression and/or recoiling from transgression signal pathology of that being. It takes a lot of effort to produce that pathology, but few if any of the efforts made throughout history, from a neighbourhood watch monitoring daily routine to the state-run concentration camps, from policing bodies to policing thoughts, have quite succeeded in reaching the aim. Besides, were it not for the ability to imagine a life different from the one lived – and the resulting disrespect for limits, coupled with an urge to trespass – the urge and passion to keep in place the stubbornly restless limits, to seal the notoriously leaking borders and to bar transcendence would hardly have been born.

The urge to transcend is the most stubbornly present, nearest to universal, and arguably the least destructible attribute of human existence. This cannot be said, however, of its articulations into 'projects' – that is, into cohesive and comprehensive programmes of change, complete with a vision of the life that the change is hoped to bring about. For the constantly present urge to transcend to be articulated into 'projects', special and much less common conditions must arise – and the nature of such conditions defines the forms of feasible articulations. Utopia is one of the forms such articulations may take. The conditions that defined that form were those of modernity in its initial 'solid' stage. That particular form was marked and set apart from other articulations of the transgression urge by two remarkable attributes: territoriality and finality.

## The sedentary imagination

The first attribute is captured in the name itself, coined by Thomas More but subsequently adopted as a family name for a long series of articulations that punctuated the historical itinerary of the modern era. 'Utopia' refers to *topos* – a *place*. However imagined, visions of a different and on the whole better life portrayed in the description of Utopias were always 'territorially defined': associated with, and confined to, a clearly defined territory.

Their essential dissimilarity to the ordinary world known thus far to readers from their daily practice was insinuated by their enormous physical distance from the explored and mapped lands, and further emphasized by locating the site of the good life on a faraway island or at the far end of a yet undiscovered and untrodden, testing and treacherous, sometimes downright impassable track. The trials and tribulation the lonely travellers suffered before reaching or accidentally straying into the land of Utopia signalled the lack of obvious, let alone easy, passages from the world of everyday life to the 'good life' that the newly discovered land incarnated. And whatever happiness could be relished within the territorial confines of Utopia could not be exported beyond its borders, could not be transplanted let alone strike roots in a different soil and clime, as for instance the hapless voyagers to James Hilton's Shangri La discovered much to their despair.

The world of 'solid modernity' was sedentary. It was a world of heavy, bulky, firmly dug in, immobilized objects. It was a blatantly and self-consciously *territorial* world. All identities, as well as differences, contradictions and antagonisms, were *glebae adscripti*. They all brandished, whether as a badge of honour or a brand of shame, fixed and registered addresses, themselves inventions of the emergent modern idea of administration. In that idea, 'running things' meant arresting things in their 'natural' places, or transporting them to more suitable places 'where they belonged' and keeping them there. Power and sovereignty were measured and evaluated with the help of spatial metaphors like 'scope' and 'volume', and defined by their physical boundaries.

In that sedentary and 'solid' phase of modernity there was an intimate correspondence between space and power. Power was a spatial, realm-fixed notion. Powers were named after the territory over which their authority extended. And vice versa: the space was divided, and its divisions were circumscribed, according to the powers that ruled over it. 'States', which replaced the dynastic realms with the advent of modernity as the seats of supreme authority, were *territorial* entities. It was over its territory that the state prevailed, *superiorem non recognoscens*.

The power of the state was measured by the size of its territory and supposed to grow (or diminish) in parallel with territorial acquisitions (or losses). As Roberto Toscano aptly puts it, 'territory means resources, population, and strategic control. Territory constitutes the very body of the state, so that every loss is perceived as a mutilation, every gain as vital growth (or, more often, recovery of previously detached limbs).'[1] Given the way the integrity of state-owned territory is seen and felt, 'the insignificant paring of a fingernail' tends to be represented as 'the painful mutilation of an arm'.

The extent of territory was coeval with the extent of sovereignty. 'Sovereignty' (according to Carl Schmitt's synthesis of modern practice, as recently reexamined by Giorgio Agamben[2]) was all about the power to include or exempt. The sovereign is he who *decides on the state of exception*. But let us note that it is precisely the territoriality of power that makes of the capacity to exempt such an awesome weapon of the sovereign authority – indeed the constitutive factor of its 'materiality'. In as far as power is and stays coextensive with the territory over which its sovereignty spreads, the act of exemption does not mean the law's withdrawal, but on the contrary – its stepping in; not legal indifference or neutrality, but a most active engagement and 'taking a stand'. Exempting (stripping of duties, but also of rights) does not place the exempted beyond the reach of the long arm of the law – but on the contrary, exposes the exempted, now bared, disarmed and helpless, to the law's unmitigated power. Decreeing a state of exemption (by definition focused, sorting out its objects and setting them apart from the rest) is the most awesome and terrifying of the weapons of punishment the sovereign can wield with its legal arm. The right to decree, distribute and reshuffle exemptions is the true stake in all power struggle.

The sovereign is a sovereign in as far as he controls admission to the House of Law. Whoever happens to be bodily present inside the territorial boundaries of the sovereign state falls under that control. Inside a territory in which every subject is allocated its rightful place, an entity that is exempted from allocation and so denied a place of its own is stripped of rights – it carries none of the rights that other subjects have the (state-imposed and state-policed) obligation to respect. Among the subjects all dressed in uniforms sewn of legal categories, its life is *la vita nuda*, a 'bare', purely corporeal life denied all legally woven significance. A 'sovereign territory' is the artefact of its own map: an impression left on a physical space full of human bodies by a tightly woven canvas of legal categories.

As long as it is armed with the ultimate sanction of exemption the sovereign power turns its law into a cage, making the exit from the cage into a fate feared, shunned and far too horrifying to be contemplated as an acceptable price of freedom, and the entry to the cage into a privilege that needs to be earned, and once earmed, cherished. The captives have every reason to view the cage as shelter (uncomfortable maybe, yet secure). This is a cage to which most would-be internees clamour to be admitted, and which those refused entry dream of as the ultimate redemption.

It was inside the cage of law that the life of a subject of the sovereign was to flow; the whole of it, from cradle to the grave. Having left no alternative, except a life fit solely, as Aristotle warned, for a beast or a god, to subjects who were neither, the sovereign could count on the subjects' obedience. The few daring enough to fancy themselves as godlike could easily be certified out into invisibility or censored off into inaudibility, while most subjects-that-be and would-be subjects would resent the plight of beasts and prefer the cage to the wilderness.

Sovereignty being territorial, the wilderness most resented and feared was that exception-generated one inside the cage: both wilderness and individual or categorial lot, conjured up by the law's power to forbear its rule, and particularly the responsibility that comes with the rule. The stateless inside the state, the *sans-papiers* among passport holders, were to be the modern incarnations of *homo sacer* – the forcefully desocialized and de-ethicized, adiaphorized 'bared bodies', exempt from human and divine law, bodies that can be destroyed with impunity and whose destruction would have neither human nor divine significance.

The sovereign has the power to exempt. The sovereign also has the power to refrain from exemption. Above all, the sovereign has the power to set the conditions that separate the first from the second. It can be said that the ultimate meaning of 'order', that supreme goal of all modern endeavour, was the drawing of that distinction in an unambiguous fashion, unquestionable and immune to controversy – and then rendering it invulnerable to dissent and contest. It was not so much the law-making, as the law-suspending or law-withdrawing power that was the principal weapon of modern order-building and order-protection. Unless flanked by the power of exclusion, territorial inclusion would not suffice. There wouldn't be territorial sovereignty were the sovereign impotent to choose between granting and withholding admission to the cage/ shelter of law. And there would be little to set apart order from un-order, the rule of law and the absence of law.

The presence of the sovereign despot was taken for granted by all concerned with the building and preservation of order; the question of how to enlighten (read: tame and domesticate) the despot natur-ally followed. At the heart of the idea of the 'enlightened despot' was a state of affairs in which the sovereign would hardly ever – only in truly exceptional circumstances – resort to his power of exception. More to the point, a state of affairs in which the number and frequency of 'exceptional circumstances' would be reduced to a minimum, perhaps eliminated altogether, so that there could be but few if any occasions calling for acting in a 'non-enlightened' way.

Bringing such a situation about and making it durable had to be a joint accomplishment of the sovereign and his subjects. Or, rather, such a situation would be most likely to emerge in a setting in which the subjects were unlikely to make moves provoking/unleashing de-ployment of the sovereign's power of exception, and so the sover-eign despot would be unlikely to deploy it. The 'enlightenment' of the despot should express itself in the despot using his sovereign power to bring such a situation about and to make it permanent.

The sovereign could not forbear his potency of exclusion without forfeiting his sovereignty. But his awesome powers could be held in check in a roundabout way: through the subjects steering clear of such transgression as carried the penalty of exclusion. Whatever conditions of enlightened power could be conceived of, all and any of them were to bind the sovereign and the subjects alike. All visions of well-tempered human cohabitation assumed *permanent mutual engagement* between the rulers and the ruled and the capacity of each side to circumscribe and cut down the range of options the other side might be tempted to choose from.

Like the rest of the thought of the time, utopian thought took the territoriality of all order, also of the 'good order' it struggled to model and engrave on to social reality, for granted. Models differed in many respects (though less than their inventors imagined), but they were all planted in a *topos* – a territory set apart and insulated from the rest of space, while simultaneously internally integrated – courtesy of the power that was sovereign inside its boundaries, *superiorem non recognoscens*. Each utopian society had a fixed address in the distinctly and emphatically physical, even if imaginary space, and the undivided sovereignty of a council of elders or a benevolent Sun-King that set the rules of the life game for all its members was the foundation of its fixity and the guarantee of its durability.

For all practical intents and purposes, a good life meant a life lived in a good society, while a 'good society' translated in turn as a population inhabiting a territory plotted and mapped, and then projected upon the physical space, by the wise and benevolent powers of a good state.

The utopian imagination was essentially architectural and urbanistic. Most of the attention of the model builders was devoted to plotting and mapping, leaving the job of the projection of the map over the territory (or more to the point the job of remaking reality in the likeness of the map) to the rulers of the *topos*. The purpose was to design a spatial arrangement in which there would be a right and proper place for everyone for whom a right and proper place would have been designed.

In the sketching of the anticipatory map of Utopia, both (inseparable, as it were) edges of the power sword were adumbrated. The construction of good order was, invariably, an exercise in inclusion and exclusion: in the unconditionality of law and the unconditionality of its exemptions.

The exemption built into the masterplan of the Utopia was, however, envisaged on the whole as a one-off act. Once the right places had been allocated to everyone inside, and once those for whom no place was reserved had died out, had left of their own accord or had been forced out of the city, no further exercise of the power of exemption would be needed. The sword of power would be kept permanently in its sheath, preserved for the illumination of the new happy generations mostly as a museum piece, a relic of bygone, 'pre-good-society' times.

This hope has been, one may guess, the main reason why the term 'utopian' acquired in the course of modern history the semantic flavour of a fanciful, perhaps inane pipe-dream and found itself in modern thesauruses in the company of such terms as 'figmental', 'chimerical', 'impractical' or 'dreamy-eyed'.

## The transfixing imagination

And so we come to the second of the two ubiquitous attributes of utopian thought: finality.

As if taking a hint from the schoolman Anselm's admittedly faulty proof of God's existence (some beings are better than others, so there must be a being better than *all* other beings, the perfect being that cannot be bettered: God), drafters of Utopia took it for granted that the long series of improvements on social reality, whether scattered over a long stretch of time or condensed revolutionary-style, must at some point reach its natural conclusion: not just a better society, but the best society conceivable, the *perfect* society, society in which any further change could be only a change for the worse. The passage from any 'really existing reality' to the perfect society would consti-tute a gigantic leap and a truly formidable change, but no more leaps would need to be made after that, and no further change, with its usual vexing accompaniment of risk, apprehension and a discom-fort no less painful and harrowing for being 'transitional', would be called for or desired.

There are but so many injustices on the long list of human wrongs; only so many blank spots on the maps of the universe and only so many unknown quantities in the equation of the human condition; only so many tools and tricks as yet not invented or still undiscovered in the unstoppable progress of humans to full control over human fate; only so many paragraphs in the code of the happy life as yet not articulated, spelled out and added to the book of law; only so many human needs still unsatisfied because of supply lag-ging behind demand and industrial plants lagging behind the needed volume of supply. And so one can hope (be sure) that all blank spots in human know-how will be eventually filled, all wrongs excised from social life one by one, all needs satiated, all precepts of the happy life revealed and joyfully embraced. The march to perfection is admittedly long and arduous, but somewhere in the misty far-away there is a clearly marked, even if as yet barely visible, *finishing line*. Utopia was that *topos* which rewarded the hardship of the travellers: that end of the pilgrimage that would (albeit retrospect-ively) make the past trials and tribulations worth the pains they once brought and the exertions needed to fight back against them and overcome them.

At the time the blueprints of Utopias were penned, the world seemed to have entered a state of permanent revolution. The most harrowing adversities and setbacks of modern order-building were the perpetual dislocations, seemingly without end, resembling earth-quakes following volcanic eruptions and followed by tornados. The crumbling of familiar landscapes, cutting the bonds of friendship, care and mutual support, made the customary ways and the learning of them useless, while new and untried ways, for the reason of being new and untried, appeared treacherous, risky and untrustworthy. Utopia was to put an end to all that.

Utopia was to be the fortress of certainty and stability; a kingdom of tranquillity. Instead of confusion – clarity and self-assurance. In-stead of the caprices of fate – a steady and consistent, surprise-free sequence of causes and effects. Instead of the labyrinthine muddle of twisted passages and sharp corners – straight, beaten and well-marked tracks. Instead of opacity – transparency. Instead of ran-domness – a well-entrenched and utterly predictable routine.

In a nutshell: the sufferings of modern revolution caused by the vexing inconstancy and seeming randomness of the modernized and modernizing life it brought in its wake derived from the unfamiliar state of exhilarating/frightening freedom carrying the fear of the unknown together with the joys of novelty. Utopias were the antici-pated end-products of the skilful deployment of both the plasticity of the world and the new (genuine or supposed) freedom to remould human conditions for the purpose of constructing a world free from the bane of uncertainty and insured against all further remoulding: a world resistant to all further change.

In other words, Utopias were blueprints for the routine hoped to be resurrected. But the routine that this time, in its new incarnation, would be immune to the crosswinds and earth tremors that shook and devastated the routine of yore, and prevented it from being rebuilt. Utopias were visions of a life in which freedom was but necessity understood and obediently, willingly and gratefully accepted; thanks to the absence of a clash between the possible and the real, between the desired and the feasible, no occasion would then arise to experience necessity as a burden or an oppres-sion. Once the desires were gratified, nothing would be coveted except what could be obtained. In the utopian world of the perfect balance between the 'ought' and the 'must', life would be accident-free and all the deviations from the expectable and the regular would be but momentary irritants, easy to isolate and repair.

Utopia is a vision of a closely watched, monitored, administered and daily managed world. Above all, it is a vision of a predesigned world, a world in which prediction and planning stave off the play of chance. The vision of Utopia was that of a world made to order, closely monitored in its day-by-day operation and regularly serviced.

Such a world would not be conceivable if not for the team of sages carefully and meticulously calculating the setting in which thoughts are thought and deeds done, and daily scrutinizing the results – so that adjustments and corrections could be made before the errors of design rebounded as threats to the smooth operation of the whole. And so Utopia had to be a world of tight and intimate, day in day out engagement between the rulers and the ruled: stern yet benevolent rulers and their obedient yet happy subjects. And a world of sages – whose job it was to secure the benevolence of the rulers and the happiness of the ruled.

The rulers could afford to be benevolent since in the properly designed setting the subjects were led by their own free will to do what they had to do, while the chances of wishing to do something different from what had to be done were minimal, if not nil. In other words, the ruled could feel happy because in such a carefully worked out setting they would always wish to do what do they must and nothing else – and so never come to experience the coercive power behind the rule and never suffer the punishment lying in store for the recalcitrant. In the perfect society of Utopia philosophers need not be kings, but no kings could do without wise men, the philosophers. Like God of the late-medieval schoolmen, philosophers – the wise men – conjured up the clockwork of the perfect society and then revealed and imparted to the kings and their servants the wisdom of winding it up daily and keeping it free of rust and dust.

Utopia was the product of the Age of Engagement and Commitment. A tripartite engagement – between the princes, the people, and men of knowledge. Engagement in and to the territory – jointly, continually and for a foreseeable 'forever' inhabited by all three. Commitment to a purpose – the purpose being the establishment and the preservation of the accident/risk/uncertainty free, ultimate order of the perfect society.

## The nomadic imagination

It was not always like that – nor, once it came about, was it to last for long. As Peter Scott put it recently: 'The wandering scholar of the Middle Ages may have been replaced by the jet-setting conference-hopper, who in turn may be in the process of being superseded by the information technology revolution with its potential for teleconferencing, the stay-at-home but intercontinental conference and so on.'[3] These two forms, separated by centuries, of the *extraterritoriality* of scholars are 'manifestations of the same basic idea: that science and scholarship know no frontiers.'

The first case of the two comes from the pre-engagement/precommitment era; the second comes from the present condition of a fast globalizing world of crumbling state borders and a worldwide supranational network of capital, knowledge and knowledge capital. Squeezed between the two periods whose total length is as yet unknown but certainly much greater, the engagement/commitment era, that time of a sedentary and transfixing imagination and an ensuing utopian profligacy, seems increasingly to have been a brief episode, a momentary departure from the normal or prevalent historical tendency, rather than a steady trend or an augury of things to come. That brief episode was the time of nation-building and state-building, of the two mutually prodding and reinvigorating processes converging on the most remarkable and fateful of modern social inventions: the nation-state.

The two intertwined processes were set in motion by the growing inefficacy and imminent collapse of the *ancien régime*, with its powers-that-be construed in the likeness of gamekeepers rather than gardeners and confined by and large to the creaming off of the surplus product, while leaving the ways the product came to be produced to the ancient and inscrutable, better-left-alone laws of custom and tradition and studiously refraining from all managerial-style interference.

The modern idea of a *designed* and *managed* order was born beside the death-bed of such routine, self-reproducing un-selfconsciously, by default rather than by design, with a feeling of 'without us, the deluge' in the midwife's role. The conception of a 'good society' run by the friendly yet demanding, state-centred powers of the sharing/caring nation, and the prospect of bringing under daily control and management the erratic forces of chaos currently untamed by either the dead hand of tradition or the armed hand of the police, were twin ideological glosses over that confluence of necessity and apprehension. Self-reliance and self-confidence resting on trust in the unlimited powers of human reason and resolve were to accomplish the feat that providence and the 'blind forces of history' evidently failed to conjure up. That change of guard was to be recorded subsequently, and so only retrospectively, as 'the project of modernity'.

The desire for a better life focused on the search for the model of a good *society* – a society more likely to satisfy the totality of human needs than all its conceivable alternatives and offering a setting for human life more solid, reliable and resistant to corruption than any other model could provide. Utopian blueprints were the findings of that search. In unison with the boisterous proclamations and bold undertakings of the nascent nation-states, they tried to explore the limits to which the nation-state could go if it traversed to the end the whole length of the trail blazed by human reason; and to find out to where it might lead a humanity orphaned by/emancipated from the 'divine chain of being', once believed to be tied up in the six-day-long Act of Creation with an (unfulfilled) mandate to last for eternity.

By now, however, with the nation-state in a double-bind of pressures coming simultaneously 'from above' and 'from below', the bottom fell out of the barrelful of utopian blueprints. No barrel can hold its contents if there is a gaping hole where the bottom used to be.

Today, as Masao Miyoshi put it, having surveyed the worldwide developments of recent years, the nation-state 'no longer works; it is thoroughly appropriated by transnational corporations.'[4] Transnational corporations, in their turn, 'are unencumbered with nationalist baggage... They travel, communicate, and transfer people and plants, information and technology, money and resources globally.' 'They operate over distance.' They 'remain aliens and outsiders in each place, faithful only to the exclusive clubs of which they are members'. In Sheila Slaughter's summary of the neoliberal credo of our times,[5] market forces that are 'impersonal, disembodied, and inexorable' supplant 'national economies with a global market', and the territorial nation-states are expected, and pressed, to free capital and corporations from regulation and allow them 'to operate unfettered'; 'the only acceptable role of the state is that of global police officer and judge, patrolling the edges of the playing field and adjudicating trading infractions and transgressions.'

We may say that the power to make and unmake, to alter and reforge the conditions of human life has deserted the nation-state's controlling towers, having been carried away beyond the limits of the state's sovereign territory and beyond the reach of the state's sovereignty – locked in the securely sealed briefcases of the new free-floating, extraterritorial, transnational (or, as it prefers to call itself, flatteringly, 'multicultural') elite. The demise of the nation-state coincides and blends with the *expropriation* of old, local power elites that now count for little as long as they stay local, and the *secession* of a new global power elite that truly counts, and counts ever more, as long as it stays global: an elite that is not rooted in, and not fixed to or tied by, any of the nominally sovereign political entities.

A powerless or insufficiently empowered nation-state has little allure. With whatever creative potential the human race might be endowed, the nation-state, progressively reduced to police-precinct functions, has few if any marks of being its likely carrier. Under the circumstances, the recent eruption of tribal sentiments in all their forms – of ethnicism, communitarianism or fundamentalism – is an expectable, if misguided reaction to the collapse of the nation-state and of the kind of politics it embodied, or at least promised to embody, as a secure investment for the hopes of a better life.

Ethnicism is not 'early modern nationalism reborn'. It is, in fact, the opposite of nationalism – 'a kind of mirrored reflection' (as Makler, Martinelli and Smelser put it)[6] 'of the decline of the viability of nationalism as a political unifying force.' The self-assertive interethnic wars, squabbles and reconnaissance sorties are loud, often gory manifestations of a withdrawal of trust from nationalist projects; of an abandonment of early modern ambitions, of a loss of courage and of confidence that courage, if guided by reason, may bear fruit. In Miyoshi's words, 'the fragmenting and fragmented' ethnicist movements 'are newly awakened agents not for the construction of autonomous nations but for the abandonment of the expectations and responsibilities of the politicoeconomic national projects'. Those movements are neither fit nor willing to take over the burden of responsibilities falling from the shoulders of nation-states. Most conspicuously, they are neither willing nor able to serve as new frames in which the self-confident ambitions of rationally managed happiness could be inscribed and securely fixed. The utopian hopes tied closely to the era of state-and-nation building are unlikely to obtain a second lease of life from the born-again tribes.

If the products of the modern, emboldened and self-confident imagination that came to be known as 'Utopias' invoked an expectation of a perfectly orderly society and trust in the sovereign territorial power of the nation-state as its vehicle, the contemporary imagination fails on both counts. Territorially confined powers look anything but sovereign and most certainly do not hold out the promise of designing, let alone effectively managing, any kind of stable order, while the very idea of the finality of any arrangement of human togetherness has lost most of its past credibility, together with its attraction and mobilizing power.

## The disengaged imagination

Whoever thinks of doing something about the state of the world, of improving the current shape of the human condition, adding something to human possessions or altering the mode in which they are used – would rather look elsewhere. Focusing hopes and efforts on the orthodox, hopelessly local tools of joint action seems uncannily like a waste of time and energy. One would be better to move to where action has moved: and the name of this new place is no-place, no-land, no-territory. Unlike that orthodox world of sovereignty, with border-poles erecting and border-passages guarding nation states, the new transnational and trans-state global space is (at least for the time being) 'whole and uniform', unmarked by legible signs and full of unanchored, floating meanings, vainly seeking (or keenly avoiding?) fixed locations. It is in such a space that the new powers reside.

Like the powers of yore, they demand loyalty and discipline. But the targets and condensation points of loyalty are thoroughly stripped of all association with place; their seductive/mobilizing power rests in their very out-of-placeness. They symbolize the continuity of forever inconclusive travel, not the finality of arrival. They invoke movement, and not 'being always there', 'since time immemorial and ever hence'. Having identified yourself with a commodity brand, a gadget, a globetrotting celebrity, a cult or a faddish lifestyle currently in the limelight, you are not taking an oath of loyalty to any of the political units of the globe. If anything, such acts of identification help you to shake off locally focused obligations and feelings of indebtedness to the 'natives'.

The new global elite is floating, skating, surfing – often physically, but at all times spiritually. Its members do not 'relate to' the once (and not so long ago) universal territorial sense. Their points of orientation are as mobile as they – bodily or spiritually – are, and as short-lived as their self-identifying loyalties. In the cyberspace they inhabit there are no geographically fixed *topoi*, no borders and no border posts. Their addresses are registered on the internet providers' servers (as extraterritorial as their owners), not in the files of local police precincts, nor in the rosters of state subjects. Membership of the global elite is defined by their *disengagement*, and by freedom from binding territorial commitments.

Members of the global elite meet mainly each other and communicate mainly with each other. Their idiosyncrasies appear small and insignificant, amusing variations on a theme common to all, none of them affecting the easily discernible tune. Such peculiarities do not impede mutual understanding; there is an expectation of reciprocity of perception, and of willing, if temporary retention, built into every dialogue. Multiculturalism, polyvocality, hybridity, cosmopolitanism are the verbal glosses through which members of the global elite struggle to grasp and convey that uncanny experience of variety as but so many little and shallow ripples on the uniform surface of a common lifestyle, or as peculiarities of accents or styles that each shared language easily takes in its stride.

The necessary (and for all practical purposes sufficient) condition of the genuine or putative unity of the global elite is the 'transnationality' of all its members. Cutting local ties and treating differences between one's own and other partners' traditional make-ups as minor only, and above all tractable and transient irritants, is the precondition of membership. Unlike their ancestors of the nation-building era, these global elites have no mission to perform; they do not feel the need nor do they intend to proselytize, to carry the torch of wisdom, to enlighten, instruct and convert. Their earth-bound, and now left-behind compatriots, too deeply engrossed in their worries about daily survival to ponder the valours of polyculturalism and impotent to relish its joys, may have to look up to the globals as role models – but the globals hardly consider themselves as teachers and even less as examples to be followed. Through their actions the global elite may shape, more by default than by design, the life conditions in which the rest are cast, their horizons, dreams and images of a good life – but the actions are not calculated to bring about that effect and so the actors do not feel obliged to assume responsibility for the consequences their actions may have on others; particularly on such others as have failed to follow them so far, and are most unlikely to follow them in the future, on to the global circuits. The present-day global elite has no managerial ambitions and order-building is nowhere to be found on its agenda.

The imagination of the global elite is, like their own life-setting and conduct, disengaged and unattached – not territorially embedded, let alone entrenched and circumscribed or otherwise confined by locality. Fixity, durability, bulk, solidity or permanence, those supreme values of the sedentary mentality, have all been degraded and have acquired an unambiguously negative flavour. They are all conditions to beware of and to avoid. It is not for their naivety but for being misguided from the start, not for their limitations but for their ambitions – for the original sin of pursuing a once-and-for-all predesigned order meant to bar change and substitute routine for contingency – that the Utopias of yore stand condemned in the new global elite's *Weltanschauung* and life philosophy. Their two most crucial attributes – territoriality and finality – disqualify past Utopias and bar in advance all future attempts to re-enter the line of thinking they once followed.

This devaluation of territorial engagement and resentment of all finality is manifested in the new mistrust of 'society' and in the exasperation caused by all suggestions of society-bound, society-promoted and society-managed solutions to jointly or individually experienced human problems. Hopes and dreams have flown elsewhere; they are instructed to steer clear of societal harbours and on no account cast their anchors there.

## Imagination privatized

Our world, as Paul Virilio put it when interviewed by John Armitage, 'is constantly on the move. Today's world no longer has any kind of stability; it is shifting, straddling, gliding away all the time.'[7] Borders may still be in place, but they do not matter as much as they used to a mere half century ago. Most certainly, they are not an obstacle for the drifting and gliding, skating and surfing that fills the *Lebenswelt*. The messages, images, genuine or mock representations of places that fill the *Lebenswelt* have mostly an electronic or cyberspatial, not geographic, address. Were there a 'society' in the sense of self-enclosed and self-sustained totality, it would find it difficult to cut itself off and isolate itself, territorially, from the global whirlwind. Even totalitarianism, as Virilio caustically observed, can no longer be credibly adumbrated as a localized phenomenon. We live in the era of *globalitarianism*, when there are no more plots left to which one could escape and in which one could hide. Distance is no defence. We are under watch and at people's beck and call everywhere, obediently carrying in our pockets the imponderables of our captivity in the form of cellular telephones, portable internet-connected computers or credit cards.

For the Utopia drafters of the solid modern era, imagining a far-away *topos* not yet found, penetrated, ingested and assimilated by the rest of the *oikoumene* was the easiest part of the task. It was also the most plausible and convincing, 'realistic' part of the story, however fantastic it might seem. Maps of the continents and the oceans were spattered by numerous blank spots, while many of the mountain ranges, rainforests, deserts and swamps already mapped defied the endurance of all but a few of the most courageous and adventurous travellers. The earth appeared to be filled with as yet undiscovered and unexplored places, while stretches of wilderness seemed to offer natural shelter for anyone who felt uneasy, or would not be allowed to settle, in the parts of the globe already 'under management' by a sovereign and recognized power.

If the good life was to be a new *beginning*, it seemed obvious that it called for a new *place*. All known forms of life – good or bad, enjoyed or resented, tranquil or troublesome, full of promise or prospectless – were 'territorial', as had to be, in consequence, all schemes for their improvement. *Politics*, an activity aimed at designing, guarding, correcting and repairing the conditions under which people pursue their life purposes, derived its name from the Greek name of the *city* – and whatever else the city might have been, it was always a *place*. Sharing lives was always a *territorial* affair. And so were human identities, hopes and fears, dreams and nightmares, resolves to make the human world better or surrenders to its indomitable evil. Human rights and obligations, as well as the routines to follow, the boons and bonuses to expect from following them and the penalties threatening the routine-breakers, were also territorial. Through thick and thin and apparently till death them do part, the fates of politics and of the territories were linked: indeed, inseparable.

For better or worse... In our fast globalizing world, while territory is fast losing its importance, it is acquiring a new significance: a symbolic and ghostly shadow of the gravity lost. No wonder that the 'grounded politics' of past ages is rapidly running out of substance, even if, like territory bereaved of its past importance, it is gaining in spectacularity and emotional value. Territorial powers offer no secure, reliable, trustworthy supports for rights and obligations. As Virilio put it in conversation with Chris Dercon, these days 'a state of rights is not connected with a state of place, to a clearly determined locality.'[8]

Besides: the globe is full. There are no undiscovered places left and no places where one could hide from the order (or for that matter disorder) ruling (or for that matter misruling) in the places already known and mapped, criss-crossed by beaten tracks, administered and managed. In this world, there is no 'outside' any more. Each *polis* is but a pale shadow of the old sovereign realm, but *il n'y a pas hors de cité*, no place outside the city, anywhere on the planet. 'Utopia' – in its original meaning of a *place* that does not exist – has become, within the logic of the globalized world, a contradiction in terms. The 'nowhere' (the 'forever nowhere', the 'thus-far nowhere', and the 'nowhere-as-yet' alike) is no longer a *place*. The 'U' of 'Utopia' bereaved by the *topos*, is left homeless and floating, no longer hoping to strike roots, to 're-embed'.

Frontier-land – the warehouse of opportunities, the greenhouse of dreams and the plot singled out as a building site of happiness – is not a place either. These days frontier-land cannot be plotted on any map; it is not a geographical notion anymore. As the network of human interdependencies tightly wrapped the whole of the globe, 'frontier-land' expanded to embrace the whole of the *Lebenswelt*, leaving few if any of its nooks and crannies off-limits. It is 'the whole life', lived as it is from one project to another, each of the projects aimed at expanding the range of similarly one-off and short-lived projects and none of the projects aimed at terminating the obsessive search for projects, that has become the updated, liquid modern version of the solid modern frontier-land.

The mood of liquid modern times has recently found an articulation (though admittedly confined to narrowly pragmatic concerns) in quarters not particularly notorious for profundity of reflection or the urge to fathom the deeper layers of the human condition: among the American military bosses and their political animators. The occasion was the need to develop a strategy of military action in the new global frontier-land, like all frontier-lands in the past inhospitable to durable commitments and lasting alliances and notorious for the tendency of its colonizers to tear up the papers on which peace or armistice treaties were written before the ink of the signatures had dried, and for untiringly redrawing the boundary between confederates and foes. As Paul Wolfowitz, the US deputy defence secretary, informed America's Nato allies,[9] in the war declared on terrorists[10] (one that George Bush Jr proudly yet ominously dubbed 'the first war of the twenty-first century') there will be 'shifting coalitions', 'in which some nations might help with certain operations, and others could be called upon in a different capacity'. 'To be effective, we have to be flexible,' Wolfowitz hammered home the message. 'We have to be adaptable.' A day later Donald H. Rumsfeld, Wolfowitz's immediate boss, added gravity to the vision.[11] No 'grand alliance united' this time, he announced: 'Instead it will involve floating coalitions of countries, which may change and evolve.' The enemy's cyberspace, rather than its territory, will be invaded (meaning: the enemy's communication circuit). 'There may not be as many beachheads stormed as opportunities denied.' All in all, 'we have no fixed rules how to deploy our troops.'

In a frontier-land friends are priceless; but once their usefulness has been exhausted their exile to the realm of shooting targets is swift, as swift as their escape to the enemy camp once their extant friends are no longer of use. Everyone knows this when tying the friendship bonds – and many players are careful to leave the knots only loosely fastened, ready to be untied instantaneously by one pull of the string. Building permits are sought and issued together with the permits of anticipated – imminent – demolition.

As at the level of global extraterritoriality, so at the level of life politics. At least in their broad structural outlines the two settings are remarkably similar, and so are, expectedly, the strategies – the outcomes of the rational actors' calculations. Shifting/drifting alliances and coalitions seem to be the precepts of reason. The turbulent setting in which life tasks are pursued makes a helping hand precious – but also makes one wary of the moment when the loving caress becomes more like an iron grip. Friendship, particularly a friendship cemented by an irrevocable oath of loyalty and an 'until death us do part' kind of commitment, may turn at any time from an asset into a liability. One may guess that the ambivalence that haunts contemporary interhuman bonds and the resulting uncertainty about the benefits and dangers of mutual commitments are at the roots of the current renaissance of the 'friendship ideology'. Indeed, we tend to think most keenly and to feel most strongly about the things that cause the most acute anxiety – anxiety because they elude clear-cut demarcation, defy unambiguous evaluations and carry promises and threats mixed in unknown and unknowable proportions.

In consequence, the utopian model of a 'better future' is out of the question. It fails on two counts. First, on account of its fixity. Whatever else the 'better' as imagined by our contemporaries may be, it cannot be 'once and for all', determined to last forever – and utopian models, tying their vision of happiness to a settled population of a geographically defined, immovable city, present precisely such a concept of the 'better future'. Secondly, the by now old-fashioned Utopias fail to excite on account of their tendency to locate the secret of a happy life in social reform – an operation to be performed on society as a whole and resulting in a 'steady state' of the life-setting. They propose an improvement meant to put paid to all further improvement – a gigantic leap perhaps, but followed by cadaverous odour of *stasis*.

A third factor acting against the old-style Utopias may be named: the undefined 'future' itself. Liquid modernity detached trust from the future – by detaching faith in progress from the flow of time. The passage of time is no longer measured by movement from an inferior to a superior state – but by the passing of, the vanishing of the chances of improvement which each moment of time entails in an essentially similar quantity and which sink into the unrecoverable past together with that moment. With the early modern 'delay of gratification' decisively out of fashion and at odds with 'rational choice', and with credit cards replacing saving books as weapons of self-assertion, seductive power shifted from the indefinite series of 'tomorrows' to the fully tangible, securely within reach 'today'. Happiness and more happiness are desired now as they used to be in the bygone times of Utopia-writing; but happiness means now a *different today* rather than a more felicitous tomorrow.

And so happiness has become a *private affair*, and a matter for *here and now*. The happiness of others is no longer – or had better be no longer – a condition of one's own felicity. Each moment of happiness is, after all, lived through in a company that may be, but more likely may not be, around when the next moment of happiness arrives. The settings in which moments of happiness are staged are not to be cultivated after the pattern of fields that bring ever more profuse crops the longer they are tended to, ploughed and fertilized. The paradigm of the search for happiness is mining, rather than agri- or horticulture. The mines are emptied of their useful contents and then promptly abandoned – when the deposits have been exhausted or when their further exploitation becomes too cumbersome or costly.

Unlike the utopian model of the good life, happiness is thought of as an aim to be pursued individually, and as a series of happy moments succeeding each other – not as a steady state. If places appear in that thinking, they do so mostly in the capacity of sites where the succession of happy moments is believed to acquire velocity and density unattainable in other sites. This capacity is not related (not necessarily at any rate) to previous investment in the place. On the contrary, as the novelty of a place wears off and the pleasures it offers turn tediously familiar, the 'law of diminishing returns' begins to operate and each next moment of happiness may require an increased investment of time and effort – a waste of resources, considering the profusion of still unexplored places and still untested excitements. Hence the attraction of the modicum of happiness known to be on offer in places already visited and familiar needs to compete with the magnetic power of 'virgin lands' and 'new beginnings' whose promises are all the more believable and seductive for having been untested – and more often than not the old faithful and trusty sites do not emerge from that competition victorious. Whatever attraction prevails, though, one option looks definitely unappetizing: the prospect of 'fixity', of the chance that mobility will be cut out and that alternative sites where happier sensations could be sought will be declared out of bounds.

In the contemporary equivalent of solid modern Utopias, happiness is linked to mobility, not to a place. More often than not, places are ushered into the dream of happiness by a hankering after change-of-place: as the projected far end of homesickness or as an imagined destination of a pining to 'get away from it all'. The liquid modern equivalents of the Utopias of yore are neither about time nor about space – but about *speed* and *acceleration*.

# Notes

## Introduction

1 Cf. Giorgio Agamben, *Homo Sacer: Sovereign Power and Bare Life*, trans. Daniel Heller-Roazen (Stanford University Press, 1998), p. 11.
2 Ibid., p. 9.
3 Ibid., pp. 120, 122.
4 Jean-Pierre Dacheux, 'Balcaniser l'Europe?', *Lignes*, Oct. 2001, p. 78.
5 See the chapter 'Community' in my *Liquid Modernity* (Polity, 2000).
6 Paul Virilio, *Virilio Live: Selected Interviews*, ed. John Armitage (Sage, 2001), pp. 84, 71.
7 Constantin von Barloewen, 'La culture, facteur de la Realpolitik', *Le Monde Diplomatique*, Nov. 2001, p. 22.

## 1 Chasing the Elusive Society

1 From Max Weber, *Theory of Social and Economic Organization*, see *Max Weber*, ed. J. E. T. Eldridge (Nelson, 1971), pp. 102, 93.
2 From Émile Durkheim, *Les règles de la mèthode sociologique* (*Rules of the Scientific Method*), see *Émile Durkheim: Selected Writings*, ed. Anthony Giddens (Cambridge University Press, 1972), p. 59.
3 C. Wright Mills, *The Sociological Imagination* (Oxford University Press, 1959), pp. 100, 32.
4 Robert S. Lynd, 'The science of inhuman relations', *New Republic*, 27 Aug. 1949.
5 *The Sociological Imagination*, p. 117.

6   Daniel Cohen, *Nos temps modernes* (Flammarion, 1999), pp. 48, 56, 60.

7   Luc Boltanski and Éve Chiapello, *Le nouvel esprit du capitalisme* (Gallimard, 1999), pp. 143ff.

8   Ulrich Beck, *Risk Society: Towards a New Modernity*, trans. Mark Ritter (Sage, 1992), p. 137.

9   'The new thinking', in *Franz Rosenzweig: His Life and Thought*, presented by Nahum Glatzer (Schocken, 1961), p. 200.

10  Franz Rosenzweig, *Understanding the Sick and the Healthy*, trans. Nahum Glatzer (Harvard University Press, 1999), p. 59.

11  'The new thinking', p. 199.

12  Quoted after Steven E. Prokesh, 'Mastering chaos at the high-tech frontier: an interview with Silicon Graphics' Ed MacCracken', *Harvard Business Review*, Nov.–Dec. 1993, pp. 142–4.

13  Norman R. Augustine, 'Reshaping an industry: Lockheed Martin's survival story', *Harvard Business Review*, July–Aug. 1997, p. 85.

14  Richard Sennett, *Corrosion of Character: The Personal Consequences of Work in the New Capitalism* (W.W. Norton, 1998), p. 51.

15  Andrei Schleifer and Larry Summers, 'Corporate takeovers as breach of trust', in A. Auerbach (ed.), *Corporate Takeovers: Causes and Consequences* (University of Chicago Press, 1988).

16  F. Dubet, *Sociologie de l'expérience* (Seuil, 1994), p. 52.

17  Cohen, *Nos temps modernes*, p. 91.

18  Mary Jo Hatch, Monika Kostera and Andrzej Koźminski, 'Myths and managers', ch. 3 of 'Managers, artists, priests', MS.

19  Nigel Thrift, 'The rise of soft capitalism', *Cultural Values*, Apr. 1997, p. 52.

20  Boltanski and Chiapello, *Le nouvel esprit du capitalisme*, p. 151.

21  Richard Rorty, *Achieving our Country: Leftist Thought in Twentieth-Century America* (Harvard University Press, 1998), p. 85.

22  In *Le Monde Diplomatique*, May 2000, pp. 6–7.

23  Quoted after *Émile Durkheim: Selected Writings*, p. 64.

24  Keith Tester, *Moral Culture* (Sage, 1997), p. 6.

25  Harvie Ferguson, 'Watching the world go round: atrium culture and the psychology of shopping', in Roy Shields (ed.), *Lifestyle Shopping: The Subject of Consumption* (Routledge, 1992), pp. 34–5.

26  Michael Allen Gillespie, 'The theological origins of modernity', *Critical Review*, 13: 1–2 (1999), pp. 1–30.

27  Quoted from the *Portable Renaissance Reader*, ed. James Bruce Ross and Mary Martin McLoughlin (Viking, 1953), p. 478.

28  Max Horkheimer, *Critique of Instrumental Reason*, trans. Matthew J. O'Connor et al. (Seaburg Press, 1974), p. 29.

29  Max Horkheimer, *Critical Theory: Selected Essays*, trans. Matthew J. O'Connor et al. (Herder and Herder, 1972), pp. 229, 207.

30  Hannah Arendt, *Men in Dark Times* (Harcourt Brace, 1995), pp. 8, ix.

## 2   The Great Separation Mark Two

1   Aristotle, *Politics*, trans. John Warrington (Everyman, 1959), pp. 11, 25.
2   Ibid., p. 8.
3   Ibid., pp. 7–8.
4   Ibid., pp. 67–8.
5   Here quoted after Eithne Wilkins and Ernst Kaiser's translation, *The Man without Qualities* (Capricorn Books, 1965), vol. 2, p. 174 ('entrollt der Zug der Ereignisse seine Gleise vor sich her, und der Fluß der Zeit reißt seine Ufer mit sich').
6   Jacques Ellul, *L'illusion politique*, 1965; here quoted after Konrad Kellen's translation, *The Political Illusion* (Random House, 1972), pp. 186, 185.
7   Ernst Cassirer, *The Myth of the State* (Doubleday, 1955), pp. 362–3.
8   Ibid.
9   Erich Fromm, *The Fear of Freedom* (Routledge and Kegan Paul, 1960), p. 23.
10  Cassirer, *The Myth of the State*, p. 351.
11  Theodor W. Adorno, *Eingriffe. Neun kritische Modelle*, 1963, and *Sichworte. Kritische Modelle 2*, 1969 (both Suhrkamp Verlag); here quoted from Henry W. Pickford's translation, *Critical Models: Interventions and Catchwords*, (Columbia University Press, 1998), pp. 118, 139.
12  See *L'Express*, 5 May 2001, p. 64.
13  Ignazio Ramonet, 'Big Brother', *Le Monde Diplomatique*, June 2001, pp. 1 and 24–5.
14  See 'The Editor', *Guardian*, 2 June 2001.
15  This characterization comes from Michael Allen Gillespie, 'The theological origins of modernity', *Critical Review*, 13: 1–2 (1999), pp. 1–30.
16  Peter F. Drucker, *The New Realities* (Mandarin, 1990), pp. 9–15.
17  Hannah Arendt, *The Origins of Totalitarianism* (André Deutsch, 1951), p. 438.
18  Pierre Bourdieu, *Contre-feux. Propos pour servir à la résistance contre l'invasion néo-libérale* (Raisons d'Agir, 1998), p. 117.
19  Pierre Bourdieu, *Contre-feux 2. Pour un movement social européen*, (Raisons d'Agir, 2001), p. 30.
20  Ibid., p. 46.
21  Ulrich Beck, *Risikogesellschaft. Auf dem Weg in eine andere Moderne*, 1986; here quoted after Mark Ritter's translation, *Risk Society: Towards a New Modernity* (Sage, 1992), pp. 135–7.
22  Richard Sennett, *The Corrosion of Character: The Personal Consequences of Work in the New Capitalism* (W. W. Norton, 1998), pp. 43, 31, 25.

23   Alain Peyrefitte, *La société de confiance. Essai sur les origines de développement* (Odile Jacob, 1998), pp. 514–17, 539.
24   See my *Liquid Modernity* (Polity, 2000).
25   Laurent Fabius, 'Le temps des projets', *Le Monde*, 1 June 2001, pp. 1, 16.
26   'I can already hear some commentators asking: why, for heaven's sake, is the French Minister for the Economy and Finance thinking about the long term. Shouldn't he be concentrating on running things now...?'
27   Luc Boltanski and Éve Chiapello, *Le nouvel esprit du capitalisme* (Gallimard, 1999), p. 144.
28   See, for instance, his *Contre-feux* (Raisons d'Agir, 1998).
29   See Judith Doyle and Max Nathan, 'The hypermobile must not be allowed to rule roost', *Guardian*, 23 Apr. 2001, p. 23.
30   See *The Complete Prose of Woody Allen* (Picador, 1980).

### 3   Living and Dying in the Planetary Frontier-land

Part of this chapter was published earlier in *Tikkun* (Mar.–Apr. 2002).

1   Eric le Boucher, 'Le 11 September, tournant dans le mondalisation', *Le Monde*, 25 Oct. 2001, p. 17.
2   Donald H. Rumsfeld, 'Creative coalition-building for a new kind of war', *International Herald Tribune*, 28 Sept. 2001, p. 6.
3   See 'US keeps NATO outside', *International Herald Tribune*, 27 Sept. 2001.
4   Gary Younge, 'Lots of wars on terror', *Guardian*, 10 Dec. 2001, p. 17.
5   Jean Baudrillard, 'L'esprit du terrorisme', *Le Monde*, 3 Nov. 2001, p. 11.
6   Madeleine Bunting, 'The raging colossus', *Guardian*, 19 Nov. 2001.
7   William Pfaff, 'The war on terror turns into war on Afghanistan', *International Herald Tribune*, 3–4 Nov. 2001.
8   George F. Will, 'A lesson for America from an Israeli attack on Saddam', *International Herald Tribune*, 3–4 Dec. 2001.
9   Knud Løgstrup, *Opgør med Kierkegaard* (*Opposing Kierkegaard*, 1968; here quoted from the translation by Susan Dew and Kees van Kooten Niekerk).
10   See Marwan Bishara, 'L'ère des conflits asymmétriques', *Le Monde Diplomatique*, Oct. 2001, pp. 20–1.
11   As defined by the American military handbooks (see Noam Chomsky, 'Terrorisme, l'arme des puissants', *Le Monde Diplomatique*, Dec. 2001, pp. 10–11).
12   See 'Unfinished business', *Observer*, 9 Dec. 2001, pp. 15–18.

13   Quoted after Arundhati Roy, 'Ben Laden, secret de famille de l'Amér-
     ique', *Le Monde*, 14–15 Oct. 2001.
14   Jacques Derrida, *Cosmopolites de tous les pays, encore un effort!*
     (Galilée, 1997), p. 42: 'Hospitality is culture itself, not just one ethic
     among others...ethics is hospitality.'
15   As Giorgio Agamben discovered, see his *Homo Sacer: Sovereign
     Power and Bare Life*, trans. Daniel Heller-Roazen (Stanford University
     Press, 1998).
16   Quoted in Marc Ferro, *Histoire des colonisations* (Seuil, 1994).
17   A charge eagerly resorted to, with great profit, by an ever-widening
     range of contemporary politicians across the political spectrum, from
     Le Pen of France, Pia Kjersgaard of Denmark or Vlaam Bloc of Bel-
     gium on the far right, to a growing number of such as define them-
     selves as 'left of centre'.
18   *Guardian*, 26 Nov. 2001.
19   See Michel Foucault, 'Of other spaces', *Diacritics*, 1 (1986), p. 26.
20   See Loïc Wacquant, 'Symbole fatale. Quand ghetto et prison se
     ressemblent et s'assemblent', *Actes de la Recherche en Sciences
     Sociales*, Sept. 2001, p. 43.
21   See Norbert Elias and John L. Scotson, *The Established and the Out-
     siders: A Sociological Inquiry into Community Problems* (Frank Cass,
     1965), esp. pp. 81 and 95.
22   See Loïc Wacquant, 'The new urban color line: the state and fate of
     the ghetto in postfordist America', in Craig J. Calhoun (ed.), *Social
     Theory and the Politics of Identity* (Blackwell, 1994); also 'Elias in the
     dark ghetto', *Amsterdams Sociologisch Tidjschrift*, Dec. 1997.
23   Michel Agier, 'Entre guerre et ville. Pour une anthropologie urbaine
     des camps de réfugiés', *Ethnography*, 1 (2002).
24   The first stage consisting in the dismantling of the old identity, the
     third and last in assembling the new one: see Arnold van Gennep, *The
     Right of Passage* (Routledge and Kegan Paul, 1960); Victor W. Turner,
     *The Ritual Process: The Structure and Anti-Structure* (University of
     Chicago Press, 1969).


4   (Un)Happiness of Uncertain Pleasures

This chapter was published earlier in *Sociologisk Arbejdpapir*, 10 (2001),
Aalborg University.

1   Władysław Tatarkiewicz, *O szczesciu* (PWN, 1965; originally pub-
     lished 1939).
2   'On the shortness of life', translation by C. D. N Costa of *De
     Brevitate Vitae*, see Seneca, *Dialogues and Letters* (Penguin, 1997),
     pp. 77–8.

3   Arthur Schopenhauer, 'On the vanity of existence', in *Essays and Aphorisms*, trans. R. J. Hollingdale (Penguin, 1978), p. 51.

4   Arthur Schopenhauer, 'On the suffering of the world', in ibid., p. 46.

5   Schopenhauer, 'On the vanity of existence', p. 54.

6   Pascal, *Pensées*, trans. A. J. Krailsheimer (Penguin, 1966), p. 48.

7   Ibid., pp. 67–8.

8   Michel de Montaigne, *The Complete Essays*, trans. M. A. Screech (Penguin, 1991), pp. 1211–12.

9   Seneca, 'On the shortness of life', p. 77.

10  Piero Camporesi, *The Fear of Hell: Images of Damnation and Salvation in Early Modern Europe*, trans. Lucinda Byatt (Pennsylvania State University Press, 1991), p. 36, quoting Carl Ambrogio Cattaneo.

11  Quoted after ibid., p. 53.

12  See Émile Durkheim, *L'Éducation morale*, here quoted from *Émile Durkheim: Selected Writings*, ed. Anthony Giddens (Cambridge University Press, 1972), p. 110.

13  See Émile Durkheim, *Sociologie et Philosophie*, quoted from *Selected Writings*, p. 115.

14  See Émile Durkheim, 'La science positive de la morale en Allemagne', quoted from *Selected Writings*, p. 94.

15  George L. Mosse, *The Fallen Soldiers: Reshaping the Memory of the World Wars* (Oxford University Press, 1991), pp. 35ff.

16  See John Bowker, *Problems of Suffering in Religions of the World* (Cambridge University Press, 1970), pp. 16, 21, 35–7, 94.

17  'When I consider the brief span of my life absorbed into the eternity which comes before and after...the small space that I occupy and which I see swallowed up in the infinite immensity of spaces of which I know nothing and which knows nothing of me, I take fright'; Pascal, *Pensées*, p. 48.

18  See Schopenhauer, *Essays and Aphorisms*, pp. 41, 52, 53, 45, 43.

19  See Jacques Ellul, *Métarmophose du bourgeois* (La Table Ronde, 1998; first published Calman-Lévy, 1967), pp. 81, 90, 97–8, 102–3.

20  Ibid., p. 275.

21  Luc Ferry, 'Une menace pour l'Humanisme?', *Le Monde des Débats*, June 2001, p. 27.

22  Jacques Ellul, *La technique ou l'enjeu du siècle*, here quoted from John Wilkinson's translation, *The Technological Society* (Vintage Books, 1964), pp. 134, 390.

23  Nigel Thrift, 'Performing cultures in the new economy', *Annals of the Association of American Geographers*, 4 (2000), pp. 674–92.

24  A. Muoio, 'Idea summit', *Fast Company*, 31 (2000), pp. 150–94.

25  Max Weber, *The Protestant Ethic and the Spirit of Capitalism*, trans. Talcott Parsons (George Allen and Unwin, 1976), pp. 58–61.

26  Harvie Ferguson, *The Science of Pleasure: Cosmos and Psyche in the Bourgeois World-View* (Routledge, 1990), p. 47.

27   Richard Sennett, *The Corrosion of Character: The Personal Conse-quences of Work in the New Capitalism* (W. W. Norton, 1998), pp. 61–2.
28   Max Scheler, 'Ordo amoris', in *Schriften aus dem Nachlass. Zut Ethik und Erkentnisslehre*; here quoted from *Selected Philosophical Essays*, trans. David R. Lachterman (Northwestern University Press, 1973), p. 110.
29   Jean-Paul Sartre, *L'Être et le Néant* (1943), here quoted from Hazel E. Barnes's translation, *Being and Nothingness: An Essay on Phenomeno-logical Ontology* (Methuen, 1969), pp. 608–11.
30   See Frank Mazoyer, 'Consommateurs sous influence', *Le Monde Dip-lomatique*, Dec. 2000, p. 23.
31   Ferguson, *The Science of Pleasure*, p. 205.
32   See Philippe Pons, 'La culture furita, ou le nomadisme au travail', *Le Monde*, 13 Apr. 2001, p. 14.
33   Quoted from Jim McClellan, 'New media gets the message', *Guardian Online*, 21 June 2001, p. 2.
34   Quoted from *Guardian Weekend*, 16 June 2001, p. 66.

## 5   As Seen on TV

This chapter was first published in *Ethical Perspectives*, 2–3 (2000).

1   Jacques Attali, *Dictionnaire du XXI^e siècle* (Fayard, 1998), p. 318.
2   Jean Baudrillard, *Simulacra and Simulation*, trans. Paul Foss, Paul Pat-ton and Philip Beitchman (*Sémiotexte*, 1983), pp. 1–13. Simulacrum is 'a map that precedes the territory', that 'engenders the territory'. While 'feigning or dissimulating leaves the reality principle intact', simulation 'threatens the difference between "true" and "false", between "real" and "imaginary" . . . It is no longer a question of a false representation of reality (ideology).'
3   Bruno Latour, *Petite réflexion sur le culte des dieux Faitiches* (Synthé-labo, 1996), p. 16. The word 'fetish' was coined by Portuguese mis-sionaries appalled by the sight of clay or wooden objects to which the natives of Guinea ascribed divine potency. They reproached the hea-then for failing to see the difference: 'Vous ne pouvez pas à la fois dire que vous avez fabriqué vos fétiches et qui'ils sont de vrais divinités, *il vous faut choisir*, c'est l'un ou bien s'est l'autre' ('You cannot at one and the same time say that you have made your fetishes and that they are true gods, you have to choose, either it's one or it's the other'). A simulacrum is neither *l'un* nor *l'autre*, neither the real thing nor its man-made model: or it is both.
4   Pierre Bourdieu, *Sur la télévision* (Raisons d'Agir, 1996), pp. 30–1.
5   Simon Hoggart, 'Beethoven Blair pounds kettle drums for Britain', *Guardian*, 29 Mar. 2000, p. 2.

6 Nick Lee, 'Three complex subjectivities: Borges, Sterne, Montaigne', paper to ESRC seminar, Jan. 2000.

7 Richard Sennett, *The Corrosion of Character: The Personal Consequences of Work in the New Capitalism* (W. W. Norton, 1998), pp. 62–3.

8 Alain Ehrenberg, *L'Individu incertain* (Calman-Lévy, 1995), ch. 4.

9 Ulrich Beck, *Risk Society: Toward a New Modernity*, trans. Mark Ritter (Sage, 1992), pp. 133–7.

10 Anthony Giddens, *The Transformation of Intimacy: Sexuality, Love and Eroticism in Modern Societies* (Polity, 1992), pp. 197–8.

11 Sennett, *The Corrosion of Character*, p. 22.

12 Bourdieu, *Sur la télévision*, p. 28.

13 Ivan Klima, *Between Security and Insecurity*, trans. Gerry Turner (Thames and Hudson, 1999), p. 44.

14 Published by Paris-Méditerranée, 1998.

15 François Brune, 'De la soumission dans les têtes', *Le Monde Diplomatique*, Apr. 2000, p. 20.

16 Pierre Bourdieu, 'La précarité est aujourd'hui partout', in *Contre-feux* (Raisons d'Agir, 1998), pp. 98, 97.

### 6   Consuming Life

This chapter was published earlier by the *Journal of Consumer Culture*, 1:1 (June 2001).

1 Michel de Montaigne, *The Complete Essays*, trans. M. A. Sareech (Penguin, 1991), pp. 298–9.

2 Pascal, *Pensées*, trans. A. J. Krailsheimer (Penguin, 1966), pp. 67, 70.

3 Montaigne, *The Complete Essays*, p. 85.

4 Søren Kierkegaard, *Either/Or*, trans. David F. Swenson and Lilian Marvin Swenson (Princeton University Press); here quoted after David L. Norton and Mary F. Kille (eds), *Philosophies of Love* (Helix Books, 1971), pp. 45–8.

5 Max Scheler was to spell out later the creed in which Kierkegaard sought support for hope: there is fate, which no human being can freely choose: and there is destiny – which is that being's own, even if poorly controlled and seldom fully planned, product.... [T]he individual destiny of man is not his fate. Only the assumption that fate and destiny are the same deserves to be called fatalism... Fatalism could gain currency only as long as men *reified* fate... However, environmental structure and fate... have a natural and basically comprehensible origin... Fate, for sure, cannot be freely chosen... Nevertheless, fate *grows up* out of the life of a man or a people... Fate shapes itself for the most part in the life of the individual.

Environmental (social) pressures are not supernatural, and to withstand them is not a superhuman task. The destiny of the individual has to be pursued against many odds which can be overwhelming, but it *can* be pursued, pursued steadfastly, even seen through to the end; the dissolution of destiny in fate is in no way a foregone conclusion, even if all too often it looks as if it was. The possibility of separating destiny from fate makes life a moral choice. If Don Juan was, in Kierkegaard's opinion, 'outside morality' it was because he would not allow for that possibility. See Max Scheler, 'Ordo amoris', in *Selected Philosophical Essays*, trans. David R. Lachterman (Northwestern University Press, 1973), pp. 105–8.

6  See ibid.
7  Harvie Ferguson, *The Lure of Dreams: Sigmund Freud and the Construction of Modernity* (Routledge, 1996), p. 205.
8  Harvie Ferguson, 'Watching the world go round: atrium culture and the psychology of shopping', in *Lifestyle Shopping: The Subject of Consumption*, ed. Rob Shields (Routledge, 1992), p. 31.
9  George Ritzer, *The McDonaldization Thesis* (Sage, 1998), p. 68.
10  See Pierre Bourdieu, *Contre-feux* (Raisons d'Agir, 1998), pp. 97–9.
11  Barbara Czarniawska, *Writing Management: Organization Theory as a Literary Genre* (Oxford University Press, 1999), p. 53.
12  Émile Durkheim, 'La science positive de la morale en Allemagne', *Revue Philosophique* (1987); here quoted from *Émile Durkheim: Selected Writings*, ed. and trans. Anthony Giddens (Cambridge University Press, 1972), pp. 93–4.
13  Alain Peyrefitte, *La société de confiance* (Odile Jacob, 1998), pp. 514–16.
14  Richard Sennett, *The Corrosion of Character* (W. W. Norton, 1998), p. 31.
15  Niklas Luhmann, *Observations on Modernity*, trans. William Whobrey (Stanford University Press, 1998), p. 3.
16  Ulrich Beck, *Risk Society*, trans. Mark Ritter (Sage, 1992), pp. 135–7.
17  Ritzer, *The McDonaldization Thesis*, pp. 146, 138.

## 7  From Bystander to Actor

This chapter was published earlier in *Human Rights*, 1 (2002).

1  See Stanley Cohen, *States of Denial: Knowing about Atrocities and Suffering* (Polity, 2001).
2  Ibid., pp. x, 1.
3  Petrūska Clarkson, *The Bystander: An End to Innocence in Human Relationships?* (Whurr, 1996), pp. 6–7, xviii, xvii.
4  Keith Tester, *Moral Culture* (Sage, 1997), pp. 5–6.

5  Roberto Toscano, 'The ethics of modern diplomacy', in *Ethics and International Affairs: Extents and Limits*, ed. Jean-Marc Coicaud and Daniel Werner (United Nations University Press, 2001), p. 73.
6  See Pierre Vandegiste's survey, 'Le proper de l'homme et la culture chimpanzée', *Le Monde des Débats*, June 2001, pp. 22–3.
7  Tester, *Moral Culture*, p. 17.
8  Ibid., pp. 30, 32.
9  Ryszard Kapuściński, 'Les médias reflètent-ils la réalité du monde?', *Le Monde Diplomatique*, Aug. 1999, pp. 8–9.
10  Luc Boltanski, *La Souffrance à distance*, here quoted from Graham Burchell's translation, *Distant Suffering: Morality, Media and Politics* (Cambridge University Press, 1999), p. xv.
11  Tester, *Moral Culture*, p. 22.
12  Boltanski, *La Souffrance à distance*, pp. 31, 192, 119, 182.
13  Ibid., p. 18.
14  Tester, *Moral Culture*, p. 20.
15  See Robert Fine, 'Crimes against humanity: Hannah Arendt and the Nuremberg debates', *European Journal of Social Theory*, 3 (2000), pp. 293–311.
16  Hannah Arendt, *Essays in Understanding* (Harcourt Brace, 1994), p. 132.

Conclusion: Utopia with No *Topos*

1  Roberto Toscano, 'The ethics of modern diplomacy', in *Ethics and International Affairs: Extents and Limits*, ed. Jean-Marc Coicaud and Daniel Werner (United Nations University Press, 2001), p. 50.
2  See Giorgio Agamben, *Homo Sacer: il potere sovrano e la nuda vita* (1995), here quoted from Daniel Heller-Roazen's translation, *Homo Sacer: Sovereign Power and Bare Life* (Stanford University Press, 1998), pp. 11ff.
3  Peter Scott, 'Massification, internationalization and globalization', in *The Globalization of Higher Education* (Open University Press, 2000), p. 112.
4  Masao Miyoshi, 'A borderless world? From colonialism to transnationalism and the decline of the nation-state', in *Cultural Production and the Transnational Imaginary*, ed. Rob Wilson and Wimal Dissanayake (Duke University Press, 1996), pp. 78–106.
5  Sheila Slaughter, 'National higher education policies in a global economy', in *Universities and Globalization: Critical Perspectives*, ed. Jan Currie and Janice Newson (Sage, 1996), p. 52.
6  Harry M. Makler, Alberto Martinelli and Neil J. Smelser, *The New International Economy* (Sage, 1992), pp. 26–7.

7 In *Virilio Live: Selected Interviews*, ed. John Armitage (Sage, 2001), p. 40.
8 Conversation in 1986; here quoted from ibid., p. 80.
9 'US keeps NATO outside', *International Herald Tribune*, 27 Sept. 2001, p. 1.
10 The terrorists in question have been themselves, let us remember, America's close, cherished and coveted allies. And to help to fight them, forces are enlisted that are bound to be reclassified as 'terrorists' soon after the aims of alliance are reached.
11 Donald H. Rumsfeld, 'Creative coalition-building for a new kind of war', *International Herald Tribune*, 28 Sept. 2001, p. 6.

# Index